Social and Economic Rights in Ireland

SOCIAL AND ECONOMIC RIGHTS IN IRELAND

Dr CLAIRE-MICHELLE SMYTH

Ph.D, PGCET, LL.M, LL.B, BA.

CLARUS
PRESS

Published by
Clarus Press Ltd,
Griffith Campus,
South Circular Road,
Dublin 8.
www.claruspress.ie

Typeset by
Gough Typesetting Services
Dublin

Printed by
SprintPrint Ltd
Dublin

ISBN
978-1-905536-92-4

FOREWORD

I am delighted to welcome the publication of this book by Dr Claire-Michelle Smyth on *Social and Economic Rights in Ireland*. I had the pleasure of supervising Dr Smyth's doctoral research when she was a student in the School of Law at Queen's University Belfast; it is great to see the book that has emerged.

This new work is a timely and substantial contribution to current human rights discussions in Ireland. Dr Smyth combines detailed legal analysis with informed critical assessment of law and policy. It is evident from this book that more effective protection of social and economic rights is needed in Ireland. Ways forward are suggested here, including possible reforms. Dr Smyth, however, highlights the creative use that still might be made of the existing legal framework, and the argument advanced in support of this position will be of considerable interest. Although constitutional reform would be welcome (as proposed by the Constitutional Convention), there is clearly more that could be done to maximise the effectiveness of the present arrangements (if there is a willingness to do so).

Dr Smyth is to be commended for producing an impressive book that will help to shape debates on social and economic rights in Ireland. Sustained reflection is required on why these rights continue to be treated as 'second class', in Ireland and elsewhere. This is a significant and necessary addition to the literature; it will assist all those who want to find ways to build a more robust culture of respect for human rights in Ireland.

Professor Colin Harvey,
School of Law,
Queen's University Belfast,
Belfast
March 2017

PREFACE

I recall being an undergraduate first year law student studying constitutional law and the lecturer, who also happened to be the Dean of Law, informing us that social and economic rights were non-justiciable under the Irish Constitution. With all of the arrogance that a first year law student can muster, I thought to myself he must be mistaken—surely this cannot be the case. How can it be that rights to water, food, clothing, shelter are not protected? The bare essential elements that a human being needs to remain alive are not protected by law? To me it seemed illogical that such protection would be given to rights such as those relating to participating in a democratic society, liberty, and securing fair trials when the basic preconditions of life were not protected. How can one who is homeless and hungry actively engage with their civil and political rights?

Alas, however, my lecturer was correct much to my outrage and disbelief, and this sparked an interest in a subject which continues to grow. It spurred me on to complete an LL.M in International Human Rights Law and my PhD thesis examined whether the European Convention on Human Rights could be used in Irish Courts to indirectly constitutionalise social and economic rights (it could, in my humble opinion).

This textbook was written with the hope of sparking some of the same interest as my constitutional law lecturer did in that class, by showing that there is scope to protect these rights through the courts, that Ireland is failing to live up to its international obligations and highlighting that justiciability is a legitimate aim both in theory and in practice.

Claire-Michelle Smyth,
April 2017.

ACKNOWLEDGEMENTS

I would like to extend my gratitude firstly to Clarus Press who have supported and assisted me during the drafting and editing of this publication. Further thanks to my friends and colleagues at the University of Brighton for their facilitation and encouragement.

Above all, my biggest thanks must be to my family and friends. In particular my partner Stephen and my mum Trish, this book is dedicated to them both.

TABLE OF CONTENTS

TABLES OF CASES

Court of Justice of the European Union

European Court of Human Rights

India

Inter-American Court of Human Rights

South Africa

TABLES OF LEGISLATION AND TREATIES

CHAPTER 1

Social and Economic Rights in Ireland

Introduction

Social and economic rights encompass the essential elements required for a human being to merely exist. They include, *inter alia*, the right to food, water, shelter, emergency medical care, housing and social assistance. These rights are primarily seen as being subordinate to, and less important than, civil and political rights, with little to no judicial protection in international, regional or domestic systems. At the outset of the modern human rights movement, the Universal Declaration of Human Rights (UDHR) recognised that these form an integral part of the human rights rubric.[1] However, universal agreement on this position was not forthcoming. The disunity which came to the fore during the negotiations to transpose the UDHR into one legally enforceable document resulted these most fundamental of human rights being relegated to a subservient status, to be implemented through policy rather than law.

[1–01]

Over the last two decades, appreciation of the importance of acknowledging social and economic rights as core fundamental rights forming a central element of the human rights regime has grown, and, in the face of continuing breaches, attention has been drawn towards an analysis of what role, if any, the courts should play in their protection and vindication. Put simply, should these rights be justiciable? The term 'justiciability' refers to the ability to assert rights in a court and can have two meanings, depending on interpretation: either as something upon which the court will adjudicate, or, in the normative sense, an issue upon which it ought to adjudicate.[2] According to the legalistic approach, rights are meaningless unless they can be judicially reviewed and enforced.[3] Therefore, justiciability becomes an essential prerequisite to meaningful recognition as legal rights.

[1–02]

Convincingly, it has been argued that constitutionalisation, elevating social

[1–03]

---

[1] Universal Declaration of Human Rights (adopted 10 December 1948) UNGA Res 217A (III).
[2] Geoffrey Marshall, 'Justiciability' in AG Guest (ed), *Oxford Essays in Jurisprudence* (Oxford University Press 1961) 268.
[3] JK Mapulanga-Hulston, 'Examining the Justiciability of Economic Social and Cultural Rights' (2002) 6 International Journal of Human Rights 29, 37.

and economic rights to a comparable status with their civil and political counterparts, is the optimum approach.[4] That approach, while not without its flaws, is endorsed and advocated for herein as the superlative manner in which to protect such rights, as it raises them from subordinate status and affirms their place as fundamental human rights. It is a position which is gaining acceptance within international, regional and domestic systems and has resulted in direct and indirect constitutionalisation. The emergence of such acceptance demonstrates that the remaining objections to justiciability, considered in the next chapter, are ill-conceived.

[1–04]   In Ireland, while the courts play an active role in protecting rights through robust judicial review procedures, they play an almost non-existent role in vindicating social and economic rights. This is primarily as a result of the Supreme Court's interpretation of Article 45 of the Constitution, together with its application of the separation of powers doctrine. Thus, the courts have found that these rights are more appropriately protected by the executive arm of the state.[5] While there have been isolated cases of judicial intervention, extreme care has been taken not to establish these rights generally.[6]

[1–05]   This stance has relegated the most fundamental necessities for human existence exclusively to the realm of political decisions and budgetary considerations. As a result of the economic recession in recent years, the detrimental effects of this standpoint have become apparent. With increasing regularity, reports have emerged in relation to the appalling living conditions endured by some

---

[4]   Paul O'Connell, *Vindicating Social Rights* (Routledge 2012); Conor Gearty and Virginia Mantouvalou, *Debating Social Rights* (Hart 2011); Katharine G Young, *Constituting Economic and Social Rights* (Oxford University Press 2012); Jeff King, *Judging Social Rights* (Cambridge University Press 2012).

[5]   *TD v Minister for Education* [2001] IESC 101; *Sinnott v Minister for Education* [2001] IESC 63.

[6]   For example, Laffoy J's judgment in *O'Donnell v South Dublin County Council* [2007] IEHC 204, where she determined that, in this particular case, the inadequate living conditions of the plaintiff breached the state's obligations, and awarded damages. However, she was careful to explicitly point out that nothing in her judgment should be taken to infer a positive obligation on the State to provide housing for all Traveller families. In *O'Donnell v South Dublin County Council* [2015] IESC 28, appealing the High Court decision [2008] IEHC 545, the Supreme Court awarded damages (remitted to the High Court to assess) on the basis of a breach of statutory duty, specifically in relation to one claimant and, again, refused to establish a precedent that the state has an obligation to provide housing.

council tenants,[7] the rise in homelessness,[8] and soaring poverty rates.[9] Political decisions have statistically had a disproportionate effect on the poorer sections of society.[10] A recent report suggests that poverty, particularly child poverty, is still increasing, with 18.7% of all children in Ireland now living in poverty.[11] In acknowledgement of the inadequacy of the current position and in affirmation of the emerging awareness that judicial intervention is necessary, the Constitutional Convention voted in 2014 to strengthen the legal position of social and economic rights.[12] This recommendation advocates for specific inclusion of particular social and economic rights in the text of the Constitution.[13] However,

---

[7]   International Federation for Human Rights (FIDH) lodged a collective complaint with the European Committee on Social Rights on 21 July 2014, alleging breaches of the European Social Charter for substandard accommodation in certain council properties. Full text of the complaint is available at <www.coe.int/t/dghl/monitoring/socialcharter/complaints/CC110CaseDoc1_en.pdf> last accessed 06 January 2017. This case was declared admissible in March 2015 and we are currently awaiting a decision from the Committee. See Cianan Brennan, 'Ireland is facing a human rights case over the awful state of social housing here' *Journal.ie* (Dublin, 24 March 2015) <www.thejournal.ie/social-housing-human-rights-2009407-Mar2015> last accessed 06 January 2017.

[8]   Focus Ireland estimates that there are almost 7,000 people who are officially homeless in Ireland. While the highest percentage of people accessing homeless services were single adults, there has been a significant increase (40%) in families staying in emergency accommodation. In November 2016, there were 2,549 children living in emergency accommodation, in hostels, bed-and-breakfasts and hotels. See <www.focusireland.ie/resource-hub/about-homelessness/> last accessed 06 January 2017. Census 2016 also included a section on homelessness. However, at the time of writing, this report has not been published.

[9]   Social Justice Ireland, 'Policy Briefing–Poverty, Deprivation and Inequality' (July 2016) available at <www.socialjustice.ie/sites/default/files/attach/publication/4471/2016-07-04-sjipolicybriefingpoverty2016final2.pdf> last accessed 06 January 2017.

[10]   Social Justice Ireland, 'Budget 2017 Analysis and Critique' (October 2017) available at <www.socialjustice.ie/sites/default/files/attach/publication/4566/2016-10-12-budget2017responsefinalweb.pdf> last accessed 06 January 2017.

[11]   Rory Hearne and Cian McMahon, *Cherishing all Equally 2016, Economic Inequality in Ireland* (TASC 2016) 57.

[12]   The Convention was established by Resolution of the Houses of the Oireachtas of July 2012. The Convention was tasked with examining and making proposals on specified areas of the Constitution. However, it also had scope to receive recommendations on other issues. On 17 December 2013, the Convention announced, in its press release, that it would hear submissions on social and economic rights in its final sittings and make recommendations on the amendment of the Constitution to include same. These meetings were held in February 2014. Full terms of reference can be found at <www.constitution.ie/Convention.aspx#terms-of-reference> last accessed 24 November 2016.

[13]   This recommendation was passed by 85% of the participants. The Convention also recommended specific protection for those with disabilities and recognition of cultural and linguistic rights. A full breakdown of the votes is available at <www.constitution.ie/AttachmentDownload.ashx?mid=adc4c56a-a09c-e311-a7ce-005056a32ee4> last accessed 24 November 2016.

implementation would require a referendum,[14] which does not appear to be on the political agenda at the time of writing.[15]

[1–06]   This book provides a comprehensive examination of Ireland's relationship with social and economic rights, both in the domestic system and internationally. In doing this, it seeks to determine whether the position taken by Ireland, considered in Chapter 3, has had the effect of rendering it in breach of its international obligations. The four main treaties to which Ireland is a party and which protect these rights are examined in turn. An overview is provided in the chapter outline below.

[1–07]   This book seeks to demonstrate, first, that the position taken in the domestic system is significantly lacking. Secondly, it seeks to identify the struggles experienced by international and regional systems in advancing legal protection for social and economic rights, primarily due to their perceived subservient nature. These difficulties, borne out of ill-conceived fears, budgetary concerns, and a dominant neo-liberal agenda, render the practical use of these international treaties in the domestic system of little effect. While there have been slight and important changes to these rights within the treaties examined, the caveats limit their applicability and enforceability, both within that system itself and in the member states.

[1–08]   In each of the chapters, a similar theme emerges. The force accorded to social and economic rights is lesser than that of civil and political rights. There is a lesser requirement on the state to take immediate action to ameliorate a breach of rights, there is an appreciable lack of any enforcement mechanisms where the state is found to have violated a right and further there is a paucity of remedies available.

[1–09]   As a silver lining, however, the European Court of Human Rights is emerging as somewhat of an unlikely champion of social and economic rights. The European Convention on Human Rights (ECHR) is a treaty which textually protects only civil and political rights. However, the Court has been assiduous in affirming the interdependence, interrelatedness and indivisibility of all rights and has read social and economic rights into the existing provision. Essentially,

---

14   Article 46.2 of the Constitution provides that any amendment by way of 'variation, addition or repeal' to the text of the Constitution can only be done by way of a referendum.

15   To date, there have been three Private Members' Bills introduced to the Dáil, calling for such a referendum. The Twenty-First Amendment of the Constitution (No. 3) Bill 1999, introduced by Ruairi Quinn, was defeated. The Thirty–First Amendment of the Constitution (Economic, Social and Cultural Rights) Bill 2012, introduced by Kevin Humphries, has not progressed and, most recently, the Thirty-Fourth Amendment of the Constitution (Economic, Social and Cultural Rights) Bill 2014, introduced by Thomas Pringle, was voted down on 20 May 2015. These Bills are available to view at <www. oireachtas.ie/viewdoc.asp?m=&DocID=-1&CatID=59> last accessed 24 November 2016.

the approach taken by the European Court is that if the deprivation is such that it affects a textual right, it will be justiciable within the court. The significance of this is that the European Court delivers a legally binding judgment and can also award remedies to an applicant. This may provide an avenue to advance the justiciability of social and economic rights in Ireland.

Chapter Outline

Having provided a broad overview in Chapter 1, Chapter 2 examines the [1–10] theoretical framework in which social and economic rights sit. While these rights have historically been relegated to a subordinate status to their civil and political counterparts, this chapter sets out the case for equivalent legal protection, by way of constitutionalisation. It argues that constitutionalisation, and not merely legalisation, is necessary in order to bridge the gap between the two sets of rights and to ensure conformity with all rights. It then goes on to analyse the three main arguments proffered by those opposing justiciability, namely, characterisation, capability and democratic legitimacy. This chapter establishes that, in theory, there is no barrier to constitutionalising social and economic rights.

Chapter 3 analyses the position of social and economic rights within the [1–11] constitutional framework of Ireland. The interpretation of these rights taken by the Supreme Court in *TD v Minister for Education* establishes their place in the constitutional order.[16] Despite certain isolated cases, the judgment in *TD* stands – social and economic rights are non-justiciable. This chapter identifies two ways in which the courts might make these rights justiciable, either directly, through an expansion of the existing doctrine of unenumerated rights, or indirectly, through an expansive interpretation of the right to life. Comparisons are drawn with India, Canada and South Africa in this regard to illustrate the options available to the court and their potential effects. Further, Chapter 3 argues that, by relying solely on the separation of powers to justify this stance, the court is arguably creating a situation which the doctrine was designed to prohibit. Establishing conclusively that the domestic judicial system does not protection social and economic rights in any meaningful way, the remaining chapters are dedicated to examining the international treaties to which Ireland is a party.

Chapter 4 turns to examine the International Covenant on Economic Social and [1–12] Cultural Rights (ICESCR), adopted in 1966 as a counterpart to the International Covenant on Civil and Political Rights (ICCPR), when agreement could not be reached on the incorporation of the UDHR into one legally enforceable document. The provisions of the ICESCR are (in stark contrast to the definitive, positive and immediate obligations contained within the ICCPR) to be

---

[16] [2001] IESC 101.

implemented progressively and subject to available resources. Further, there was no individual complaints mechanism for violations of the ICESCR, resulting in the Committee being involved solely in a monitoring process under the periodic review. In 2008, the optional protocol created an individual complaints mechanism, where, for the first time, violations of the ICESCR could be heard. However, as this chapter examines, the optional protocol suffers from some potentially fatal flaws. Chapter 4 goes on to examine Ireland's record under the periodic review procedure, in order to determine whether or not the Committee is of the view that social and economic rights are being adequately protected within the domestic system, by reference to its concluding observations.

[1–13]   Chapter 5 considers the European Social Charter (ESC), the Council of Europe's ICESCR. Like the difficulties faced by the UN in transposing the UDHR, the Council of Europe submitted to the same arguments, thus drafting two human rights documents. The ECHR protects civil and political rights, whereas the ESC safeguards social and economic rights. Initially, the committee overseeing the ESC did not have any purview to hear complaints, but under its revitalisation in 1996, a collective complaints mechanism was introduced to supplement the periodic reporting structure. The considerable issues with this treaty are examined as is Ireland's record, under the periodic review and the reports of the Committee and also under the cases which have been taken against Ireland.

[1–14]   Chapter 6 focuses on the Charter of Fundamental Rights for the European Union (CFR), which has the effect and status of an EU treaty, by virtue of the provisions of the Lisbon Treaty. This provides a comprehensive list of rights which ought to be protected by EU member states, including some social and economic rights. Given that two key concepts of EU law are that it is supreme to domestic provision and will have direct effect in national legal systems, it would seem that the EU was furthering justiciability of these rights. However, the potential effect of their inclusion is significantly diminished, as the CFR only applies in the application of EU law, and, given that the EU is primarily an economic institution, it rarely legislates for matters involving these rights. The interpretation adopted by the Court of Justice of the European Union to the role of the EU in protecting human rights generally is examined, along with the potential for the CFR to make real change to the status of social and economic rights in Ireland.

[1–15]   Chapter 7 examines the European Convention on Human Rights, a treaty which textually protects civil and political rights, but which has interpreted these to include social and economic rights. From its earliest cases, it refused to exclude the possibility of indirect incorporation, a position which has been consistently applied, resulting in a growing body of jurisprudence.[17] Transposed

---

[17]   Ellie Palmer, 'Protecting Socio-Economic Rights Through the European Convention

into Irish law by way of the European Convention on Human Rights Act 2003, the Convention has had a limited impact on the furtherance of rights generally within the domestic system. This is due, in part, to its incorporation at sub-constitutional level and, further, that the Constitution already provides comprehensive protection for civil and political rights.[18] A paucity of cases, and a dearth of literature in this area has limited the extent to which the potential of the 2003 Act has been tested in Irish law. While much has been written about the constitutional status of social and economic rights in Ireland, there remains a gap in the literature testing the theoretical possibilities of the 2003 Act. In interpreting the Constitution through the prism of the Act, in light of Convention jurisprudence, is indirect constitutionalisation possible?

Finally, Chapter 8 provides some concluding observations on the future   **[1–16]**
possibilities for judicially protecting social and economic rights in Ireland.

---

on Human Rights: Trends and Developments in the European Court of Human Rights' (2009) 2 Erasmus Law Review 397, 398.

[18] Fiona de Londras and Cliona Kelly, *European Convention on Human Rights Act; Operation, Impact and Analysis* (Roundhall 2010); Suzanne Egan, 'The European Convention on Human Rights Act: A Missed Opportunity for Domestic Human Rights Litigation' (2003) 25 Dublin University Law Journal 230; Ronagh McQuigg, 'The European Convention on Human Rights Act 2003 – Ten years on' (2014) 3 International Human Rights Law Review 61.

CHAPTER 2

Theoretical Perspectives on Social and Economic Rights

Introduction

As noted in Chapter 1, social and economic rights in Ireland are given virtually no legal protection. It is argued that justiciability, particularly through constitutionalisation, is the most effective way to protect social and economic rights as it elevates their status to that of their civil and political counterparts. The Irish courts have demurred from constitutionalising this category of rights, citing reasons of democratic legitimacy, given the implications for the distribution of state resources,[1] the result of which effectively insulates government action, or inaction, from judicial review in relation to social and economic rights.

[2–01]

Despite the official position in international law that the two sets of rights are universal, interdependent, interrelated and indivisible,[2] there remains deep disagreement regarding the status of social and economic rights. The subordination of these rights in international law created significant difficulties in the propagation of, and force accorded to, these rights in international, regional and domestic contexts.

[2–02]

Arguably, the debates which took centre stage between 1949 and 1966 have largely been concluded[3] with social and economic rights having been broadly recognised as human rights deserving of protection.[4] Whether or not the courts

[2–03]

---

[1] Gerard Hogan, 'Directive Principles, Socio-Economic Rights and the Constitution' (2001) 179 Irish Jurist 1; Gerry Whyte, 'A Tale of Two Cases – Divergent Approaches of the Irish Supreme Court to Distributive Justice' (2010) 1 Dublin University Law Journal 365; Paul O'Connell, *Vindicating Social Rights* (Routledge 2012).

[2] Vienna Declaration and Programme of Action (adopted 12 July 1993) UNGA A/CONF.157/23.

[3] Malcolm Langford, 'The Justiciability of Social Rights' in Malcolm Langford (ed), *Social Rights Jurisprudence: Emerging Trends in International and Comparative Law* (Cambridge University Press 2008) 3; Kristin Henrard, 'Introduction: The Justiciability of ESC Rights and the Interdependence of all Fundamental Rights' (2009) 2 Erasmus Law Review 373; Paul O'Connell, 'The Death of Socio-Economic Rights' (2011) 74 Modern Law Review 532.

[4] Langford (n 3) 3; Philip Alston and Ryan Goodman, *International Human Rights: The Successor to International Human Rights in Context* (Oxford University Press 2013) ch 4.

are the appropriate forum in which to vindicate these rights lies at the heart of contemporary disputes.

From Aspirational to Legal: Contemporary Debates on Social and Economic Rights

[2–04]   The legalistic approach to human rights determines that rights are meaningless unless they can be enforced in a court of law.[5] However, there is little agreement on whether the courts can 'competently and legitimately' adjudicate upon social and economic rights.[6] Though it is generally accepted that the state has a duty to protect the poor and vulnerable, the question remains of which branch of the state should be responsible for this.

[2–05]   Consideration must be given to whether constitutionalisation of these rights effectively usurps the power of the executive[7] and whether the failure to constitutionalise represents an abdication of the court's intrinsic role to protect and vindicate fundamental rights.[8]

[2–06]   Opposing constitutionalisation, Conor Gearty argues that, if social and economic rights are to be made justiciable, this should be done solely by way of legalisation.[9] This is an important distinction to be addressed: whether constitutionalisation is necessary to adequately protect social and economic rights or whether the court should have a limited role, prescribed by the legislature.

Constitutionalisation or Legalisation

[2–07]   Before delving into the objections generally proffered against justiciability, it is necessary to emphasise the reasons why constitutionalisation, and not merely legalisation, is crucial for effective protection. Legalisation commends issues

---

5   JK Mapulanga-Hulston, 'Examining the Justiciability of Economic, Social and Cultural Rights' (2002) 6 International Journal of Human Rights 29, 37.

6   Alana Klein, 'Judging as Nudging: New Governance Approaches for the Enforcement of Constitutional Social and Economic Rights' (2008) 39 Columbia Human Rights Law Review 351, 353.

7   This argument, as explained by Katharine G Young, *Constituting Economic and Social Rights* (Oxford University Press 2012) 134, establishes two polar extremes in the debate. If the court does adjudicate, it is usurping the powers of the executive, but if it does not, it is abdicating its duty to protect and vindicate human rights.

8   Claire-Michelle Smyth, 'Social and Economic Rights in the Irish Courts and the Potential for Constitutionalisation' in Tom Hickey, James Gallen and Laura Cahillane (eds), *Judges, Politics and the Irish Constitution* (Manchester University Press 2017) (forthcoming).

9   Conor Gearty and Virginia Mantouvalou, *Debating Social Rights* (Hart 2011) 55; Herman Schwartz, 'Do Economic and Social Rights Belong in a Constitution?' (1995) 10 American Journal of International Law and Policy 1233, also argues that constitutionalisation is not a necessity for effective judicial protection.

to the legislature, while constitutionalisation ascribes decision-making power to the courts. Within this distinction, Gearty asserts the possibility that it would be permissible, in certain circumstances, for the court to become involved in cases of social and economic rights, but only as secondary actors, leaving primary responsibility with the political arms of the state.[10] In other words, the courts can enforce the legislation, but no further. A similar argument is put forth by Ellen Wiles, who suggests that certain safeguards or qualifications should be placed on the judiciary in determining these rights.[11] This is somewhat akin to the doctrine of 'due deference', under which the courts would defer to legislative expertise.[12] This concessionary approach effectively makes social and economic rights justiciable, albeit within the confines of the legislation.

A compelling counter-argument, as identified by Jeff King, is that there is a lack of legislative focus.[13] He draws on the UK case of *Bellinger v Bellinger*, which challenged the provisions of the Matrimonial Causes Act 1973, for its failure to include the marriages of post-operative transsexuals.[14] Despite the claim being rejected in the High Court[15] and the Court of Appeal,[16] the House of Lords issued its first declaration of incompatibility under section 4 of the Human Rights Act 1998,[17] by following the jurisprudence of the European Court of Human Rights.[18] The issue of marriage for post-operative transsexuals was clearly something that the legislature had not considered during drafting.[19] **[2–08]**

Further, even in circumstances where the intention of the legislature is clear, given changing societal norms and evolving human rights standards, the court ought to have the capacity to interpret the legislation in light of emerging standards.[20] **[2–09]**

---

[10] Gearty and Mantouvalou (n 9) 55.
[11] Ellen Wiles, 'Aspirational Principles or Enforceable Rights? The Future for Social and Economic Rights in National Law' (2006) 22 American University International Law Review 35, 63.
[12] Richard A Edwards, 'Judicial Deference under the Human Rights Act' (2002) 65 Modern Law Review 859, 860.
[13] Jeff King, *Judging Social Rights* (Cambridge University Press 2012) 164.
[14] [2003] UKHL 21.
[15] [2001] I FLR 389.
[16] [2002] Fam 150.
[17] The House of Lords declared that the legislation was incompatible with Articles 8 and 12 of the European Convention on Human Rights.
[18] *Goodwin v UK* (2002) 35 EHRR 18.
[19] For further discussion of this case and surrounding issues, see Sharon Cowan, 'That Woman is a Woman! The Case of Bellinger v Bellinger and the Mysterious (Dis) Appearance of Sex' (2004) 12 Feminist Legal Studies 79; Ralph Sandland, 'Feminism and the Gender Recognition Act 2004' (2005) 13 Feminist Legal Studies 43; Hollin K Dickerson, 'Vindication without Substance: Gender Recognition and the Human Rights Act' (2005) 40 Texas International Law Journal 807.
[20] This is known as dynamic statutory interpretation. See William N Eskridge Jr, 'Dynamic Statutory Interpretation' (1987) 135 University of Pennsylvania Law Review 1479;

[2–10]   The controversy in rigidly applying legislation without regard to such considerations is evident from the case of *R (Pearson and Martinez) v Secretary of State for the Home Department*, where the court observed that:

> In deference to the legislature courts should not easily be persuaded to condemn what has been done, especially where it has been done in primary legislation after careful evaluation and against a background of increasing public concern about crime.[21]

In upholding the prohibition of convicted felons from voting in elections, the court deferred to the legislature, relying on the Forfeiture Act, a statute enacted in 1870,[22] and taking little account of any changing societal standards, a position which has been found to be in breach of the European Convention on Human Rights.[23] Practically, if the role of courts is limited to the enforcement of duly-enacted legislation, laws which violate human rights will remain unchecked, which is wholly inappropriate and a clear abdication of duty.

[2–11]   Consequently, Paul O'Connell concludes, as fundamental rights, social and economic rights should be constitutionalised and not merely provided for in legislation. He articulates two main reasons for this approach. First, legislation, which may be repealed or modified, implies that these rights are elective or non-compulsory, and are, in essence, 'charity to the deserving poor', rather than a fulfilment of an obligation. Secondly, in hierarchical terms, statutory rights are of lower rank than constitutional rights.[24] Additionally, TRS Allan questions whether fundamental values can be 'defined' in statute at all, asserting that judgments of value are inextricably linked with context, something that legislation cannot provide.[25]

[2–12]   Therefore, courts would have their efforts vitiated if the legislature could

---

William N Eskridge Jr, *Dynamic Statutory Interpretation* (Harvard University Press 1994); Anthony D'Amato, 'The Injustice of Dynamic Statutory Interpretation' (2010) 64 University of Cincinnati Law Review 1996.

[21] *R (Pearson and Martinez) v Secretary of State for the Home Department* [2001] HRLR 39 [20] (Kennedy LJ).

[22] Cases brought before the European Court of Human Rights have since held that this blanket ban on voting for convicted felons is a breach of Article 3, Protocol 1 of the Convention in *Hirst (No.2) v UK* (2006) 42 EHRR 41; *MT v UK* App No. 60041/08 and 60054/08 (ECtHR, 11 April 2011) and *McHugh & Others v UK* App No. 51987/08 (ECtHR, 10 February 2015). See Susan Easton, 'Electing the Electorate: The Problem of Prisoner Disenfranchisement' (2006) 69 Modern Law Review 443; Steve Foster, 'Reluctantly Restoring Rights: Responding to the Prisoner's Right to Vote' (2009) 9 Human Rights Law Review 489.

[23] Edwards (n 12) 861.

[24] O'Connell (n 1) 6.

[25] RTS Allan, 'Human Rights and Judicial Review: A Critique of Due Deference' (2006) 65 Cambridge Law Journal 671, 674.

simply repeal any law or policy, thereby making any ruling null and void. Identifying social and economic rights as constitutional rights affirms their status as fundamental rights which cannot be changed at the whims of succeeding governments and ministers. They 'should not be at the mercy of changing governmental policies and programmes',[26] but rather, rights to basic goods '*ought* to be above politics'.[27]

The distinction in Ireland between constitutional rights and legal rights is [2–13] important, not only because legislation may change, but also in terms of the protection that the court must afford the right. In *DPP v Healy*, Finlay CJ declared that to classify the right to legal advice as merely legal would be to 'undermine its importance and the completeness of the protection of it which the courts are obliged to give'.[28] It has been a serious normative defect to exclude an entire category of rights from the rubric of constitutional order.

However, constitutionalisation alone, while the superior option, may not be [2–14] sufficient without also engaging with the underlying political climate. The rise of neo-liberal globalisation, which is at foundational levels 'antagonistic' to the judicial protection of social and economic rights, must be addressed.[29] As globalisation of economic markets dominate political discourse,[30] the drive towards commodification and the 'transformation of all social relations to economic relations' serves the economic elite to the detriment of the imposition of obligations on the state to provide.[31] This market globalisation has permeated the judiciary to create what Anne-Marie Slaughter terms 'transjudicial communication',[32] which defines and strengthens political and economic values within the communicating states.[33] With the political discourse centring on growing markets and capitalist ideals, the judicial development of social and

---

[26] Asbjørn Eide and Allan Rosas, 'Economic, Social and Cultural Rights: A Universal Challenge' in Asbjørn Eide, Catarina Krause and Allan Rosas (eds), *Economic Social and Cultural Rights; A Textbook* (2nd edn, Martinus Nijhoff 2001) 6.

[27] Gearty and Mantouvalou (n 9) 108.

[28] [1990] 2 IR 73, 81.

[29] O'Connell, 'The Death of Socio-Economic Rights' (2011) 74(4) Modern Law Review 532.

[30] See generally, Arthur MacEwan, *Neo-Liberalism or Democracy? Economic Strategy, Markets and Alternatives for the 21st Century* (Zed Books Ltd 1999); Paul O'Connell, 'On Reconciling Irreconcilables: Neo-Liberal Globalisation and Human Rights (2007) 7 Human Rights Law Review 483.

[31] See generally, David Harvey, *A Brief History of Neoliberalism* (Oxford University Press 2005).

[32] This relates to an international judicial network established through international conferences and colloquia. See Christopher McCrudden, 'A Common Law of Human Rights? Transnational Judicial Conversations on Constitutional Rights' (2000) 20 Oxford Journal of Legal Studies 199.

[33] Anne-Marie Slaughter, 'A Typology of Transjudicial Communication' (1994) 29 University of Richmond Law Review 99.

economic rights is hampered through a reflection of values which enhance the 'transnational economic elites'.[34]

[2–15] Thus, it is not argued that the constitutionalisation of social and economic rights is free from flaws. Clearly, political considerations, particularly where judges are political appointees, will have an impact upon the interpretation and application of rights.[35] However it is the optimum manner in which they *may* be protected. Complete exclusion of the judiciary results in the relegation of these rights to the realm of policy, which is liable to change with each succeeding minister, with no recourse to any legal enforcement. Restricting the court's role to enforcement of legislation impedes the development and content of the right, taking no account of the contextual element of a given case.

[2–16] There is, however, significant opposition to the constitutionalisation of social and economic rights. Gearty, in his opposition, draws heavily on the refusal of the Joint Committee on Human Rights in the United Kingdom to recommend them as justiciable rights within a proposed Bill of Rights.[36] The Committee provided three main reasons for this approach. First, these rights could only be vaguely expressed and this would increase the potential for lengthy and boundless litigation against public bodies.[37] Secondly, the incorporation of these rights would be undemocratic in nature, as it would open matters of purely political concern to scrutiny by the judiciary.[38] Finally, any adjudication upon such rights would require judges to make decisions that they are ill-equipped to make, given the complexity of these rights.[39] In addition, Gearty discerns further difficulties and objections, centring on the competence of the courts,[40] issues of enforceability relating to the potential of on-going court supervision and threats

---

[34] O'Connell (n 29) 540.
[35] See generally, Orley Ashenfelter, Theodore Eisenberg and Stewart J Schwab, 'Politics and the Judiciary: The Influence of Judicial Background on Case Outcomes' (1995) 24 Journal of Legal Studies 257; Michael JS Moran, 'Impartiality in Judicial Appointments: An Absent Concept' (2007) 10 Trinity College Law Review 5; Jennifer Carroll, 'You Be The Judge: A Study of the Backgrounds of Superior Court Judges in Ireland in 2004, Part 1' (2005) 5 Bar Review 153; Jennifer Carroll, 'You Be The Judge Part II: The Politics and Processes of Judicial Appointments in Ireland' (2005) 6 Bar Review 182.
[36] Gearty and Mantouvalou (n 9) 60. See also, Jemima Stratford, 'Joint Committee on Human Rights Report, A Bill of Rights for the UK? Proposed Approach to Social and Economic Rights' (2009) 1 Judicial Review 35.
[37] Joint Committee of Human Rights, 'A Bill of Rights for the UK?' Twenty Ninth Report of Session 2007-8, HL165, HC 150, 183-4.
[38] ibid 185-187.
[39] ibid 188-191.
[40] Gearty and Mantouvalou (n 9) 60. The argument of the court's competence is dealt with in more detail later in this chapter as a central argument against its involvement.

of 'undesirable outcomes'.[41] Essentially, these concerns can be categorised under three headings: characterisation, legitimacy, and institutional capacity.[42]

Characterisation

The objection to the justiciability of social and economic rights in terms of their content, obligation, and cost can be classified as one based on the character of these rights, suggesting that their normative content is too vague and that they necessarily impose costly positive obligations on the state and should, therefore, remain solely within the ambit of the political sphere.[43] This is redolent of the position of those who do not deny the existence, or indeed importance, of social and economic rights, but maintain that they belong within the political arena.

[2–17]

The first argument is that social and economic rights are less specific, less concrete than civil and political right, are subject to more debate as to their substance and therefore are 'quintessentially political' in nature.[44] This is countered by Pius Langa, who argues that the reason for any vagueness is due to their exclusion from adjudication.[45] It can equally be argued that many civil and political rights were equally vague, but, through consistent judicial review ,the parameters and content of these rights have been developed.[46]

[2–18]

Gearty argues that the lack of specificity inherent in these rights would require a novel and radical shift in the style of analysis undertaken by the courts, which

[2–19]

---

41 He provides the example of such an undesirable outcome as, if courts can issue orders and enforce social and economic rights, taxes may have to be raised in order to meet the cost of fulfilling the order. Gearty and Mantouvalou (n 9) 63.

42 Aoife Nolan, Bruce Porter and Malcolm Langford, 'The Justiciability of Social and Economic Rights: An Updated Appraisal' (2007), NYU School of Law, Centre for Human Rights and Global Justice, Working Paper 15/2007 6. They are referred to as 'vague, costly and institutionally complex' by Klein (n 6) 360.

43 Mark Tushnet, 'Reflections on Judicial Enforcement of Social and Economic Rights in the Twenty First Century' (2011) 4 National University of Juridical Sciences 177, 178.

44 Gearty and Mantouvalou (n 9) 53; EW Vierdag, 'The Legal Nature of the Rights Granted by the International Covenant on Economic, Social and Cultural Rights' (1978) 9 Netherlands Yearbook of International Law 69; Michael J Dennis and David P Stewart, 'Justiciability of Economic, Social and Cultural Rights: Should there be an International Complaints Mechanism to Adjudicate the Rights to Food, Water, Housing and Health?' (2004) 98 American Journal of International Law 462.

45 Puis Langa, 'Taking Dignity Seriously–Judicial Reflections on the Optional Protocol to the ICESCR' (2009) 27 Nordic Journal of Human Rights 33.

46 This is particularly so when the court has determined and expanded upon the precise contours of what is required in order to secure the right to a fair trial. For examples and analysis, see Eva Brems, 'Conflicting Human Rights: An Exploration in the Context of the Right to a Fair Trial In the European Convention for the Protection of Human Rights and Fundamental Freedoms' (2005) 27 Human Rights Quarterly 294; Paul Mahony, 'Right to a Fair Trial in Criminal Matters Under Article 6 ECHR' (2004) 4 Judicial Studies Institute Journal 107.

could result in a backlash from other sections of society.[47] Historically, the same could be said of cases concerning civil and political rights. One salient example comes from the United States Supreme Court in *Brown v Board of Education*.[48] Here, the court departed from its reasoning of past decisions and held that racial segregation in educational facilities was unconstitutional. This decision incited a surge in activity from the white supremacist movement. Yet, the legacy of this judgment cannot be disregarded. It led to significant change in racial relations, the desegregation of public services and accommodation cascaded through the southern United States with judges declaring segregation laws invalid. Further this case acted as the catalyst for the enactments of the Civil Rights Act.[49] The conditions in the United States prior to the *Brown* decision illustrate the difficulties of placing human rights exclusively within the political sphere. Before *Brown*, segregation remained insulated from meaningful scrutiny. It was only by the intervention of the Supreme Court, declaring the unconstitutionality of the practice, that action became possible. To leave these rights solely within the remit of the political realm is to promulgate, retain, and affirm existing policies, which systematically occasion violations in the first instance.

[2–20]   Devising a distinction between civil and political rights on the one hand as worthy of judicial protection, and social and economic rights on the other as purely political, is misguided, as the two are not mutually exclusive. This divergence is often accomplished by categorising corresponding obligations as either positive or negative. In traditional terms, civil and political rights were deemed to impose negative obligations, as they act to restrain the state from certain actions, while social and economic rights were seen as imposing positive, and expensive, obligations upon the state.[50] This is clearly an oversimplification of the issue, creating a false dichotomy, as all human rights contain an amalgamation of both positive and negative obligations. Many civil rights, such as those which seek to ensure the right to a fair trial, impose positive obligations on the state (and are costly to enforce), while preventing evictions might require the state to refrain from an action.[51] Thus, the assertion that social and economic rights are naturally expensive is questionable.[52] Internationally, the notion that all rights contain both positive and negative obligations has gained broad acceptance, particularly within the European Court of Human Rights.[53] Additionally, there have been several high profile cases in different jurisdictions, which have served

---

[47]   Gearty and Mantouvalou (n 9) 48.

[48]   347 US 483 (1954).

[49]   See generally, Martha Minow, *In Brown's Wake: Legacies of America's Educational Landmark* (Oxford University Press 2010).

[50]   See generally, Alston and Goodman (n 4) 277-310; DM Davis, 'The Case Against the Inclusion of Socio Economic Demands in a Bill of Rights Except as Directive Principles' (1992) 8 South African Journal of Human Rights 475.

[51]   Examples given in Gearty and Mantouvalou (n 9) 110.

[52]   Wiles (n 11) 47.

[53]   *Airey v Ireland* [1979] 2 EHRR 305; Ellie Palmer 'Protecting Socio-Economic Rights

to confirm that vindicating social and economic rights does not always require positive action on the part of the state. Cases such as *Grootboom v Republic of South Africa*,[54] *Olga Tellis & Others v Bombay Municipal Council*[55] and *Attorney General v PHS Community Services Society (the 'Insite case')*[56] all show that this category of rights can be upheld and enforced effectively by the implementation of negative obligations.

Thus, it can be argued that it may be costly to administer rights generally. **[2–21]** Arguments relating to the characterisation of social and economic rights are misguided. Judicial intervention will concretise the scope and parameters of the right, allowing for a developmental approach. Further, once it is accepted that all rights contain an amalgamation of both positive and negative obligations, this argument loses considerable traction.

Institutional Capacity

A further argument against justiciability is the lack of expertise that judges may **[2–22]** possess in such matters. Indeed, this concern was echoed by the Constitution Review Group when they declined to recommend the inclusion of social and economic rights in 1996.[57] Those subscribing to this objection argue that there is no objective way for a judge to decide on the amount of an individual's welfare entitlement, such being political decisions.[58] However, in countering this proposition, it has been demonstrated that courts are often injected into controversies where specialist knowledge is required and this concern is without foundation, as:

> ... to suggest that economic rights issues should be dealt with exclusively by economists and others is tantamount to suggesting that civil and political rights issues should be seen as the exclusive domain of criminologists, trade unionists, psychologists, physicians, paediatricians, the clergy, communication experts and others.[59]

A critique of the court's capability to engage with this category of rights is that **[2–23]**

Through the European Convention on Human Rights: Trends and Developments in the European Court of Human Rights' (2009) 2 Erasmus Law Review 397.

54   2000 ZACC 19.
55   [1985] 2 Supp SCR 51.
56   [2011] 3 SCR 134.
57   The Constitution Review Group, *Report of the Constitution Review Group* (Dublin Stationery Office 1996).
58   Tara Usher, 'Adjudication of Social and Economic Rights: One Size Does Not Fit All' (2008) 1 UCL Human Rights Review 155, 159.
59   Philip Alston, 'US Ratification of the Covenant on Economic Social and Cultural Rights: The Need for an Entirely New Strategy' (1990) 84 American Journal of International Law 365, 375.

it is ill-equipped to determine polycentric situations.[60] Cases which involve, or will result in, budgetary allocations are classically polycentric. The fear is that adjudicating upon these types of cases will have unintended consequences, encourage unorthodox solutions, or cause courts to avoid the complexity and implications of cases in order to mould the problem into a more manageable form.[61] It has been contended that traditional adversarial court proceedings are unsuited to such disputes, which could more properly be determined through the parliamentary process.[62] However, this is not unique to matters associated with social and economic rights, and many cases of civil and political rights (for example, in ensuring access to legal aid in order to secure the right to a fair trial) involve similar polycentric issues.

[2–24]   In rejecting that polycentricity is a bar to justiciability, the South African High Court has stated that:

> The problems of polycentricity must clearly act as important constraints upon the adjudication process, particularly when the dispute has distributional consequences. But polycentricity cannot be elevated to jurisprudential mantra, the articulation of which serves, without further analysis, to render courts impotent to enforce legal duties which have unpredictable consequences.[63]

Unequivocally, King considers this the most overstated objection to the constitutionalisation of social and economic rights, as courts regularly engage in polycentric adjudication, and all constitutional rights have budgetary implications. [64]

[2–25]   Questioning the court's ability to determine these rights on the basis that they lack the capacity accordingly infers that the executive possesses the requisite expertise. It is argued that this is not necessarily the case. In December 2014, a homeless man died,[65] virtually on the steps of Leinster House,[66] as a result of which an emergency forum on homelessness was called.[67] During political

---

[60]   Polycentric, in this context, refers to the fact that the judgment will have considerable implications outside of the particular case before it. This was argued by Lon Fuller, 'The Forms and Limits of Adjudication' (1978) 92 Harvard Law Review 353, discussed in King (n 13) 190-193; JWF Allison 'Fuller's Analysis of Polycentric Disputes and the Limits of Adjudication' (1994) 53 Cambridge Law Journal 367.

[61]   King (n 13) 192.

[62]   Usher (n 58) 159.

[63]   *Rail Commuter Action Group & Ors v Transnet Limited & Ors*, High Court, Cape of Good Hope Provincial Division, Case No 10968/2001, [112].

[64]   King (n 13) 172.

[65]   Carol O'Brien and Steven Carroll, 'Campaigners warn of "grave risk" as homeless man dies near Dáil' *The Irish Times* (Dublin, 2 December 2014).

[66]   Leinster House is the name given to the building where the Dáil (Irish Parliament) sits.

[67]   Minister for the Environment Alan Kelly called the emergency meeting inviting council

discourse which followed in an attempt to achieve a solution to the growing number of homeless people, Billy Timmins, an Independent TD,[68] proposed legislation to criminalise 'sleeping rough', as a means of tackling the 'homeless problem'.[69] This shows a fundamental misunderstanding of homelessness generally and an inability, or an unwillingness, to adequately protect fundamental rights.

Evidentially, remitting these rights exclusively to the executive compounds their vulnerability. Excluding completely one category of rights from judicial review excessively restricts their development and implementation and, further, compounds their status as being inferior to their civil and political counterparts.　　**[2–26]**

Democratic Legitimacy

This argument, in essence, is that as adjudications on social and economic rights will have implications on resource allocation, such competence lies solely within the remit of the executive branch of the state. The distributive nature of remedies is central to this objection. Distributive justice is concerned with the distribution of society's wealth, supported by utilitarianism emphasising the common good and it has implications beyond the two parties to the case.[70] Conversely, commutative justice (or corrective justice), based on libertarianism, advocates and defines the protection of human rights in a negative manner.[71] Commutative justice requires the court to focus on restoring the victim to the position that they were in prior to the violating taking place.[72] It has been suggested that to engage in resource distribution usurps the role of the executive, as well as violates the comity between the separate branches of government. However, in models of deliberate democracy, adjudication enhances the democratic process by augmenting accountability. Further, once it is acknowledged that there is no clear distinction between the two sets of rights, there can be no breach of the separation of powers.[73]　　**[2–27]**

To suggest that engaging in matters which involve resource distribution is　　**[2–28]**

---

[68]　members, NGOs, representatives from the Department of Social Protection, the Health Service Executive and religious groups to discuss emergency measures to combat homelessness. This was held on 4 December 2014.

Teachta Dála is a member of Dáil Éireann, the equivalent of a member of parliament.

[69]　The full speech is available at <www.kildarestreet.com/debates/?id=2014-12-05a.5&s=speaker%3A18#g31> last accessed 8 January 2017.

[70]　Christopher Mbazira, 'Appropriate, Just and Equitable Relief in Socio-Economic Rights Litigation: Tension Between Corrective and Distributive Forms of Justice' (2008) 125 South African Journal of Human Rights 71, 78.

[71]　ibid 72.

[72]　Dinah Shelton, *Remedies in International Human Rights Law* (Oxford University Press 1999) 38. See also, Ernst J Weinrib, 'Corrective Justice in a Nutshell' (2002) 52 University of Toronto Law Journal 349.

[73]　Tushnet (n 43) 178.

undemocratic is to misunderstand the nature of democracy. In a democratic system, where decisions are made by majorities, policies which neglect social and economic rights are common. Conversely, part of the judicial role is to correct 'the deficiencies of the democratic system and their effects on the most vulnerable'.[74] This issue of failing to protect the marginalised is one that cannot reasonably be disputed by those who argue against justiciability. Instead, they reformulate the argument, stating that judicial review cannot provide an adequate remedy and therefore is not appropriate.[75] Mounting evidence shows this not to be the case. In several jurisdictions, court rulings have led to the immediate amendment or repeal of offending policy or legislation and, in the absence of immediate action, political pressure has been brought to bear on governments through public debate surrounding these rulings. Accordingly, these cases not only represent a victory for the individual who has successfully litigated her case, but also result in far-reaching change for all of those affected by the same violation.

[2–29]   As King notes, to cite concerns of democratic legitimacy as a reason to deny judicial protection for social and economic rights is to deny democracy itself, as:

> A just democracy depends on the guarantee of social human rights. In any such democracy that guarantee is delivered through a legislative programme of social rights, administered by a responsible executive and buttressed by the existence of legal accountability.[76]

While agreement has not yet been reached as to the role of the court in protecting and vindicating social and economic rights generally, the reasons given by those against justiciability evidence a fundamental misunderstanding of the nature of these rights. Objections based on characterisation, competency and democratic legitimacy have been comprehensively addressed and dismissed

Conclusion

[2–30]   The debate in relation to social and economic rights is far from settled. While its core content may have changed from its initial contours, it has not been conclusively resolved. It has been persuasively argued that justiciability, specifically through constitutionalisation, is the most favourable manner in which to protect social and economic rights.[77] The role of the court is essential, as it provides, not only accountability, but also a forum for voices to be heard,

---

[74] Gearty and Mantouvalou (n 9) 125.
[75] King (n 13) 165.
[76] ibid 187.
[77] O'Connell (n 1).

which is often absent from the political arena.[78] Legalisation by legislation unduly restricts the court's ability to expand and define the contours of rights, compounds their status as subordinate and renders them liable to repeal.

Clearly, the favoured, idealistic approach is to have social and economic rights constitutionalised in Ireland. Chapter 3 sets out the existing position in Ireland and establishes how this could, in fact, be done without the need for a referendum to explicitly include them in the text of the Constitution. With the courts reluctant to sway from their current stance, international and regional treaties are examined, in order to determine whether they can provide a solution to make these rights justiciable, if not constitutionalised. **[2–31]**

---

[78] Gearty and Mantouvalou (n 9) 116.

CHAPTER 3

Constitutional Protection of Social and Economic Rights in Ireland

Introduction

Ireland, to date, continues to subscribe to the notion that social and economic **[3–01]** rights remain beyond the purview of the judiciary. In determining that these rights are not encompassed within the rubric of fundamental rights protected by the Irish Constitution, the courts have predominantly relied on the democratic legitimacy objection. This chapter is dedicated to analysing and critiquing the legal status and judicial interpretation of social and economic rights in Ireland.

Beginning by briefly outlining the fundamental rights under the Constitution, **[3–02]** this chapter then considers their status and scope, together with restrictions and remedies. Having established that the placement of social and economic rights within the Constitution lie solely within the aspirational and non-justiciable Directives of Social Policy contained in Article 45 (with the exception of the right to free primary education), this chapter delves into their judicial interpretation. It analyses the landmark Supreme Court decisions of *Sinnott v Minister for Education*[1] and *TD v Minister for Education,*[2] before proceeding to observe the legacy of these judgments. The Supreme Court has, as will be demonstrated, taken an excessively restrictive approach to social and economic rights, resulting in inordinate difficulties for litigants bringing such claims.[3] It then proceeds to examine the potential avenues available to the court to constitutionalise without the need for a referendum.

The primary reason for the Supreme Court's refusal to engage in a meaningful **[3–03]** manner with social and economic rights centres on the democratic legitimacy objection, considering that engaging in distributive justice breaches the separation of powers. The final section of this chapter examines this rationale, identifying a number of flaws inherent in this reasoning. It further draws on comparisons with Canadian jurisprudence in order to illustrate the effective protection through the imposition of negative obligations, thereby obviating concerns in relation to expensive and resource intensive remedies.

---

[1]   [2001] IESC 63; [2001] 2 IR 545.
[2]   [2001] IESC 101; [2001] 4 IR 259.
[3]   Gerry Whyte, *Social Inclusion and the Legal System: Public Interest Law in Ireland* (Institute of Public Administration 2002) 359.

The Constitution of Ireland

[3–04]   In contrast to Ireland's first Constitution,[4] which was primarily concerned with the organisation, powers and function of the government of the Free State of Ireland, the 1937 Constitution[5] had the concept of sovereignty as its driving force.[6]

[3–05]   Of the fifty articles contained within the 1937 Constitution, five were expressly dedicated to fundamental human rights.[7] This represented advancement in the constitutional integration of human rights relative to other nations of this era and it was acclaimed as being 'ahead of its time'.[8]

[3–06]   The fundamental rights can be divided into two categories: express and implied rights. The express rights are those listed as fundamental rights within the text of the Constitution itself, while the implied rights (also known as unenumerated rights) have been created by the courts. These implied rights derived from an acknowledgment that there are additional rights protected by the Constitution although not expressly contained therein.

[3–07]   The inclusion of express rights was perceived as the incorporation of a Bill of Rights,[9] and, with the exception of education,[10] are exclusively civil and political in nature. It is debatable whether the drafters of the Constitution appreciated the importance of a legally enforceable right to education (particularly when all other social and economic rights are placed elsewhere), or whether this

---

4   Constitution of the Irish Free State (Saorstát Éireann) Act 1922. For analysis of the drafting and provisions of this Constitution, see Nicholas Mansergh, *The Irish Free State: Its Government and Politics* (George Allen & Unwin Ltd 1934); Hugh Kennedy, 'Character and Sources of Constitution of the Irish Free State' (1928) 14 American Bar Association Journal 437.

5   Bunreacht na hÉireann was approved by Dáil Éireann on 14 June 1937 and passed by referendum on 1 July 1937. See Deirdre McMahon, *Republicans and Imperialists: Anglo-Irish Relations in the 1930s* (Yale University Press 1984).

6   Tim Murphy, 'The 1937 Constitution – Some Historical Reflections' in Tim Murphy and Patrick Twomey (eds), *Ireland's Evolving Constitution 1937-1997* (Hart 1998) 12. See also, VTH Delaney, 'The Constitution of Ireland: Its Origins and Development' (1957) 12 University of Toronto Law Journal 1, 6-8; Sean Faughnan, 'The Jesuits and the Drafting of the Irish Constitution of 1937' (1988) 26 Irish Historical Studies 79.

7   Articles 40-44.

8   *A v Governor of Arbour Hill Prison* [2006] 4 IR 88, 145 (Denham CJ).

9   Michael Bertram Crowe, 'Human Rights, The Irish Constitution and the Courts' [1972] 47 Notre Dame Law Review 281, 289.

10   Article 42.4 states, 'The State shall provide for free primary education and shall endeavour to supplement and give reasonable aid to private and corporate educational initiative and, when the public good requires it, provide other educational facilities or institutions with due regard, however, for the rights of the parents, especially in the matter of religious or moral formation'.

was due to the legacy of education facilities provided under British rule.[11] The express rights include liberty,[12] equality,[13] the inviolability of the dwelling,[14] and protecting the good name and property of the person.[15] While the inclusion of a Bill of Rights was heralded as an innovative measure, the court's lack of interaction and engagement with these fundamental rights elicited criticism.[16]

Early jurisprudence testing the scope of these rights showed significant deference   [3–08]
to the legislature.[17] When considering the constitutionality of legislation which empowered the Minister to arrest and detain, without trial, persons engaging in particular behaviour,[18] the Supreme Court found that the balancing of the rights of an individual, against the rights of citizens as a whole, was a matter solely within the province of the Oireachtas.[19] Court Martials, which could impose the death penalty on civilians, established under the Emergency Powers (Amendment) (No.2) Act 1940[20] and a Special Criminal Court consisting solely of army personnel,[21] were also upheld as constitutional, with questions arising as to whether these fundamental rights would serve any useful purpose.

The 1960s saw the emergence of a Supreme Court more enthusiastic to test the   [3–09]
bounds, parameters and powers of the Constitution.[22] The revelation of implied (or unenumerated) rights in the Constitution saw unprecedented engagement with fundamental rights. It arose from an expansive interpretation of Article

---

[11] See generally, John Coolahan, *Irish Education: Its History and Structure* (Institute of Public Administration in Ireland 1981).

[12] Article 40.4.1 provides, 'No citizen shall be deprived of his personal liberty save in accordance with law.'

[13] Article 40.1 provides, 'All citizens shall, as human persons, be held equal before the law.'

[14] Article 40.5 provides, 'The dwelling of every citizen is inviolable and shall not be forcibly entered save in accordance with law.'

[15] Article 40.3.2 provides, 'The State shall, in particular, by its laws protect as best it may from unjust attack and, in the case of injustice done, vindicate the life, person, good name and property rights of every citizen.'

[16] Edward McWhinney, 'The Courts and the Constitution in Catholic Ireland' (1954) 29 Tulane Law Review 69, 70; Ronan Keane, 'Judges as Lawmakers: The Irish Experience' (2004) 4 Judicial Studies Institute Journal 1, 9, suggests an explanation for this may lie in the fact that the judiciary had been educated in the English system dominated by common law and parliamentary sovereignty.

[17] A practice continued from decisions under the 1922 Constitution, where the court did not develop the practical or normative content of fundamental rights. See Bertram Crowe (n 9) 286.

[18] Offences Against the State Act 1939 and Offences Against the State (Amendment Act) 1940.

[19] *In Re Article 26 of the Constitution and The Offences Against the State (Amendment) Bill 1940* [1940] IR 470 481 (Sullivan J).

[20] *Re McGrath and Harte* [1941] IR 68; *The State (Walsh) v Lennon* [1942] IR 122.

[21] In *Re McCurtain* [1941] IR 83, the argument that this effectively created a military tribunal was rejected and it was determined that the composition of courts was a matter entirely for the Oireachtas.

[22] Ruadhan MacCormaic, *The Supreme Court* (Penguin 2016).

40.3, where the High Court determined that it ultimately had jurisdiction to determine what rights were constitutionally protected.[23] Yet, the fact that there is no reference to unenumerated rights within the text of the document itself makes their genesis one of judicial activism.[24] The foundation of this doctrine is credited to the dictum of Kenny J in the landmark case of *Ryan v AG,* in which he stated:

> I think that the personal rights which may be involved to invalidate legislation are not confined to those specified in Article 40 but include all those rights which result from the Christian and democratic nature of the State.[25]

[3–10] This declaration, subsequently approved in the Supreme Court, of a hitherto unknown power of the court to declare rights beyond the explicit text of the Constitution, was a significant milestone.[26] This doctrine became the catalyst for the most innovative feature of Irish constitutional law, the gravity of which is one that would be difficult to overstate. While the applicant in *Ryan* was ultimately unsuccessful in her claim that compulsory fluoridation of the public water supply was a breach of her personal rights, the declaration of the unenumerated right to bodily integrity spurred a period of judicial activism, with the court discerning the existence of new fundamental rights. Among these, the right to privacy,[27] the right to earn a livelihood,[28] the right to travel,[29] the rights to marry and to found a family,[30] and the right to fair procedures were declared.[31]

[3–11] Opponents of the doctrine argue that *Ryan* was insufficiently justified and castigate it as being a deeply flawed decision, a 'legal aberration which no longer commands the authority of stare decisis'.[32] Questions were raised as to

---

[23] Article 40.3.1, 'The State guarantees in its laws to respect, and as far as practicable to vindicate the personal rights of the citizen.'

[24] Unlike the American Constitution, which expressly acknowledges the existence of unspecified rights. Amendment IX states, 'The enumeration in the Constitution of certain rights shall not be construed to deny or disparage others retained by the people'.

[25] *Ryan v AG* [1965] IR 294, 312.

[26] Gerard Hogan and Gerry Whyte, *JM Kelly: The Irish Constitution* (Bloomsbury Professional 2003) 1415.

[27] *McGee v Ireland* [1974] IR 284.

[28] First recognised by Kenny J in *Murtagh Properties v Cleary* [1972] IR 330.

[29] In *Ryan v AG* [1965] IR 294, a right to travel within the state was declared by Kenny J and broadened by Finlay P in *State (M) v AG* [1979] IR 73 to include a right to travel outside the state and to obtain a passport for this purpose.

[30] Recognised in *Ryan v AG* [1965] IR 294. See also, *Murray v AG* [1985] IR 532.

[31] *Garvey v Ireland* [1981] IR 75 elevated the common law position of procedural fairness in decision-making to an unenumerated right. See Hogan and Whyte (n 26) 1389-1494; Michael Forde and David Leonard, *Constitutional Law of Ireland* (3rd edn, Bloomsbury Professional 2013) ch 12.

[32] Desmond M Clarke, 'Unenumerated Rights in Constitution Law' (2011) 34 Dublin University Law Journal 101, 116.

how the judiciary could be trusted when using 'unpredictable ideas and sources of inspiration to justify their conclusions'.[33]

The judicial activism which created the doctrine has been condemned as *ultra* **[3–12]** *vires*, in that the power to declare new rights falls to the people, as represented by the legislature.[34] Where the courts annunciate new rights on an ad hoc basis, without explicit textual referents, this introduces elements of uncertainty into the law, leaving the state in the precarious position of not knowing precisely what rights it must respect.[35] Deemed to be 'supertextual',[36] an unprincipled expansion of judicial power[37] based upon vague and subjective rationale,[38] the introduction of implied rights into the Constitution was an unwelcome addition for many.

The initial zeal with which the courts embraced the power to declare unspecified **[3–13]** rights began to dwindle, in part due to unease with the legitimacy of the doctrine.[39] Keane CJ (dissenting), in *O'T v B,* took the view that, where there was no legislative provision in place, such:

> Did not justify the Courts in undertaking a task for which they lack, not merely the expert guidance available to the legislative arm, but also, and more crucially, the democratic mandate.[40]

Keane CJ further emphasised his point in *TD v Minister for Education,* where he surmised:

> Save where such an unenumerated right has been unequivocally established by precedent, as, for example, in the case of the right to travel or the right to privacy, some degree of judicial restraint is called for in identifying new rights of this nature.[41]

---

33 David Morgan, 'Judicial Activism – Too Much of a Good Thing?' in Murphy and Twomey (eds) (n 10) 107.

34 James Casey, 'Are there Unenumerated Rights in the Irish Constitution?' (2005) 23 Irish Law Times 123, 126.

35 John Kelly, *Fundamental Rights in the Irish Law and Constitution* (2nd edn, Oceana Publications 1967) 42.

36 Gearoid Carey, 'Police Targeting and Equality Rights' (2001) 19 Irish Law Times 8, 14.

37 Gerard Hogan, 'Unenumerated Personal Rights: Ryan's Case Re-evaluated' (1992) 25 Irish Jurist 95, 112.

38 Katharine Lesch Bodnick, 'Bringing Ireland up to Par: Incorporating the European Convention for the Protection of Fundamental Rights and Freedoms' (2003) 26 Fordham International Law Journal 396, 446.

39 Keane (n 16) 13.

40 [1998] 2 IR 321, 379.

41 [2001] IESC 101 [281]. This was an opinion reiterated by the Supreme Court in *BL v ML* [1992] 2 IR 77, where the previous High Court judgment was overruled on the basis that it purported to create a new right of a spouse to an interest in property based on work in the home, which was not supported by precedent.

[3–14] This is demonstrative of the fact that, in more recent years, the court appears to have reverted to its initial reluctance to develop fundamental rights, preferring to defer to the Oireachtas. David Morgan suggests that this is due to the difficulty in reconciling judicial activism in this area with Article 15.2.1, which gives the Oireachtas the role of sole lawmaker for the state.[42] However, there is legislative reluctance in dealing with morally or politically sensitive issues, leaving those embroiled in such potentially controversial matters with no option but to resort to the courts.[43]

The Scope of Fundamental Rights

[3–15] The fundamental rights in the Irish Constitution, both specified and unspecified, are not absolute and are subject to a number of qualifications. It has been judicially observed that 'it is difficult to identify a constitutional right that is unqualified; the right to life is not itself absolute'.[44]

[3–16] The primary restriction imposed on the fundamental rights in the Constitution is by way of a proportionality test, articulated by O'Higgins CJ as the 'circumstances in which the State may have to balance its protection of the right as against other obligations arising from regard for the common good'.[45]

[3–17] This requires the court to engage in balancing the individual's enjoyment of a fundamental right and the state's ability to restrict that freedom. There is nothing controversial or novel in this however, and, until relatively recently, the Supreme Court had given little guidance as to the precise parameters of the proportionality test.[46] In *Murphy v IRTC*, it enunciated that, in order to be proportionate, the measure must:

> (a) Be rationally connected to the objective and not be arbitrary, unfair or based on irrational considerations;
> (b) Impair the right as little as possible; and
> (c) Be such that its effects on the rights are proportional to the objective.[47]

[3–18] This test is even more nuanced where the competing rights are both constitutionally protected. Here, the Supreme Court has stated that there is a hierarchy of rights where one is characterised as superior and therefore prevails. There is some difficulty in formulating a precise list of which rights are superior

---

[42] David Morgan, 'Judicial Activism – Too Much of a Good Thing?' in Murphy and Twomey (eds) (n 10) 125.
[43] Clarke (n 32) 103.
[44] *Murray v Ireland* [1991] ILRM 465, 477 (McCarthy J).
[45] *Moynihan v Greensmith* [1977] IR 55, 71.
[46] Casey (n 34) 390.
[47] [1994] 3 IR 593, 607.

to others and this appears dependent solely on the facts of each particular case. For example, the right to life has been held to be superior to personal liberty,[48] the dissemination of information,[49] and to the inviolability of the dwelling,[50] while potentially being inferior to the right to bodily integrity.[51]

There is also restriction on who can assert and benefit from the fundamental rights. The reference in the Constitution to the 'citizen' excludes those who have not obtained this status.[52] The Supreme Court, in *Lobe and Osayande v The Minister for Justice Equality and Law Reform*,[53] was charged with determining whether the constitutional rights of a citizen child extended to the parents of that child.[54] Having regard to the legislative measures in place and upholding the deportation order, it determined that: **[3–19]**

> The state is entitled to expect that this legislative scheme will be respected. If the entire family of a failed asylum seeker is to acquire the right to continue to reside in the state as a result of the mere *"fortuity"* of a child being born in the state during, or, as in this case after the termination of the statutory procedures, this would set aside the whole carefully contrived system. It would result in the parents deriving substantial rights to which they are not entitled.[55]

Following this ruling, the practice of granting leave to remain to parents solely **[3–20]**

---

48 *DPP v Shaw* [1982] IR 1.
49 *Society for the Protection of Unborn Children Ireland Ltd v Open Door Counselling* [1988] IR 593.
50 *DPP v Delaney* [1997] 3 IR 453.
51 *AG v X* [1991] IR 1, 92 (Egan J).
52 Article 40.3.1.
53 [2003] IESC 3.
54 Article 2 previously represented a pure 'jus soli' provision of citizenship for those born within the Irish territory, stating, 'It is the entitlement and birth right of every person born on the island of Ireland, which includes its islands and seas to be part of the Irish nation.' As a result of a previous decision in *Fajujonu & Ors v Minister for Justice* [1990] 2 IR 151, wherein the Supreme Court found that the Irish child, as a citizen under the definition of Article 2, was entitled to the benefit of fundamental rights, including the care of their family. This case resulted in an appreciable number of parents obtaining legal status on the basis of having a child born in Ireland. The rise in numbers caused public concern and media storms, as detailed in Michael Breen and Eoin Deveraux, 'Setting up Margins: Public Attitudes and Media Construction of Poverty and Exclusion in Ireland' (2003) 2 Nordic Irish Studies 74, 87.
55 [2003] IESC 3 (Fennelly J). For further analysis of this case, see Bernard Ryan, 'The Celtic Cubs: Controversy over Birthright Citizenship in Ireland' (2004) 6 European Journal of Migration and Law 173; Ronit Lentin, 'Ireland: Racial State and Crisis Racism' (2007) 30 Ethnic and Racial Studies 610; Dianna J Shandy, 'Irish Babies, African Mothers: Rights of Passage and Rights in Citizenship in Post–Millennial Ireland' (2008) 81 Anthropological Quarterly 803.

on the basis of having an Irish born child ceased[56] and it was affirmed that the rights of the citizen attach to that person only and cannot extend benefit to a non-citizen relative. However, it should be noted that not all constitutional rights are inapplicable to those whose legal status has not yet been regularised. Rights, for example, to a fair trial, to fair procedures and against self-incrimination can be enforced by an asylum seeker.[57] It seems that the rights which non-citizens cannot assert are those which confer an associated benefit.[58]

[3–21]   Therefore, the fact that a right is expressed as a fundamental right in the Constitution does not mean that such a right is protected absolutely, and, as is evidenced above, must be balanced with other interests.

[3–22]   As such, should social and economic rights be incorporated into the Constitution they would be subject to the same restrictions as other fundamental rights.[59] Not only would proportionality be a key factor in determining the success of a claim, but the restriction as to who can assert constitutional rights would remain.

Remedies for Breach of Fundamental Rights

[3–23]   While the Constitution attributes the role of protecting fundamental rights to the courts, it does not specify how a given violation should be remedied.[60]

The courts have consistently articulated that for every breach of right, there must exist a corresponding remedy, otherwise a declaration would be without effect.[61]

[3–24]   Where a constitutional right is protected by way of legislation or common law, remedies for such would be contained therein. However, difficulties arise, as the courts have expressed that the Constitution protects other rights which are

---

[56] Department of Justice Press Release, 17 July 2003; for further analysis, see also, Liam Coakley and Claire Healy, 'Ireland's IBC/05 Administrative Scheme for Immigrant Residency, the Separation of Families and the Creation of Transnational Familial Imaginary' (2012) 50 International Migration 1.

[57] See *ED v DPP* [2011] IEHC 110.

[58] For further analysis of this point, see Liam Thornton, 'The Rights of Others: Asylum Seekers and Direct Provision in Ireland' (2014) 3(2) Irish Community Development Law Journal 22.

[59] See *Bringing ESC Rights Home: The Case for Legal Protection of Economic Social and Cultural Rights in Ireland* (Amnesty International 2014) 35-37.

[60] Article 34.1 states, 'Justice shall be administered in Courts established by law and by judges appointed in the manner prescribed in this Constitution.' Article 40.3 states, 'The state guarantees in its laws to respect and as far as practicable by its laws to defend and vindicate the personal rights of the citizen.'

[61] *Byrne v Ireland* [1972] IR 241.

not regulated by law and for which no legal provision exists, either to prohibit an anticipated infringement or to compensate for a past one.[62]

In *Meskell*, the court held that: **[3–25]**

> A right guaranteed by the Constitution or granted by the Constitution can be protected by action or enforced by action even though such action does not fit into any of the ordinary forms of action in either common law or equity and that a Constitutional right carries within it its own right to a remedy or the enforcement of it.[63]

The court can, therefore, fashion a remedy appropriate to the breach. While this is still subject to the restrictions outlined above, it evidences the power that the court possesses to award damages, or injunctive relief.[64]

Where a violation has caused loss or damage which can be quantified in monetary terms, and where the breach can be remedied with an award of compensation, courts exhibit a strong presumption in favour of awarding damages. **[3–26]**

Injunctive relief is also available to restrain an apprehended or continuing breach of a constitutional right, or to compel positive action to remedy the violation.[65] Such a remedy, however, is only available where the applicant can satisfy the court that injunctive relief is the only way to protect the right and damages are an inadequate remedy.[66] **[3–27]**

The simplified position is, therefore, that once one can establish the existence of **[3–28]**

---

[62] *W v Ireland (No.2)* [1997] IEHC 212; [1997] 2 IR 141.
[63] *Meskell v CIE* [1973] IR 121, 132.
[64] This applies both horizontally and vertically. See Sibo Banda, 'Taking Indirect Horizontality Seriously in Ireland: A Time to Magnify the Nuance' (2009) 31 Dublin University Law Journal 263; Stephen Gardbaum, 'The Horizontal Effect of Constitutional Rights' (2003) 2102 Michigan Law Review 387. Aoife Nolan argues that this horizontal effect could potentially apply to the enforcement of social and economic rights against non-state actors. An exploration of this is beyond the scope of this book, however, it is a logical conclusion that should they be constitutionalised, based on cases such as *Educational Company of Ireland v Fitzpatrick (No.2)* [1961] IR 345 that these rights could potentially be enforced against private entities, albeit in a negative manner. See Aoife Nolan, 'Holding Non-State Actors to Account for Constitutional Economic and Social Rights Violations: Experiences and Lessons from South Africa and Ireland' (2014) 12 International Journal of Constitutional Law 61.
[65] Hilary Delaney, *Equity and the Law of Trusts in Ireland* (5th edn, Roundhall 2011) 611-613; Ronan Keane, *Equity and the Law of Trusts in the Republic of Ireland* (2nd edn, Roundhall 2011) 292-295.
[66] *Lovett v Gogan* [1995] 3 IR 132. See also, James Roche, 'The Relevance of Constitutional Rights to the Granting of an Interlocutory Injunction' (2013) 12 Hibernian Law Journal 64.

a right, judicial intervention and vindication by means of an appropriate remedy will follow, subject to any restrictions which may apply.

Social and Economic Rights

[3–29]   While there is a relatively comprehensive catalogue of fundamental rights protected under the Constitution, these are, with the exception of the right to education, exclusively civil and political rights. Many newer European constitutions contain explicit protection for social and economic rights.[67] The Croatian Constitution,[68] the Charter of Fundamental Rights and Freedoms of the Czech Republic (which is justiciable under the Constitution of the Czech Republic)[69] the Constitution of Finland,[70] the Constitution of Moldova,[71] the Constitution of Hungary,[72] the Constitution of Poland,[73] the Constitution of Serbia,[74] and the Swiss Constitution,[75] provide express protection for various social and economic rights and for their judicial enforcement. In November 2016, the Slovenian Constitution was amended to include a justiciable right of everyone to 'drinkable water'.[76] Within the Irish Constitution, the only reference to social and economic rights is found within the Directive Principles of Social Policy, the non-justiciable Article 45. Thus, while acknowledging the existence of social and economic rights, the Constitution excludes them from the remit of judicial review,[77] and rather views them as a statement of moral principles

---

[67]   Identification of these provisions has been made by a search of world constitutions on <www.constitution.org/cons/natlcons.htm> last accessed 4 April 2015.

[68]   Entered into force on 22 December 1990, protecting the right to social assistance (Article 58), the right to healthcare (Articles 59 and 70) and the right to education (Article 66).

[69]   Entered into force on 1 January 1993, protecting the right to social assistance (Article 30), the right to health (Article 31) and the right to education (Article 33).

[70]   Entered into force on 1 March 2000, protecting the right to social security and housing assistance (s 19) and the right to education (s 16).

[71]   Entered into force on 29 July 1994, protecting the right to education (Article 35), the right of health security (Article 36), the right to live in a healthy environment (Article 37) and the right to social assistance to include food, clothing, shelter and medical care (Article 47).

[72]   Entered into force on 25 April 2011, protecting the right to education (Article XI), social security (Article XIX) the right to health (Article XX) and the right to decent housing conditions (Article XXII).

[73]   Entered into force on 2 April 1997, protecting the right to health (Article 68).

[74]   Entered into force on 8 November 2006, protecting the right to health (Article 68), the right to education (Article 71) and Social Protection (Article 69).

[75]   Entered into force on 18 April 1999, protecting the right to social assistance (Article 12) and the right to basic education (Article 19).

[76]   Article 70a of the Slovenian Constitution.

[77]   Gerard Quinn, 'Rethinking the Nature of Economic, Social and Cultural Rights in the Irish Legal Order' in Cathryn Costello (ed), *Fundamental Social Rights, Current European Legal Protection and the Challenge of the EU Charter on Fundamental Rights* (Trinity College 2001) 49.

which do not create positive rights.[78] Judicial attitudes toward their justiciability have developed against this backdrop and the resultant jurisprudence supports a clear division of rights.

In 2015, the UN Committee on Economic, Social and Cultural Rights, as part [3–30] of the periodic review process, raised questions in relation to the application of social and economic rights before the domestic courts in Ireland.[79] In response, Ireland stated that these rights are litigated through the Constitution and that 'the courts do not operate a rigid classification of rights which puts economic, social and cultural rights beyond their reach'.[80] This statement is at variance with the Supreme Court's interpretation of these rights.

The first case to test the position of social and economic rights within the [3–31] constitutional framework was *O'Reilly v Limerick Corporation*.[81] This case was brought by members of the Travelling community, who resided in an unofficial halting site in conditions of extreme poverty and deprivation. Their claim was that the Corporation had an obligation to provide them with a minimum standard of living, including access to sanitation. Costello J found that this matter was a non-justiciable political one which involved distributive and not commutative justice. He relied heavily on the distinction between the two in concluding:

> What could be involved in the exercise of the suggested jurisdiction would be the imposition by the Court of its view that there had been an unfair distribution of national resources. To arrive at such a conclusion it would have to make an assessment of the validity of the many competing claims on those resources ... in exercising those functions the Court would not be administering justice as it does when determining an issue relating to commutative justice, but it would be involved in an entirely different exercise, namely an adjudication of fairness or otherwise of the manner in which other organs of the State had administered public resources.[82]

While somewhat paradoxically affirming that the Constitution exhibits concepts [3–32]

---

[78] Gerard Hogan, 'Directive Principles, Social and Economic Rights and the Irish Constitution' (2001) 36 Irish Jurist 174, 177.

[79] United Nations Committee on Economic Social and Cultural Rights, 'List of Issues in relation to the Third Periodic Report of Ireland' E/C.12/IRL/Q/3 (17 December 2014) [3].

[80] Committee on Economic Social and Cultural Rights, 'List of Issues in relation to the Third Periodic Report of Ireland, Addendum, Replies of Ireland to List of Issues' E/C.12/IRL/Q/3/Add.1 (8 April 2015) [2].

[81] [1989] ILRM 181.

[82] ibid 195.

of distributive justice,[83] Costello J found that the court was not in a position to make determinations on competing state resources and, in the absence of legislation conferring such power, it was a matter entirely within the remit of the Oireachtas.[84] The fact that there was no legislation in the area appeared central to this decision, as, in a similar case involving deplorable living conditions, he found that there was a breach of the right to bodily integrity, granting a mandatory order compelling the local authority to provide three serviced sites.[85] In the latter case, he grounded his ruling on the provisions of the Housing Act 1988,[86] a ruling that now appears at odds with the current position of the Supreme Court, which endorsed his previous reasoning in *O'Reilly*.

[3–33]   Beginning in the mid-1990s, a plethora of cases involving minors with varying degrees of behavioural and psychological impairments requiring specialist support and secure accommodation came to be determined by the High Court. In both *FN v Minister for Education*[87] and *DG v Eastern Health Board*,[88] the court had advised the relevant authorities to take the appropriate steps to remedy the situation, stopping short of making the mandatory orders that were asked of it.

[3–34]   The High Court emphatically affirmed the availability of a legal remedy in cases of inaction on the part of the state in *DB v Minister for Justice*, where an exasperated Kelly J considered the case of a fourteen year old minor diagnosed with a severe personality disorder.[89] Orders had previously been made in relation to his care and custody, and an order was sought, compelling the Minister to build a unit for the applicant and others like him in need of secure accommodation. Kelly J outlined, with reference to previous case law, that the court did have the jurisdiction to make the orders sought, should they be required to ensure the personal rights of the citizen:

> The Court must have available to it any power necessary to do so in an effective way. If that were not the case this Court could not carry out the obligation imposed upon it to vindicate and defend such rights. This power exists regardless of the status of a respondent. The fact that in the present case the principle respondent is the Minister for Health is no reason to believe that he is in some way immune from orders of

---

[83]   [1989] ILRM 181, 195, 'I am sure that the concept of justice which is to be found in the Constitution embraces the concept that the nation's wealth should be justly distributed'.

[84]   Claire McHugh, 'Socio Economic Rights in Ireland: Lessons to be Learned from South Africa and India' (2003) 4 Hibernian Law Journal 109, 113.

[85]   *O'Brien v Wicklow Urban District Council* (HC, 10 June 1994).

[86]   s 13 of the Housing Act provides that the local authority 'may' provide, manage and control sites for Traveller families. It does not compel them to do so.

[87]   [1995] 1 IR 419.

[88]   [1997] 3 IR 511.

[89]   [1999] 1 ILRM 93.

this Court in excess of mere declarations if such orders are required to vindicate the personal rights of the citizen.[90]

Observing that the separation of powers, while an important doctrine, is not immutable and, in the face of continued and unjustifiable procrastination, the court reserved the right to make mandatory orders. **[3–35]**

Having regard to recommendations and declarations previously made, the court held that the state's obligation had been identified and the Minister had still not made provision for secure places for minors. In these circumstances, the court granted a mandatory order compelling the Minister to complete the facilities, stating that it was not 'dictating policy' (and thereby breaching the separation of powers doctrine), rather the order would 'ensure that the Minister who has already decided on the policy lives up to his word'.[91] **[3–36]**

This case was regarded as a turning point in the vindication of social and economic rights and an affirmation of the court's ability to grant mandatory orders against the state to protect and vindicate such rights.[92] **[3–37]**

Kelly J considered an almost identical issue in *TD v Minister for Education*.[93] TD was the first named minor applicant,[94] with special educational and welfare needs, who required urgent residential treatment in a secure unit, akin to those required by the appellant in *DB*. In the aftermath of the *DB* ruling, the state had complied with the order without appeal and provided facilities within the Dublin area.[95] *TD* centred on the expansion of these facilities beyond Dublin and the state offered detailed plans to the court regarding such development. As a result, the court granted lengthy adjournments, however the plans were not implemented. **[3–38]**

In opposing the granting of a mandatory order, the state contended that it would be inherently vague, an argument rejected on the grounds that the previous injunction granted in *DB* had not been appealed.[96] **[3–39]**

Kelly J set down four criteria to be considered in determining whether or not the court should grant a mandatory injunction in cases such as this: **[3–40]**

---

90 ibid 102.
91 ibid 105.
92 Blathna Ruane, 'The Separation of Powers and the Granting of Mandatory Orders to Enforce Constitutional Rights' [2000] 5 Bar Review 416.
93 [2000] 2 ILRM 321.
94 Also joined in the case were DB, MB, GD, GD, PH, BJ, TL and ST.
95 In *DB,* the order specifically required the State to provide for the facilities in Portrane and Lucan, both of which are located within Dublin.
96 [2000] 2 ILRM 321, 335.

(a) Whether a declaratory order has already been granted in a case of this type affording the Government an opportunity to put matters right;

(b) The need to act quickly in order to secure rights for applicants before they attain the age of majority and lose their entitlement to those rights;

(c) The effect of a failure to provide the appropriate facilities on the lives of those who are entitled to them (including risk of harm);

(d) Due regard is to be had to the efforts of the Government to address the difficulties to date, if all reasonable efforts have been made then normally no order of this type should be made.[97]

[3–41]   These conditions are quite restrictive and clearly only apply in the most extreme cases, leaving the primary responsibility with the executive.[98] It acknowledges that the court should only intervene where the choice before the court is 'observing the separation of powers or vindicating a constitutional right',[99] and, in those circumstances, according to Kelly J, the court should always choose the latter. The High Court in these circumstances granted the order sought, which was appealed to the Supreme Court.

[3–42]   In 2001, the Supreme Court delivered two rulings which copper-fastened the extent to which social and economic rights could be judicially enforced. These cases evidence clearly that the Constitution, as interpreted, does not protect social and economic rights which, though 'laudable aspirations', are properly left to the executive branches.[100] The first of those was the case of *Sinnott v Minister for Education,* involving the right to education as contained in Article 42 of the Constitution.[101] Initially, it was understood that this provision was restricted to mainstream education. However, in *O'Donoghue v Minister for Health*,[102] O'Hanlon J held that the obligation was to provide basic elementary education to all children, to enable them to make the best use of their inherent potential capabilities, determining that this:

> Involves giving each child such advice, instruction and teaching as will enable him or her to make the best possible use of his or her inherent and potential capabilities, physical, mental or moral, however limited these capacities may be.[103]

---

[97]   ibid 343.

[98]   Conor O'Mahony, 'A Deficit of Protection – Economic Social and Cultural Rights in Ireland' (Amnesty International Conference, Dublin, November 2012) 8 <www.amnesty. ie/sites/default/files/HRII/Conor%20O%27Mahony%20Paper.pdf> last accessed 19 October 2016.

[99]   ibid 8.

[100]   Paul O'Connell, *Vindicating Socio-Economic Rights* (Routledge 2012) 151.

[101]   [2001] IESC 63.

[102]   [1996] 2 IR 20.

[103]   ibid 65.

Consideration of the extent of this obligation was at the core of the *Sinnott* case.[104] **[3–43]**
Mr Sinnott was an autistic man who claimed that he was entitled to free primary
education for as long as he could benefit from it.[105] Barr J in the High Court,
having regard to the decision in *O'Donoghue,* agreed, and held that the right
to education was need-based and not age-based. The court awarded damages
and ordered that education facilities be provided to the plaintiff for as long as
he could benefit from them. The state partially appealed this determination to
the Supreme Court. It conceded that Mr Sinnott's right to education had been
breached and as such the appeal sought to have the Supreme Court determine
the general rights of persons with disabilities to be provided with education
beyond the age of 18.[106] As Article 42 does not, itself, place any age limitation
on the provision of free primary education, the Supreme Court was tasked with
determining whether any restriction did in fact apply. Murphy J interpreted the
provision in light of the Education Act 1892, which required children to attend
school up to the age of 14, concluding that the right to receive primary education
ceases at the age of 12.[107] This interpretation leaves the educational obligations
on the state in a 'permafrost' of 1892 and takes no account of the developments
in education since.[108] The majority of the Supreme Court focused on the age
at which one ceases to be a child. Geoghegan J observes that 'the arbitrary
choice by the state of the age 18 is not necessarily illogical. In the perception
of most people a child becomes an adult at 18'.[109] Hardiman J, through an
examination of both the English and Irish texts of the Constitution, determined
that the word 'leanbh' in the Irish text suggests that the framers had intended
the clause to be restricted to children. Ultimately he decided, concurring with
Murray and Fennelly JJ, that the age of 18 was 'the latest at which a person
could be regarded as a child'.[110] Accordingly, the state is not obliged to provide
free primary education for persons over the chronological age of 18, regardless
of their intellectual age.[111]

With that decided, the separation of powers argument became somewhat of a **[3–44]**
moot point. Nonetheless, opinions were expressed in relation to the ability of
the court to issue mandatory orders in such cases.[112]

---

[104] [2001] 2 IR 545.
[105] At the time of the application, Jamie Sinnott was 22, and evidence was adduced that he
had received less than three years of primary education.
[106] See Shivaun Quinlivan and Mary Keyes, 'Official Indifference and Persistent
Procrastination: An Analysis of Sinnott' (2002) 2 Judicial Studies Institute Journal 163,
166-167.
[107] [2001] 2 IR 545, 675.
[108] Quinlivan and Keyes (n 106) 168.
[109] [2001] 2 IR 545, 720.
[110] ibid 696.
[111] Claire-Michelle Smyth, 'The Constitution at 75; Time for a New Interpretation?' (2012)
30 Irish Law Times 130.
[112] Quinlivan and Keyes (n 106) 181.

[3–45] Hardiman J relied on the judgment in *O'Reilly v Limerick Corporation*[113] to determine that the judiciary has no role in granting mandatory orders to command expenditure for the purpose of upholding constitutional rights.[114] This view, it would seem, is at odds with the view expressed in *Meskell v CIE*.[115]

[3–46] The opinion was advanced in *O'Reilly* that such orders should only be granted in rare and exceptional circumstances, and where a previous declaratory order had been flouted.[116] In this regard, it is worth observing that five years had elapsed since the court's ruling in *O'Donoghue* and the state had completely failed to implement the recommendations made. As such, it would appear that the *Sinnott* case had met the criteria and was instead decided on the basis of policy.

[3–47] Shortly after this ruling, the Supreme Court delivered its judgment on the appeal case of *TD*.[117] When this appeal came before the Supreme Court, it effectively had a choice of two High Court decisions which it could endorse: the carefully considered test set down by Kelly J, or that of Costello J, established in *O'Reilly*, a position from which he subsequently publicly[118] and judicially resiled.[119]

[3–48] The majority of the court relied on the latter. Costello J's dictum in *O'Reilly* and the distinction between distributive and commutative justice was expressly approved of. It was held that, by granting such an order, the High Court was breaching the separation of powers, as such issues of resource distribution were solely a matter for the Oireachtas.[120]

[3–49] Murray J confirmed that there is no constitutional obligation on the state to provide medical and social services. He subsequently reaffirmed this position in *North Western Health Board v HW*, where he stated that 'there are no provisions of the Constitution cognisable to the courts expressly requiring or permitting the State to provide medical services or social welfare of any kind'.[121] Hardiman J was of the opinion that relief for cases such as this ought to be advanced in Leinster House and not in the Four Courts.[122] In justifying this position, he reiterates the reasons, previously espoused in *Sinnott*, why this is so:

---

[113] [1989] ILRM 181.
[114] [2001] 2 IR 545.
[115] [1973] IR 121.
[116] [1989] ILRM 181.
[117] [2001] IESC 101; [2001] 4 IR 259.
[118] *The Irish Times* (Dublin, 14 November 1998), referred to in Liam Thornton, 'Declan Costello (1926-2011) and Irish Socio-Economic Rights Jurisprudence' *humanrights.ie* (8 June 2011) available at <humanrights.ie/constitution-of-ireland/declan-costello-1926-2011-and-irish-socio-economic-rights-jurisprudence/> last accessed 9 April 2015.
[119] Conor O'Mahony, 'Education, Remedies and the Separation of Powers' (2002) 24 Dublin University Law Journal 57, 76.
[120] [1989] ILRM 181.
[121] [2001] 3 IR 622, 729.
[122] [2001] 4 IR 259, 357.

Firstly, to do so would offend the constitutional separation of powers. Secondly, it would lead the courts into the taking of decisions in areas in which they have no special qualifications or experience. Thirdly, it would permit the courts to take such decisions even though they are not, and cannot be, democratically responsible for them as the legislature and the executive are. Fourthly, the evidence based adversarial procedures of the court, which are excellently adapted for the administration of commutative justice, are too technical, too expensive, too focused on the individual issue to be an appropriate method for deciding on issues of policy.[123]

In addition, Hardiman J was fearful that this would encourage cases being advanced in the courts rather than in the political arena, which would downgrade the power of the political arms of the state and involve the court in politics.[124]   **[3–50]**

The majority of the Supreme Court concurred, finding that these rights should remain firmly non-justiciable. However, they do not appear able to advance a consistent logic to defend this position.   **[3–51]**

The decision was not unanimous and, in her dissenting judgment, the now Chief Justice Denham took the position that expenditure is not a sufficient reason to abdicate the responsibility of the court in deciding the constitutionality of an issue, reasoning that was more in line with the High Court judgment.[125]   **[3–52]**

The decision in *TD* has been labelled as one overwhelmingly harmful to the protection of rights, as it does not limit the right on grounds of practicality or proportionality as had been done in the past, but rather fetters the power of the judiciary to grant a remedy for the violation of rights.[126] The court did accept that there may be certain exceptional circumstances[127] in which it would intervene, but its failure to clarify these 'exceptional circumstances' further hampers the development of this area.[128]   **[3–53]**

Subsequent cases seeking mandatory orders must fall within the narrow exception accepted by the Supreme Court in order to succeed.[129] The elusive   **[3–54]**

---

[123] (n 1) 710 reiterated in (n 2) 361.
[124] Ciaran Lawlor, 'Conscience of the Nation: Socio-Economic Rights and the Irish Constitution' (2005) 5 University College Dublin Law Review 34, 52.
[125] (n 2).
[126] Francis Kieran, '*TD* Re-Considered; Constructing a new approach to the enforcement of rights' (2004) 7 Trinity College Law Review 62, 69.
[127] A position reiterated in *Re Article 26 and the Health (Amendment)(No.2) Bill 2004* [2005] IESC 7.
[128] O'Connell (n 100) 160.
[129] ibid 159.

'exceptional circumstances' principle sets an excessively high barrier,[130] with cases involving education rights and housing conditions generating the most jurisprudence.

[3–55] In relation to education, the reluctance to grant mandatory orders (save in exceptional circumstances) is particularly troublesome, given its textual nature. Where *Sinnott* examined education rights beyond school-going age, in *Cronin v Minister for Education,* the High Court was tasked with determining whether the right to education extended to pre-school age.[131] A mandatory injunction was sought and the state argued that the obligation commenced at the attainment of school going age. In granting the order, Laffoy J found that her decision did not fall foul of the *TD* and *Sinnott* cases, as it was limited to this particular plaintiff and merely extended a programme already sanctioned by the state.[132]

[3–56] In a carefully constructed judgment, Laffoy J did not establish a precedent that all pre-school children with autism were generally entitled to these services, but rather, in the right circumstances, the right to education can be invoked at the pre-school stage.

[3–57] The extent of the right to education was tested further in the case of *O'Carolan v Minister for Education*, where the parents of a profoundly autistic child contended that the placement being offered by the state was inadequate to meet their son's educational needs.[133] They claimed that his right would only be vindicated if the state funded a place in an institution in Bangor, Wales. This is the first time a litigant claimed to have a right to have education abroad paid for by the state. In deciding against the plaintiff, McMenamin J clarified that the case centred on whether or not the place offered was appropriate, and not whether an alternative placement would be best or better. So long as the placement in question was appropriate to meet the needs of the child, it did not violate his rights.[134]

[3–58] This reasoning appears at odds with *O'Donoghue*, where it was interpreted that the obligation was to enable the child make the best possible use of his or her inherent and potential capabilities, a position approved of in subsequent cases.[135]

---

130 Whyte (n 3) 359.
131 (HC, 6 July 2004).
132 ibid (Laffoy J).
133 [2005] IEHC 296.
134 ibid [46].
135 *O'Donoghue v Minister for Health* [1996] 2 IR 20, 65, approved in *Comerford v Minister for Education* [1997] 2 ILRM 134 and in *O'Sheil v Minister for Education* [1999] 2 ILRM 241, 275, where Laffoy J states that 'it is inconceivable that the framers of the Constitution intended that the State should be under a duty to fund primary education to a "certain minimum" level only. Such an intention is not manifested by the words used in Article 42 or indicated by its purpose'.

The failure to explain this departure from the previously approved interpretation undermines this decision.[136]

The more recent case of *AMCD v Minister for Education & Ors* seems to require a deliberate and conscious disregard of the Plaintiff's rights and in this case the mere lack of available places did not reach the required threshold.[137]   **[3–59]**

The right to education has been interpreted in a restrictive manner, with *Sinnott* significantly limiting its potential in two ways. First, it establishes, arbitrarily, that the obligation on the state to provide free primary education ends when a person attains the age of 18. Secondly, in deference to the separation of powers, it determines that only in the rarest of circumstances should the court issue mandatory orders. Where the courts do grant these orders, they are in isolated and carefully worded judgments, reflective of the general hostility towards the constitutionalisation of social and economic rights.   **[3–60]**

The second area which has generated an appreciable amount of jurisprudence is the right to housing. Many recent cases have alleged breaches of rights contained in the European Convention of Human Rights. However, for the purpose of this section, which considers constitutional protection, Convention cases are omitted, analysed separately in Chapter 6. With no express or implied right to housing or shelter, it has been left to the state to decide how best to implement, and vindicate, this right.[138] In order to achieve this, the state created a social housing policy,[139] which has since been codified into legislative obligations.[140]   **[3–61]**

These provisions are decidedly weak and do not impose individual enforceable rights, but rather, require the implementation of a programmatic response. Few national constitutions refer specifically to housing rights, and, where they do, they primarily impose the programmatic approach as contained in the ICESCR.[141]   **[3–62]**

---

[136] O'Mahony (n 98) 10.

[137] [2013] IEHC 175.

[138] Article 43 of the Constitution protects private property. However, this provision has been interpreted as protecting existing ownership of private property and not tenants or those in need of housing. For example, in *Blake v Attorney General* [1982] IR 117, rent restrictions were deemed to impose an undue attack on the property rights of landlords.

[139] Mairead Considine and Fiona Dukelow, *Irish Social Policy, A Critical Introduction* (Gill and Macmillan 2009).

[140] The Housing Act 1966 confirms that there is an obligation on local authorities to provide housing. The Planning and Development Act 2000 requires that developers cede a portion of their land for social housing by the local authority. This provision was the subject of a constitutional challenge in *Re Art 26 and Part V of the Planning and Development Bill 1999* [2000] 2IR 321, where the constitutionality was upheld on the basis of requirements of the common good. See Brid Cannon, 'Constructing a House of Cards? Social and Affordable Housing in Ireland: Policy and Practice' (2007) 10 Trinity College Law Review 21.

[141] Deborah Mabbeth, 'The Development of Rights-Based Social Policy in the European

Individually enforceable rights, where they do exist, generally extend no further than the provision of homeless services or emergency accommodation.[142] Initial attempts to create such a justiciable right against homelessness in Ireland were met with considerable opposition on the basis that it would be unduly costly (in the context of the provision and subsequent litigation) and that it would interfere with the allocation based on prioritisation of particular groups.[143] As such, legislation, rather than creating an obligation, constructs an expectation that the local authority will implement the policy.[144]

[3–63]   In contrast, Scottish law takes a more legalistic approach (as opposed to a policy approach), placing a positive duty and legal obligation on local authorities to provide for sustainable accommodation,[145] not merely emergency accommodation, making it unique.[146] The legislation clearly places a legal duty on the local authority and provides a framework whereby this can be executed. Notably, it authorises the local authority to compel registered landlords to house homeless persons.[147] The system provides a transparent process, which places the individual need above policy considerations and limits discretion based on any perceived notions of deservedness. The absence of any legal obligation in Ireland necessarily allows the local authority to consider additional factors. Concerns in relation to balancing policy and strategic objective appears to trump need. The creation of a right to housing in Scotland not only has statistically a greater impact in tackling homelessness, when compared with Ireland's policy-based approach, but further, it has had a considerable impact on lessening the associated stigma. Beth Watts describes Scottish people asserting their rights and, importantly, feeling that they were entitled to housing, whereas their Irish counterparts expressed gratitude and felt lucky to have been given a short term and often substandard accommodation.[148]

[3–64]   As there is no legal right to housing, the majority of cases arise as a result of living conditions, the obligation to provide an adequate standard of accommodation and procedural safeguards in relation to eviction. The first

---

142 Suzanne Fitzpatrick and Elizabeth Watts, 'The "Right to Housing" for Homeless People' in Eoin O'Sullivan, Volker Busch-Geertsema, Deborah Quilgars and Nicholas Pleace (eds), *Homelessness Research in Europe* (FEANTSA 2010) 105.
143 Brian Harvey, 'Homelessness, the 1988 Housing Act, State Policy and Civil Society' in Dáithí Downey (ed), *Perspectives on Irish Homelessness: Past Present and Future* (Dublin Homeless Agency 2008) 11.
144 Eoin O'Sullivan, 'Sustainable Solutions to Homelessness: The Irish Case' (2008) 2 European Journal of Homelessness 205, 206.
145 Housing (Scotland) Act 2001.
146 Beth Watts, 'Rights, Needs and Stigma: A Comparison of Homelessness Policy in Ireland and Scotland' (2013) 7 European Journal of Homelessness 41, 42.
147 ibid 52.
148 ibid 56.

Union: The Example of Disability Rights' (2005) 43 Journal of Common Market Studies 97, 98.

cases to establish the constitutional position of social and economic rights in Ireland, *O'Reilly v Limerick Corporation*, dealt with conditions in which members of the travelling community were living.[149] This unsuccessful case set the precedent, later endorsed by the Supreme Court, that these rights are beyond the court's jurisdiction. Nevertheless, in extreme circumstances, the living conditions can amount to a breach of rights. As a result of this position, the crisis of homelessness in Ireland has steadily escalated over the last 10 years, exacerbated by austerity measures imposed due to the economic crash. With no legal right to be housed, many found themselves sleeping in tents, on streets and in doorways due either to a lack of available beds, or to a lack of suitable beds.[150] In response to this situation, a group of activists occupied a NAMA owned building, Apollo House, to house the homeless during the winter period.[151] Apollo house, an abandoned office building was transferred to NAMA in 2012 and has remained vacant since. Shortly after the occupation, the receivers for NAMA sought an injunction in the High Court, which was heard on 21 December 2016 and which was granted by Gilligan J, compelling the residents to vacate the building by 11 January 2017.[152] In granting the injunction, the judge accepted evidence presented by an officer of Dublin City Council that there was sufficient beds to accommodate all residents of Apollo House and that no person would be forced to sleep on the streets. This appeared to be pivotal to the judge's decision, as, if the order would result in them being without shelter, this would reach the threshold of exceptional circumstances in which he would not grant the order.[153]

In relation to the standard of accommodation provided, in *County Meath VEC v Joyce*, it was held that there is an obligation to provide for the needs in a 'fair and reasonable manner'.[154] However, there have been no consistent rulings as to what precisely this obligation entails. In *O'Donoghue v Limerick Corporation*, it was held that the Corporation had failed in its obligation to provide a site for the caravan of the applicants, who were living in unsanitary conditions having refused an offer of housing accommodation.[155] In contrast, in *Doherty v South Dublin County Council,* the Council were found not to have breached **[3–65]**

---

[149] [1989] ILRM 181.

[150] There has been a plethora of media reports relating to serious safety issues, drug abuse, violence and sub-standard conditions in emergency accommodation, leaving people with little choice but to sleep on the streets.

[151] The National Assets Management Agency (NAMA) was created by legislation (the NAMA Act 2009) to essentially function as a bad bank, taking over distressed loans. As a result, NAMA acquired numerous developments and buildings into its ownership.

[152] (HC, 21 December 2016).

[153] See Aodhan O'Faolain and Kitty Holland, 'Apollo House: Judge says occupants must vacate in January' *The Irish Times* (21 December 2016) available at <www.irishtimes.com/news/ireland/irish-news/apollo-house-judge-says-occupants-must-vacate-in-january-1.2913959> last accessed 5 January 2017.

[154] [1997] 3 IR 402.

[155] [2003] 4 IR 93.

their obligations where an elderly couple were living in unsanitary conditions, having refused an offer of alternative accommodation.[156]

The case law, therefore, is sporadic and inconsistent, providing no clear definition of any obligation.

[3–66]   Where accommodation is provided, the court, in *Siney v Dublin Corporation,* declared that there was an implied warranty that it be fit for human habitation.[157] Further, in *Burke v Dublin Corporation,*[158] the Supreme Court found that there was a continuing obligation to inspect and to fix any defects, and that there was an implied warranty that the property would be capable of being healthily, safely and properly heated.[159] However, in the absence of a recognised right to adequate housing, the precise parameters of this implied condition are uncertain. Regulations which govern private rented accommodation do not apply equally to tenants of social housing,[160] and lower standards in relation to heating, food preparation and laundry are permitted.[161] Even within these lower standards, it does appear that the court requires minimum standards to be maintained. In February 2016, in an unreported Circuit Court case, the court awarded damages to a family who suffered significant and recurring illnesses as a result of their living conditions in a council property.[162]

[3–67]   The judicial interpretation of social and economic rights has been consistent in its opposition to constitutionalisation. Save for the most extreme and exceptional circumstances, these rights have not been judicially enforced. The Supreme Court has consistently maintained that they remain within the exclusive remit of the executive. It does appear that, in recent years, public opinion towards these rights has shifted in a more favourable direction. In 1996, the Constitution Review Group, despite acknowledging the levels of poverty in Ireland, dismissed the possibility of including social and economic rights in the text of the Constitution, for fear of 'distorting democracy'.[163] In more recent years,

---

[156] [2007] IEHC 4.

[157] [1980] IR 400.

[158] [1991] 1 IR 341.

[159] ibid 349.

[160] s 3(2) of the Residential Tenancies Act 2004 expressly excludes application to a dwelling let by a public authority.

[161] Padraic Kenna, *Housing Law, Rights and Policies* (Clarus Press 2011) 749. See also, Housing (Standards for Rented Houses) Regulation 2008, SI 2008/354, Housing (Standard for Rented Houses) Regulation 2009, SI 2009/462.

[162] Ray Managh, 'Dublin City Council ordered to pay family medical damages due to the state of their home' *Journal.ie* (11 February 2016).

[163] The Constitution Review Group, *Report of the Constitution Review Group* (Dublin, Stationery Office 1996) 210, a decision criticised heavily in Jerome Connolly, *Re-righting the Constitution: The Case for New Social and Economic Rights: Housing, Health, Nutrition, Adequate Standard of Living* (Irish Commission for Peace and Justice 1998).

the Constitutional Convention was established,[164] which was given the scope to examine and make recommendations on issues outside of those specified in its terms of reference.[165] A significant number of submissions were received, requesting an examination of social and economic rights, and, on 23 February 2014, following its ninth and final meeting, members of the Convention voted on the issue, with 85% agreeing that the Constitution should include protection for these rights.[166] This outcome evidences a clear shift in opinion from the 1996 report, showing an increasing desire to have these rights protected by law. The recommendation of the Convention to amend the Constitution to include specific social and economic rights has been put to the government, and would require a referendum to implement. Speaking on this issue, Professor Whyte opined that the likelihood of a referendum being called on this matter is virtually non-existent.[167]

As evidence emerges that public opinion increasingly favours the constitutional inclusion of social and economic rights, a motion by way of Private Member's Bill, was initiated in Dáil Éireann to call for a referendum.[168] This bill was brought to second stage on 20 May 2015, where it was voted against.[169] However, there are avenues by which these rights could form part of the Constitution's fundamental rights, without the need for express incorporation by way of referendum.   [3–68]

The Potential for Constitutionalisation

When faced with determining cases of social and economic rights, the Supreme Court had, and, it is argued, still has, two main ways it could constitutionalise these rights. If the court were to declare them as unspecified rights, they would become a textual part of the Constitution. Alternatively, the court could have interpreted existing fundamental rights with reference to the Directive Principles of Social Policy in Article 45 to indirectly constitutionalise them. Both would require a significant element of judicial activism not seen since the 1960s and   [3–69]

---

[164] By Resolution of the Houses of the Oireachtas of July 2012.

[165] Full terms of reference can be found at <www.constitution.ie/Convention.aspx#terms-of-reference> last accessed 20 February 2017.

[166] See the report of the Convention at <www.constitution.ie/AttachmentDownload.ashx?mid=adc4c56a-a09c-e311-a7ce-005056a32ee4> last accessed 20 February 2017.

[167] Professor Gerry Whyte speaking at Trinity College Dublin (FLAC Annual Socio-Economic Event, Dublin, 18 February 2015).

[168] Thirty-Fourth Amendment of the Constitution (Economic Social and Cultural Rights) Bill 2014, Bill No. 115 of 2014 introduced by Deputy Thomas Pringle on 17 December 2014. Full text of the Bill is available at <www.oireachtas.ie/viewdoc.asp?fn=/documents/bills28/bills/2014/11514/document1.htm> last accessed 05 January 2017.

[169] The introduction of the Bill to the Dáil by Deputy Pringle is available at <www.thomaspringle.ie/thomas-introducing-his-economic-social-and-cultural-rights-bill-2014/> last accessed 17 January 2017.

70s, which could be justified by reference to changing international standards and by using certain national jurisdictions as persuasive authority, as alluded to later in this section.

Direct Constitutionalisation as an Unspecified Right

[3–70]   The superior courts have the task of declaring which rights fall within the Constitution and, thus, which are to be protected by the law. When it comes to deciding which rights are encompassed within this category, social and economic rights have not yet found favour with the judiciary, despite the clear link with many of the unenumerated rights.

[3–71]   Cases such as *Ryan v AG*[170] and *McGee v AG*,[171] which created the unenumerated rights to bodily integrity and marital privacy respectively, had strong links with the right to health, although the court did not frame them in those terms.[172] What appeared to be a declaration of a right to health, where O'Flaherty J opined that it was 'beyond debate that there is a hierarchy of constitutional rights and at the top of that list is the right to life, followed by the right to health', has remained relatively undeveloped.[173]

[3–72]   An explanation for this may be found in the fact that judicial support for the doctrine of unenumerated rights and its associated activism was waning by the time cases involving social and economic rights fell to be decided. In *TD v Minister for Education*, Keane CJ, while not expressly discounting this category of rights, made clear his dissatisfaction with their entire premise:

> I would also share the unease which has been expressed as to the somewhat dubious premises on which the doctrine of unenumerated rights rests and the dangers for democracy of unrestrained judicial activism in the area.[174]

[3–73]   Not only was the court loath to declare new unspecified rights, but it was also extremely reluctant to expand existing express or implied rights. Keane CJ

---

[170] [1965] IR 294.
[171] [1974] IR 284.
[172] In *Ryan*, the plaintiff ultimately failed, as she did not show sufficient evidence that fluoridation of the water supply would cause adverse effects to her health. The *McGee* case challenged a criminal prosecution for importing contraception, grounded on medical advice. The court accepted that the decision whether to reproduce was a matter for the married coupled and created the unenumerated right to marital privacy.
[173] See *Re Art 26 and the Health (Amendment) (No 2) Bill 2004* [2005] IESC 7, where the Supreme Court accepted that there may be particular circumstances where the state may have to maintain patients free of charge. However, it rejected the argument of an entitlement to free healthcare.
[174] (n 2) 5.

concluded that even those who are in agreement with the decision of in *Ryan* (that the Constitution protects some rights other than those expressed) would concede that judicial restraint is required in order to preserve the 'delicate balance' of the separation of powers.[175]

Concerns that the inclusion of social and economic rights into the Constitution **[3–74]** (through either a reinvigoration of the doctrine of unenumerated rights, or, equally, by virtue of inclusion following a referendum) would result in excessive financial burdens on the state, are unfounded. These rights, as with any other constitutional right, would be subject to the same rigorous and legitimate restrictions. South Africa provides the foremost example of a domestic system which enshrines social and economic rights within their constitution[176] and confers full justiciability on them.[177] Rights such as housing,[178] healthcare, food, social security and shelter[179] are of equal rank and dignity to civil and political rights, a measure intended to transform the post-apartheid nation.[180]

The first substantive case[181] on the issue of social and economic rights before **[3–75]** the Constitutional Court was *Soobramoney v Minister for Health, KwaZulu-Natal,* which challenged the denial of dialysis treatment to prolong life.[182] The applicant relied on the provision that 'no one may be refused emergency

---

[175] ibid 6.

[176] The Constitution of the Republic of South Africa 1996 was approved by the Constitutional Court on 4 December 1996 and entered into force on 4 February 1997.

[177] For an in-depth analysis of the debate on constitutionalising social and economic rights in the South African Constitution, see Craig Scott and Patrick Macklem, 'Constitutional Ropes of Sand or Justiciable Guarantees? Social Rights in a New South African Constitution' (1992) 141 University of Pennsylvania Law Review 1-148; Sandra Liebenberg, *Social and Economic Rights: Adjudication under a Transformative Constitution* (Juta 2010)

[178] s 26 states, '(1) Everyone has the right to have access to adequate housing. (2) The state must take reasonable legislative measures and other measures within its available resources, to achieve the progressive realisation of this right. (3) No one may be evicted from their home, or have their home demolished, without an order of the court made after considering all the relevant circumstances. No legislation may permit arbitrary eviction'.

[179] s 27 states, '(1) Everyone has the right to: (a) Healthcare Services, including reproductive healthcare; (b) Sufficient food and water, and; (c) Social security, including if they are unable to support themselves and their dependants, appropriate social assistance. (2) The state must take reasonable legislative and other measures, within its available resources, to achieve the progressive realisation of these rights. (3) No one may be refused emergency medical treatment'.

[180] Marius Pieterse, 'Beyond the Welfare State: Globalisation of Neo-Liberal Culture and the Constitutional Protection of Social and Economic Rights in South Africa' (2003) 14 Stellenbosch Law Review 3, 9.

[181] The first case, *Re Certification of the Constitution of the Republic of South Africa* 1996 (4) SA 744 (C), found that the inclusion of social and economic rights in the Constitution did not breach the separation of powers and was constitutional. See Jeremy Sarkin, 'The Drafting of South Africa's Final Constitution from a Human Rights Perspective' (1999) 47 American Journal of Comparative Law 67.

[182] 1997 (12) BCLR 1696 (CC).

medical treatment',[183] which was rejected by the court. It was determined that the provision could not be extended to prolonging the life of terminally ill patients. The right had to be weighed against the limited resources of the state,[184] and it was justified in restricting this treatment to non-terminal patients. This decision was measured and caused concern about the future of social and economic rights jurisprudence, as it appeared to defer excessively to the executive.[185]

[3–76] The case of *Government of the Republic of South Africa v Grootboom*, considered five years post-*Soobramoney*, injected fresh hope.[186] This case sought to enforce the right to housing under s 26.[187] It arose when the applicant and several hundred other residents of an informal settlement left due to dismal living conditions, settling, instead, on private land. An eviction order was granted by the court and, during its enforcement, the temporary shelters and possessions of the applicants were destroyed, forcing them to return to the original informal settlement. The High Court found that the Constitution did not confer an enforceable individual right to a minimum entitlement to temporary shelter. However, it did find that, where parents were unable to provide basic shelter, s 28 imposed an obligation on the state to provide 'tents, portable latrines and a regular supply of water',[188] and made declaratory orders in that regard, requiring the respondents to provide, within three months, temporary accommodation, particularly for the children.[189]

---

[183] s 27(3).

[184] This is expressly provided for in s 27(2), which states, 'the state must take reasonable legislative and other measures, within its available resources to achieve progressive realisation'.

[185] Eric C Christiansen, 'Adjudicating Non-Justiciable Rights: Socio-Economic Rights and the South African Constitution' (2007) 38 Columbia Human Rights Law Review 321, 364; Darrel Moellendorf, 'Reasoning about Resources: *Soobramoney* and the Future of Socio-Economic Rights Claims' (1998) 14 South African Journal of Human Rights 327; Albie Sachs, 'Social and Economic Rights: Can They be Made Justiciable?' (2000) 53 Southern Methodist University Law Review 1381. In contrast, see Craig Scott and Philip Alston, 'Adjudicating Constitutional Priorities in Transnational Context: A Comment on *Soobramoney's* Legacy and *Grootboom's* Promise' (2000) 16 South African Journal of Human Rights 206, 268. The authors argue that the decision should not be seen as limiting the potential of future jurisprudence, but rather, as the court's first attempt at litigating these rights and, as such, its approach was tentative.

[186] 2000 (11) BCLR 1169 (CC).

[187] s 26 states, '(1) Everyone has the right to have access to adequate housing. (2) The state must take reasonable legislative and other measures, within its available resources to achieve the progressive realization of this right. (3) No one may be evicted from their home or have their home demolished without an order of the court made after considering all the relevant circumstances. No legislation may permit arbitrary evictions.'

[188] High Court judgment of Davis J, referred to in 2000 (11) BCLR 1169 (CC) [25]-[26].

[189] For a full history of the case, see Rosalind Dixon, 'Creating Dialogue about Socio-Economic Rights: Strong-Form Versus Weak-Form Judicial Review Revisited' (2007) 5 International Journal of Constitutional Law 391, 395-397.

In upholding the decision in the Constitutional Court, Justice Yacoob articulated   **[3–77]**
the reasonableness test to be applied in such matters:

> Reasonableness must also be understood in the context of the Bill of
> Rights as a whole. To be reasonable, measures cannot leave out of
> account the degree and extent of the denial of the right they endeavour
> to realise. Those whose needs are the most urgent and whose ability
> to enjoy all rights therefore is most in peril, must not be ignored by
> the measures aimed at achieving realisation of the right. It may not be
> sufficient to meet the test of reasonableness to show that the measures
> are capable of achieving a statistical advance in the realisation of the
> rights. Furthermore, the Constitution requires that everyone must be
> treated with care and concern. If the measures, though statistically
> successful, fail to respond to the needs of those most desperate, they
> may not pass the test.[190]

In applying this test of reasonableness, which falls just short of a proportionality   **[3–78]**
test,[191] the court found that the state was in breach of s 26(2), as its housing plan
failed to provide reasonable measures 'to provide for relief for people who have
no access to land, no roof over their heads, and who are living in intolerable
conditions or crisis situations',[192] and that 'it is essential that a reasonable
part of the national housing budget be devoted to the homeless'.[193] However,
it merely granted declaratory orders and did not assert what measures would
satisfy this reasonableness test. As such, it has been argued that this decision is
weak, in that it lacks both substance and effective remedy.[194] In contrast, it has
been contended that the case demonstrates the balancing act performed by the
court, by forcing compliance with the Constitution, while allowing discretion
in the manner of compliance.[195]

The limits of enforceability for social and economic rights remained in question   **[3–79]**
following this judgment[196] However, its paramount significance is in confirming

---

[190] 2000 (11) BCLR 1169 (CC) [44].
[191] Linda Stewart, 'Adjudicating Socio-Economic Rights Under a Transformative
Constitution' (2010) 28 Penn State International Law Review 487, 495.
[192] 2000 (11) BCLR 1169 (CC) [99].
[193] ibid [66].
[194] Mark Tushnet, 'New Forms of Judicial Review and the Persistence of Rights and
Democracy Based Worries' (2003) 38 Wake Forest Law Review 813; Mark Tushnet,
'Social Welfare Rights and the Forms of Judicial Review' (2004) 84 Texas Law Review
1895; Mark Tushnet, 'Enforcing Socio-Economic Rights: Lessons from South Africa'
(2005) 6 ESR Review: Economic and Social Rights in South Africa 2.
[195] Mark S Kende, 'The South African Constitutional Court's Construction of Social and
Economic Rights: A Response to Critics' (2004) 19 Connecticut Journal of International
Law 617, 620.
[196] Christiansen (n 185) 368; Marius Pieterse, 'Coming to Terms with Judicial Enforcement
of Socio-Economic Rights' (2004) 20 South African Journal of Human Rights 383, 395.

that they contain both negative and positive dimensions and obligations. While not imposing positive obligations, cases such as *Jaftha v Schoeman & Ors*,[197] *City of Johannesburg v Rand Properties Ltd*,[198] and *Abahlali BaseMjondolo Movement SA and Ors v Premiere of the Province of Kwazulu and Others*,[199] saw the courts striking down legislation and procedures which allowed for arguably arbitrary eviction. This approach has not been confined to cases of housing, and, in *Khosa v Minister for Social Development*, the court found unconstitutional the exclusion of permanent residents from receiving certain social assistance benefits.[200]

[3–80]   While the court in *Grootboom* did not elaborate on the specifics of the positive obligations, it did confirm that the Constitution placed such a duty on the state to ameliorate the lamentable living conditions.[201] It would appear from the judgment that what is required is a demonstration that effort has been made to achieve realisation, taking into account society as a whole. Policy which excludes sections of society cannot be deemed reasonable.[202] Where this requirement has not been met, the court reserves the right to enforce such through the use of mandatory orders. These mandatory orders were granted in the High Court in the *Treatment Action Campaign* case.[203] This case challenged the policy restricting a drug called Nevirapine to certain pilot areas.[204] At first instance, the High Court ordered that the drug be made available to all infected mothers giving birth in state institutions, and that the state develop a comprehensive plan, reporting back to the court within three months in relation to its development and implementation.[205] On appeal to the Constitutional Court, the ruling of the High Court was upheld, affirming the state's duty to remove restrictions. However, in terms of the obligation to develop and implement the plan, the court preferred to grant declaratory relief with no time frame for completion.[206] Thus while the court has competence to adjudicate on social and economic rights, it appears to be endorsing an element of deference to the state in the implementation of the rights, which has been seen as a preference for a 'weak rights and weak remedies' approach.[207]

---

[197] 2005(1) BCLR 78 (CC).
[198] Unrep Case No 04/10330 (3 March 2006).
[199] 2010 (2) BCLR 99 (CC).
[200] 2004 (6) BCLR 569 (CC).
[201] 2000 (11) BCLR 1169 (CC) [93].
[202] Pierre de Vos, 'Grootboom, The Right of Access to Housing and Substantive Equality as Contextual Fairness' (2001) 17 South African Journal of Human Rights 258, 273.
[203] *Treatment Action Campaign v Minister for Health and Others* 2002 (4) BCLR 356.
[204] This drug dramatically reduces the risk of HIV infection for the child during childbirth. At this time, South Africa was in the midst of a HIV epidemic and the manufacturers had agreed to freely provide the drug to the state for five years. See generally, Christiansen (n 185) 368-372 for background.
[205] 2002 (4) BCLR 356 [85]-[87].
[206] *Minister of Health v Treatment Action Campaign (TAC)* (2002) 5 SA 721 (CC), 135.
[207] Dixon (n 189) 398.

This deference was again evident in the *Mazibuko* case, which involved a **[3–81]** challenge to the introduction of pre-pay water meters in the poverty stricken area of Soweto.[208] There were two key issues to this challenge: the first was whether the free allocation of 6 kilolitres of water per month per housekeeper was a breach of the right of access to sufficient water contained in s 27 of the Constitution and the second was whether the installation of meters to charge residents for water in excess of the free allowance was unlawful. In the High Court, Justice Tsoka held that the installation of the pre-paid water meters constituted a violation of the right to water, in that, 'To deny the applicants a right to water is to deny them the right to lead a dignified human existence'.[209] In examination of the decision, it was noted that the court linked the right to water with the principles of democracy, equality and freedom and, as such, the importance of the right was enhanced by its relation to others.[210] Further, it held that the allocation of free water was insufficient and that each resident should have access to 50 litres of water per day. The case was subsequently appealed to the Supreme Court of Appeal. It upheld the order of the High Court, stating that the city had no authority to install pre-paid meters and, *a fortiori*, that the discontinuance of water when the free limit had been reached was unlawful.[211] It did however slightly vary the order, holding that 42 litres of water per day was an adequate amount. It suspended its order for two years to allow the government revise its water policy, but, in the interim, each person was to receive their 42 litres of water per day.

The case was appealed once more to the Constitutional Court, which overturned **[3–82]** the previous orders issued by the High Court and the Supreme Court of Appeal.[212] It determined that the installation of meters did not breach any rights and it further refused to declare what amount of water was a sufficient daily allowance. It held that:

> it is clear that the right does not require the state upon demand to provide every person with sufficient water without more; rather it requires the state to take reasonable legislative and other measures progressively to realise the achievement of the right of access to sufficient water, within available resources.[213]

The Constitutional Court was at pains to stress the balancing act to be undertaken **[3–83]** when determining social and economic rights and the reasonableness of the

---

[208] *Mazibuko & Ors v The City of Johannesburg & Ors* High Court of South Africa 30 April 2008, Case No. 06/13865. For background to the case, see Stewart (n 191) 496-497.
[209] ibid 160.
[210] Russell Langford, 'Case Commentary: The Mazibuko Case' (2008) 19 Water Law 77.
[211] 2009 8 BCLR 781.
[212] 2010 (4) SA 1.
[213] ibid.

steps taken by the state.[214] It made clear that, although the Constitution protects and makes justiciable social and economic rights, positive obligations will not be imposed on the state to fulfil immediately and wholly, the requirements of each person.[215] The position of the South African court appears to be one which endorses the approach of the ICESCR, one that advocates for progressive (rather than immediate) realisation subject to the available resources of the state.

[3–84]   Thus, while South Africa explicitly protects social and economic rights and is not constrained as to the remedies it can order, it has been careful to determine the parameters of these rights within the context of available state resources. As is common in judicial determinations, they are balanced against competing interests and concepts of reasonableness. This jurisdiction shows that constitutionalising social and economic rights does not mean that in each case these rights will trump the arguments of the state, but rather that they will be treated to the same level of judicial scrutiny as civil and political rights. By adopting the South African framework, it is clear that constitutionalisation does not automatically equate to success in all cases. The court can legitimately examine competing claims on resources in order to determine whether to extend a service, a matter with which the proportionality test is well equipped to deal.

Indirect Constitutionalisation through Article 45

[3–85]   The placement of social and economic rights specifically within the non-justiciable clause of the Constitution is viewed as another stumbling block to justiciability. However, despite the lack of explicit protection, Article 45 does present an opportunity for indirect constitutionalisation. The potential of using this article to indirectly give effect to other rights is evidenced in *Murtagh Properties Ltd v Cleary*.[216] Here, Kenny J held that the preamble to Article 45 does not 'involve the conclusion that the courts may not take [this article] into consideration when deciding whether a claimed constitutional right exists'.[217] Thus, this provision is not legally irrelevant and can be used to interpret the content and existence of other rights, and further, can assist in the interpretation of legislation.

[3–86]   Former Chief Justice Keane has referred to Article 45 as a 'particular problem' in relation to the judicial determination of social and economic rights in Ireland.[218]

---

[214] This balancing act is also evident in the case of *Soobramoney v Minister for Health* 1997 (12) BCLR 1696 (CC). Here, emergency medical care covered life saving, but not life extending treatment and the state could prioritise resources in all non-emergency cases.

[215] This has been evident in recent decisions of the court, including *Nokotyana v Ekurheleni Metropolitan Municipality* [2009] ZACC 33, where the court dismissed claims for ventilated latrines, enhanced lighting and access.

[216] [1972] IR 330.

[217] ibid 337.

[218] Keane (n 16) 6.

In agreement with this sentiment, Justice Niall Fennelly distinguishes between legal rights and desirable policy. Legal rights, he states, infer a corresponding obligation cognisable in law, declared in objective legal terms by the text of law, while policy is for the politicians and is not justiciable, save where it conflicts with legally justiciable rights.[219] Thus, these vague concepts, contained within Article 45, seek to guide the politicians in their policy making,[220] serve no more than pious aspirations,[221] and remain beyond the purview of the courts.[222] Conversely, the inclusion of Directive Principles of Social Policy as non-justiciable has been criticised as undermining the purpose and supremacy of the Constitution itself.[223]

The potential for Article 45 to indirectly constitutionalise social and economic [3–87] rights can be demonstrated by considering the Indian Supreme Court's interpretation of an identical provision. Article 37[224] of the Indian Constitution was inspired by the Irish Constitution's Article 45.[225] However, the 'particular problem' which perplexes certain members of the Irish judiciary does not seem to have the same effect on the Indian Supreme Court, which has embraced these principles to interpret and expand existing textual fundamental rights.[226] Through this expansive and activist approach, the Indian Supreme Court has earned the accolade as the most assiduous court in protecting social and economic rights.[227] A pivotal moment in this regard came when it expanded Article 21[228] to make their Directive Principles of State Policy justiciable, and thus initiated an era of social and economic rights jurisprudence.[229] This unprecedented activism was

---

[219] Justice Niall Fennelly, 'Judicial Decisions and Allocations of Resources' (2010) 23 Advocate 48.

[220] Seval Yildirim, 'Expanding Secularism's Scope: In Indian Case Study' (2004) 52 American Journal of Comparative Law 901.

[221] Gary Jeffrey Jacobsohn, 'The Permeability of Constitutional Borders' (2004) 82 Texas Law Review 1763, 1772.

[222] As Hogan (n 78) 196 points out, the Supreme Court has not given a definitive ruling on this issue. The cases of *Sinnott v Minister for Education* (n 1) and *TD v Minister for Education* (n 2) did not raise Article 45 in their claims.

[223] Jeffrey Usman, 'Non-Justiciable Directive Principles: A Constitutional Design Defect' (2007) 15 Michigan State Journal of International Law 643, 645.

[224] Article 37 states, 'The Provisions contained in this part shall not be enforced by any Court, but the principals therein laid down are nevertheless fundamental in the governance of the country and shall be the duty of the State to apply these principals in making laws.'

[225] Usman (n 223) 647.

[226] Emma Keane, 'Socio-Economic Rights and National Law' (2008) 36 Irish Law Times 62.

[227] Khosla Madhav, 'Addressing Judicial Activism in the Indian Supreme Court; Toward an Evolved Debate' (2009) 32 Hastings International and Comparative Law Review 55.

[228] 'No person shall be deprived of his life or personal liberty except according to procedure established by law'.

[229] The court had previously engaged the right to life to determine cases involving bail (*Maneka Ghandi v Union of India* AIR 1978 SC 597) and treatment in custody (*Mullin v Union Territory of Delhi* AIR 1981 SC 746).

led primarily by the judiciary itself, which instigated public interest litigation by actively encouraging claimants to petition the court.[230]

[3–88] The first case to test the position of social and economic rights in the Indian Constitution came in *Olga Tellis v Bombay*, where issues involving housing and shelter were laid before the court.[231] This public interest litigation was brought on behalf of pavement dwellers against eviction, without notice or compensation, to the outskirts of the city. They argued that this eviction deprived them of their livelihood, and that this displacement from their source of income would infringe their right to life under Article 21 of the Constitution. Chief Justice Chandrachud observed that it would be 'sheer pedantry to exclude the right to livelihood from the content of the right to life'.[232] He noted that, while there was no obligation on the state to provide work for citizens, any unlawful deprivation of livelihood may be challenged as offending the right to life.

[3–89] In *Shantistar Builders v Narayan Khimalal Totame*, the court further entrenched its position, observing that the rights to food, clothing and reasonable accommodation were encompassed under the right to life.[233] Originally deemed to be a right restricting state action in terms of arbitrary arrest and detention,[234] the court interpreted the right to life as being a right to live with dignity, and to flourish intellectually and materially.[235] The court's theme of protecting poverty stricken and vulnerable sections of society in relation to housing issues continued in *Chameli Singh v State of Uttar Pradesh*,[236] where it upheld a policy which infringed on the rights of the privileged for the benefit of the marginalised[237] and, again, in *Ahmedabad Municipal Corp v Nawab Khan Gulab Khan*, where the court granted an injunction restricting the removal of makeshift huts unlawfully present on a public footpath until alternative accommodation could be sourced.[238]

[3–90] As the court advanced housing rights, its activism continued in expanding the parameters of the right to life in order to guarantee the right to health. In *Consumer Education and Research Centre v Union of India*, it held that the right to health and medical care was an integral part of the right to life.[239] This

---

[230] PN Baghwati, 'Judicial Activism and Public Interest Litigation' (1985) 23 Columbia Journal of Transnational Law 561.
[231] AIR 1986 SC 180.
[232] ibid 194.
[233] (1990) 1 SCC 520.
[234] Lauren Birchfield and Jessica Corsi, 'Between Starvation and Globalisation: Realising the Right to Food in India' (2010) 31 Michigan Journal of International Law 691, 709.
[235] Jessie Hohmann, 'Mumbai; the Struggle for the Right to Housing' (2013) 13 Yale Human Rights and Development Law Journal 135.
[236] (1996) 2 SCC 549.
[237] Hohmann (n 235) 140.
[238] AIR 1997 SC 152.
[239] (1995) 3 SCC 42.

ruling established the foundations of a positive obligation on the part of the state to ensure certain standards of good health.[240]

In *Parmanand Katara v Union of India*, the issue of emergency medical care   **[3–91]**
as an iteration of the right to life was addressed.[241] Here the court ordered that legal impediments which prevented hospitals treating medico-legal cases be removed, following the death of a man who had been refused hospitalisation on this basis. The court further ordered that its decision be publicised, thereby creating a general awareness of the state's responsibility to provide emergency medical care.[242] In *Paschim Banga Khet Mazdoor Samity v State of West Bengal*, the court reiterated the duty to provide emergency medical care as an integral part of the preservation of life.[243] Undeterred by the significant cost implications, it ordered that equipment and facilities be provided to ensure the preservation of life in emergency medical situations.[244]

However, resource implications have been considered and accepted as a   **[3–92]**
legitimate reason to restrict access in certain limited circumstances. When faced with the question of whether a reduction in the entitlement to be reimbursed for medical expenses breached Article 21, the court accepted the state's contention that such was necessary in light of financial constraints.[245] Arguably, this outcome may have differed if the benefit was entirely removed, rather than reduced, as medical care must be affordable so as to be within the reach of all.

The case of *Laxmi Mandal v Deen Dayal Harinagar Hospital & Ors* expands   **[3–93]**
again on the *Paschim Banga* judgment.[246] The case, brought on behalf of a woman who had died as a result of carrying a dead foetus in her womb, was the first case worldwide to recognise preventable maternal mortality as a human rights violation.[247] She had been refused access to emergency maternal care as her husband was unable to show a valid ration card, to which he was entitled. The court found that there had been a systematic failure on the part of the state. Declaring that it was the responsibility of the state to ensure that valid ration cards were circulated, the court ordered an overhaul of the system. This included

---

[240] Shah Skeetal, 'Illuminating the Possible in the Developing World; Guaranteeing the Human Right to Health in India' (1999) 32 Vanderbilt Journal of Transnational Law 435.
[241] AIR 1989 SC 2039.
[242] Sarvapelli Radhakrishnan, 'Development of Human Rights in an Indian Context' (2008) 36 International Journal of Legal Information 303, 315.
[243] 1996 3 SCJ 25.
[244] Jennifer Sellin, 'Justiciability of the Right to Health- Access to Medicines – The South African and Indian Experience' (2009) 1 Erasmus Law Review 445, 462.
[245] *State of Punjab v Ram Lubhaya Baga* (1998) 4 SCC 117.
[246] WP (C) 8853/2008.
[247] Sukti Dhital and Jayshree Satpute, 'Claiming the Right to Safe Motherhood Through Litigation: The Indian Story' in Helena Alviar Garcia, Karl Klare and Lucy A Williams (eds), *Social and Economic Rights in Theory and Practice: Critical Inquiries* (Routledge 2014) 159.

requiring the state to actively seek out those in need of ration cards. Moreover, it mandated the establishment of monitoring systems to ensure that its orders were being fully implemented.

[3–94]   Since this judgment, a plethora of cases involving maternal healthcare have arrived before the court.[248] The court's initial activism in this area has not diminished, and in 2010, on its own motion, it brought a case against the Union of India, following reports of a destitute woman who died several days after giving birth on the street.[249] After a preliminary hearing, the court ordered the Government of Delhi to open five homes exclusively for pregnant or lactating destitute women, establish a helpline to promote the homes, make food and medical care available 24 hours per day in the shelters, disseminate information about the shelters, host awareness camps, mobilise medical units to bring women to the shelters, and to involve NGOs. The state took issue with the expansive nature of the orders and filed objections to this effect. Nevertheless, and pending final determination of the appeals process, they were ordered to implement immediately two of the shelters, with food and medical care.[250] In 2013, the conditions of those shelters were brought before the court following the death of a baby.[251] Following a thorough inspection of the facility, and a finding of unsatisfactory conditions,[252] the court ordered several remedial measures, including a dedicated space for ante-natal check-ups, supplemental nutrition, and adequate hot water and heating in winter.[253]

[3–95]   These extensive measures taken by the court to assure fundamental rights in relation to emergency medical care and maternity care are not without precedent. The ongoing public interest litigation in *People's Union for Civil Liberties* is a stark illustration of the dramatic measures taken to protect social and economic rights.[254] Despite the right to food being articulated as forming an integral part of the right to life, it had not been formally enforced.[255] This case, instigated in 2001,

---

[248] ibid 164. It is noted here that 25 cases were lodged between 2010 and 2013.

[249] *Court on its own Motion v Union of India* WP 5913/2010.

[250] Dhital and Satpute in Garcia, Klare and Williams (eds) (n 247) 165.

[251] *Priya Kale v NCT of Delhi* WP (C) 641/2013.

[252] Fact Finding Report: *Priya Kale v NCT of Delhi* WP (C) 641/2013 available at <www. hrln.org/hrln/reproductive-rights/reports/1632-fact-finding-report-priya-kale-vs-gnct-of-delhi-and-ors-w-p-c-6412013.html> last accessed 5 January 2017.

[253] Dhital and Satpute in Garcia, Klare and Williams (eds) (n 247) 165.

[254] *People's Union for Civil Liberties & Ors v India* WP 196/2001.

[255] The only case prior to *People's Union for Civil Liberties & Ors v India* WP 196/2001 was *Kishen Pattnayak v State of Orissa* 1989 AIR 677, where the court was petitioned by way of letter to intervene in circumstances where people were dying from starvation and being forced to sell their children. The court made some orders in terms of irrigation projects to alleviate drought and price fixing, but did not recognise the right to food. Jayna Kothari, 'Social Rights and the Indian Constitution' (2004) Law, Social Justice and Global Development Journal 1, observes that these orders did not ameliorate the immediate needs of the petitioners.

initially sought an order on behalf of those dying from starvation in the state of Rajasthan to compel the government to release food stocks.[256] The underlying principle that this case establishes is that the right to food is intrinsically linked with the right to life as protected by the Constitution. The litigation continues, and a plethora of orders have issued (and continue to issue) from the Supreme Court, including orders in relation to grain allocation, implementing a midday meal scheme in schools, ration cards those living below the poverty line and directions for the operation of ration shops. In addition, orders have issued for a price-setting mechanism for grain, and for grain allocation in the 'work for food' scheme to be doubled and financial assistance for these schemes to be increased.[257]

More exemplary still are the unparalleled enforcement steps that the court has taken in order to ensure the execution of its orders. In 2002, two Commissioners were appointed specifically to enquire into breaches of any of the orders made. They act with the full authority of the Supreme Court to whom they report and may also seek further interventions of the court beyond the initial orders, as necessary.[258]   **[3–96]**

This activism has been criticised by those who argue that the court is pursuing its own political agenda, acting outside of its mandate and breaching the separation of powers.[259] Equally, the efficacy of its orders have been scrutinised, and, in many instances, found wanting.[260] However, in a system rife with corruption, it has helped to ensure, at least in part, that these directive principles are followed in implementing law and policy.[261]   **[3–97]**

India, while the most activist, is not the only jurisdiction to have indirectly constitutionalised social and economic rights. In Bangladesh, protection against forced eviction of slums without rehabilitation and resettlement was deemed to be a breach of the right to life.[262] In Latin America, several states have made significant moves to protect these rights, including making orders with considerable resource implications. In Argentina,[263] the *Viceconte* case centred   **[3–98]**

---

[256] For a full background to the case, see Birchfield and Corsi (n 234).

[257] See Birchfield and Corsi (n 234) 718-729; Kothari (n 255) 1.

[258] Jayna Kothari, 'Social Rights Litigation in India' in Daphne Barak-Erez and Aeyal M Gross (eds), *Exploring Social Rights: Between Theory and Practice* (Hart 2007) 180.

[259] Tara Usher, 'Adjudication of Socio-Economic Rights: One Size Does Not Fit All' (2008) 1 UCL Human Rights Law Review 155, 166.

[260] ibid.

[261] Jamie Cassels, 'Judicial Activism and Public Interest Litigation in India: Attempting the Impossible?' (1989) 37 American Journal of Comparative Law 495, 516.

[262] *Ain O Aalish Kendra and Others v Government of Bangladesh and Others,* Supreme Court of Bangladesh (Writ Petition No. 3034 of 1999) (1999) 2 CHRLD 393.

[263] The Argentinian Constitution does expressly protect social and economic rights by giving the ICESCR constitutional rank. It also allows for 'Amparo' action under Article 43, which provides for a constitutional review in the public interest. See generally, Horacio Javier

on the lack of availability of a vaccine against hemorrhagic fever, which was 95% effective in a population of 3.5 million 'at risk' of contracting the disease.[264] The Court of Appeal ordered the state to manufacture and distribute the vaccine and imposed fines and personal liability on the Minister when the order was not complied with. Here, the court interpreted existing constitutional provisions in light of obligations under the ICESCR to indirectly constitutionalise the right to health. [265]

[3–99]   Brazil has recognised the justiciability of social and economic rights, in particular the rights to education and health,[266] with more HIV / AIDS sufferers receiving treatment due to court orders than government treatment programs.[267] It is estimated that there are approximately 40,000 lawsuits claiming violations of the right to health on a yearly basis, and most of these will succeed.[268] Similar approaches have been taken in Colombia,[269] Costa Rica[270] and Venezuela, among others.[271] The developments in Latin America further serve to strengthen the legitimacy of judicial activism on the indirect constitutionalisation of social and economic rights.

[3–100]   The position outlined above is not one which has found favour within the Irish judiciary to date. While retaining the option, and the ability, to use Article 45 to interpret existing provisions in a manner conducive to the indirect constitutionalisation of social and economic rights, it remains unlikely, given

---

Etchichury, 'Argentina: Social Rights, Thorny Country: Judicial Review of Economic Policies Sponsored by the IFIs' (2006) 22 American University International Law Review 101.

[264] *Viceconte, Mariela Cecelia v Argentinian Ministry of Health and Social Welfare* Case No. 31.777/96 (2 June 1998).

[265] The Supreme Court has expanded this to require that states make access to medical care available in a timely fashion. See *Asociacion Benghalensis v Ministry of Health and Social Welfare* Case No. 16.986 (13 August 2000).

[266] These rights are textually recognised in Articles 6 and 196 of the Brazilian Constitution. Article 6 provides 'Education, health, nutrition, labour, housing, leisure, social security, protection of motherhood and childhood and assistance to the destitute are social rights as set forth in this constitution'. Article 196 states 'health is the right of all and the duty of the State and shall be guaranteed by social and economic policies aimed at reducing the risk of illness and other maladies by universal and equal access to all activities and services for its promotion, protection and recovery'.

[267] Octavio Luiz Motta Ferraz, 'Harming the Poor Through Social Rights Litigation: Lessons from Brazil' (2011) 89 Texas Law Review 1643, 1651.

[268] Keith S Rosen, 'Separation of Powers in Brazil' (2009) 47 Duquesne Law Review 839, 861.

[269] Manuel Jose Cepeda-Espinoza, 'Transcript: Social and Economic Rights and the Colombian Constitutional Court' (2011) 89 Texas Law Review 1699.

[270] Bruce M Wilson, 'Rights Revolutions in Unlikely Places: Colombia and Costa Rica' (2009) 1 Journal of Politics in Latin America 59.

[271] Malcolm Langford, *Social Rights Jurisprudence: Emerging Trends in International and Comparative Law* (Cambridge University Press 2009) Part 1.

the current composition of the Supreme Court, which appears to follow the view that 'poverty is a misfortune for which the law cannot take any responsibility at all'.[272] It is unlikely, given previous judicial opinions, that the far-reaching, positive obligations imposed by the Indian Supreme Court would find favour in Ireland. Arguably, in such circumstances, the separation of powers doctrine would prevail and the measures would be regarded as an inappropriate intrusion into the domain of the executive. Notwithstanding this point, indirect constitutionalisation allows the court to develop incrementally the content and scope of the right on a case by case basis. This approach not only affirms the international accepted stance in relation to the indivisibility and interrelatedness of all fundamental rights, but it allows judicial freedom unfettered by arbitrary restrictions.

Distributive Justice and the Separation of Powers

The Irish Supreme Court has primarily justified its refusal to adjudicate on social and economic rights on the basis of the separation of powers doctrine, considering that, to engage with matters of distributive justice is to go beyond its sanctioned function. [3–101]

The Constitution itself does not mention the phrase 'separation of powers'. Rather, article 6 acknowledges three separate and distinct limbs of the state: the executive, the legislature and the judiciary. The court has explained that the: [3–102]

> Separation of Powers involves for each of the three constitutional organs not only rights but duties also, not only areas of activities and functions but boundaries to them as well with regard to the legislature the right and duty of the Court to intervene is clear and express.[273]

Despite the court acknowledging that it has not only a role, but a duty to intervene to protect the constitutional rights of individuals, the position is that it should not revisit the current doctrine of separation of powers in order to address violations of social and economic rights.[274] The separation of powers has been interpreted in a rigid manner, one which is inflexible and precisely delineated. [3–103]

In essence, the central contention is that cases which involve distributive justice breach the separation of powers doctrine and that they are, as such, beyond the scope of the judicial review and enforcement. The reason for this, according to Gerard Hogan, is that social and economic rights are resource dependent, [3–104]

---

[272] Jeremy Cooper, 'Poverty and Constitutional Justice: The Indian Experience' (1993) 44 Mercer Law Review 611.

[273] *Crotty v An Taoiseach* [1987] ILRM 400, 449 (Finlay CJ).

[274] Quinlivan and Keyes (n 106) 163.

whereas civil and political rights are not.[275] This evidences the continuing and fundamental misconception by the Irish judiciary as to the cost implications surrounding the protection of rights, effective conservation of all fundamental rights necessarily requires both positive and negative obligations.[276]

[3–105] To dispel the notion that social and economic rights inevitably require expensive positive obligations, and thus to counter this particular argument, a brief examination of Canadian jurisprudence is warranted. In Canada, the courts have indirectly constitutionalised these rights and, while not imposing positive obligations on the state, have managed to adequately safeguard many rights by the imposition of negative ones.

[3–106] The main instrument protecting human rights in Canada is the Charter of Rights and Freedoms 1982,[277] which incorporates seven classes of rights and freedoms.[278] There is no explicit provision for social and economic rights. However, ss 73, guaranteeing equality, and 15, ensuring life, liberty and security of the person,[279] have been interpreted as encompassing social and economic rights, a possibility apparent from the earliest cases. [280]

[3–107] One of the defining cases for social and economic rights in Canada was *Victoria City v Adams,* which challenged the constitutionality of a bye-law enacted to prohibit temporary shelters in a public park.[281] In seeking to enforce the prohibition and remove the temporary structures which had been erected by homeless people, the city argued that this was a justified measure to prevent

---

[275] Hogan (n 78) 178.

[276] Conor Gearty and Virginia Mantouvalou, *Debating Social Rights* (Hart 2011) 110; Ellen Wiles, 'Aspirational Principles or Enforceable Rights? The Future for Social and Economic Rights in National Law' (2006) 22 American University International Law Review 35, 47; Sandra Liebenberg, 'The International Covenant on Economic Social and Cultural Rights and its Implications for South Africa' (1995) 11 South African Journal of Human Rights 359, 362.

[277] The Constitution Act 1982, Schedule B to the Canada Act 1982 (UK) 1982, c 11. See Patrick Macklem, 'Social Rights in Canada' in Daphne Barak-Erez and Aeyal M Gross (eds), *Exploring Social Rights: Between Theory and Practice* (Hart 2007) 213-242.

[278] s 2, fundamental freedoms; ss 3 to 5, democratic rights; s 6, mobility rights; ss 7 to 14, legal rights; ss 15 and 28, equality rights; ss 16 to 22, language rights; and s 23, minority language education rights.

[279] s 7 states, 'everyone has the right to life, liberty and security of the person and the right not to be deprived thereof except in accordance with the principles of fundamental justice'. s 15(1) states, 'every individual is equal before the law and has the right to equal protection and equal benefit of the law without discrimination and, in particular, without discrimination based on race, national or ethnic origin, colour, religion, sex, age or mental or physical disability'.

[280] Martha Jackman and Bruce Porter, 'Justiciability of Social and Economic Rights in Canada' in Malcolm Langford (ed), *Social Rights Jurisprudence, Emerging Trends in International and Comparative Law* (Cambridge University Press 2008).

[281] 2008 BCSC 1363.

damage. Evidence was adduced as to the overcrowding and lack of availability in homeless shelters in the city.[282] Ross J, holding that sleep and shelter were necessary preconditions to life, and rejecting the contention that Charter rights could not be engaged without positive action from the state,[283] struck down the legislation as a breach of s 7 of the Charter.

While this judgment does not impose positive obligations on the state to provide for adequate shelter, it does impose negative obligations.[284] The court did not order the provision of more spaces in homeless shelters, nor did it require that the park dwellers be housed in public housing. Rather, where these were not available, the state could not arbitrarily remove the temporary structures, which were deemed to be essential to life.   **[3–108]**

Early cases involving applications to have the state fund healthcare under s 7 of the Charter were unsuccessful, with the court holding that the provision did not include a guarantee to *enhance* life, liberty or security of the person.[285] However, restrictions on access to healthcare were struck down. For example, criminal restrictions on therapeutic abortions were regarded as unconstitutional,[286] as was the denial of sign language support in medical care, as it impeded access and resulted in inferior care.[287] There is no obligation on the state to provide for specific services, and, for example, the challenge of a refusal to fund particular types of therapy for autistic children was unsuccessful.[288]   **[3–109]**

---

[282] The case of *Chaoulli v Quebec (Attorney General)* [2005] 1 SCR 791 was relied upon in this regard. Here, the Supreme Court struck down a provision which prohibited individuals from obtaining private health care. Evidence of long delays in accessing medical care was adduced and the court found that the provision engaged the right to life. While it did not require the state to provide the care, it could not prevent the procurement of private treatment. See generally, Christopher P Manfredi and Antonia Maioni, 'The Last Line of Defence for the Citizen: Litigating Private Health Insurance in Chaoulli v Quebec' (2006) 44 Osgoode Hall Law Journal 249; Thomas MJ Bateman, 'Legal Modesty and Political Boldness: The Supreme Court of Canada's Decision in Chaoulli v Quebec' (2006) 11 Review of Constitutional Studies 317; Jamie Cameron, 'From the MRV to Chaoulli v Canada: The Road Not Taken and the Future of Section 7' (2006) 34 Supreme Court Law Review 105.

[283] 2008 BCSC 1363 [39], where the Attorney General claimed that the deprivation must arise from state action, and, since the government did not cause the homelessness, the Charter could not be invoked.

[284] Margot E Young, 'Rights, The Homeless and Social Change: Reflections on Victoria City v Adams (BCSC)' (2009) 164 British Columbia Studies 103, 108.

[285] *Brown v British Columbia (Minister for Health)* (1990) 6 DLR (4th) 444 BCSC.

[286] *R v Morgentaler* [1988] 1 SCR 30. The restriction required a woman to obtain the approval from a committee of an approved hospital. Failure to do so could result in criminal prosecution.

[287] *Eldridge v British Columbia* (1997)151 DLR (4th) 577 (SCC). See also, Isabel Grant and Judith Mossof, 'Hearing Claims of Inequality – Eldridge v British Columbia' (1998) 10 Canadian Journal of Women and Law 229.

[288] *Auton v British Columbia* [2004] 3 SCR 657.

[3–110]   The case of *PHS Community Services v Canada*, known as '*The Insite Case*' and decided by the Supreme Court in September 2011, has served to entrench the status of social and economic rights within the Charter.[289] The case related to a facility commonly referred to as a drug consumption room, established as a harm reduction mechanism due to an endemic addiction problem in the city. It operated under an exemption to the criminal law for an initial three years, extended by fifteen months. Following a change in government, plans were announced to discontinue the exemption and close the facility.[290]

[3–111]   Insite brought a claim to the British Columbia Supreme Court, claiming that the state would be in breach of s 7 of the Charter if the exemption was terminated and the facility closed. [291] The court found that, as the staff managed and prevented the spread of disease and provided services which amounted to healthcare,[292] the withdrawal of the exemption by the state would prevent access to healthcare and therefore engage the right to life and s 7.

[3–112]   The Court of Appeal upheld the ruling, determining that the right to life was engaged, as the service prevented death by overdose, and, further, that the injection of drugs without medical supervision posed a risk to life. [293]

[3–113]   On final appeal to the Canadian Supreme Court, it was unanimously held that the removal of the exemption would breach Charter rights. It issued an order of mandamus, directing the Minister to grant a permanent exemption allowing the facility to continue with its activities.[294] McLachlin CJ stated that, 'where the law creates a risk to health by preventing access to health care, a deprivation of the right to security of the person is made out'.[295]

[3–114]   The Canadian courts have not, to date, declared positive obligations in respect of social and economic rights. However, this possibility has not been specifically excluded. In *Gosselin v Quebec*, McLachlin J felt that the Charter should be allowed to develop incrementally and that its content should not be constricted by previous cases,[296] and, in *Insite,* the language used by the court is indicative

---

[289] 2011 SCC 44.

[290] For a full background to the case, see Margot Young, 'Context Choice and Rights: PHS Community Services v Canada (Attorney General)' (2011) 44 University of British Columbia Law Review 221; Claire-Michelle Smyth and Siobhan Kelly, 'Drug Consumption Rooms: Towards the Right to Health for Addicts' (2013) 31 Irish Law Times 197.

[291] *PHS Community Services Ltd v Canada (Attorney General)* [2008] BCSC 661.

[292] Including the provision of ante-natal classes for pregnant women who otherwise may not have received this, due to their addictions.

[293] 2010 BCCA 15, 314 DLR (4th) 209.

[294] 2011 SCC 44.

[295] ibid [93].

[296] [2002] SCC 42 [79].

of future possibilities.[297] However, a more recent attempt to impose positive obligations was struck out without hearing. The case of *Tanudjaja v Canada* was brought by a group of housing activists alleging that legislative and policy changes taken by the Ontario government resulted in inadequate housing and increased homelessness.[298] In essence, it was asking the court to determine whether ss 7 and 15 of the Charter carried a positive obligation to be housed. The petition was initially struck out and the Court of Appeal upheld this determination, as the challenge did not point to a specific piece of offending law, rather a complex matrix of policies. As the majority agreed with the lower court's decision, it did not enter into further discussion of whether or not positive obligations *could* be placed on the state on the issue of homelessness. In her dissenting judgment, however, Feldman J opined that it was too early to decide whether or not this case contained circumstances which would merit the court imposing positive obligations, advocating strongly for the case to be heard.[299] Leave to appeal to the Supreme Court in this case was rejected in 2015.

Thus, as Canada has shown, it is possible to protect social and economic rights [3–115] adequately without imposing excessively burdensome positive obligations. Extrapolating from this in the Irish context, the argument for non-justiciability based on resource implications can be dismissed if adequate protection is possible by the imposition of negative obligations. Social and economic rights may be assured through negative obligations, while, conversely, certain civil and political rights may be costly to guarantee. Further, all fundamental rights contain elements of positive and negative obligations on the state. Thus, the resource argument proffered by Ireland in this regard becomes considerably less persuasive.

On a more extensive examination of the separation of powers doctrine, it is [3–116] apparent that the rigid interpretation as determined by the Irish courts is not the sole method of interpretation. An alternative understanding of the separation of powers could be based on or more general concepts of accountability and justification.[300] This is supported by the doctrine's purpose, based on protecting the citizen from tyranny, where all power is vested in one organ of the state.[301]

---

[297] Matthew Rottier Voell, 'PHS Community Services Society v Canada (Attorney General) Positive Health Rights, Health Care Policy and Section 7 of the Charter' (2011) 31 Windsor Review of Legal and Social Issues 41, 56.

[298] 2014 ONCA 852.

[299] ibid [49].

[300] Nicholas Haysom, 'Giving Effect to Socio-Economic Rights: The Role of the Judiciary' (1999) 1 Economic and Social Rights Review 11.

[301] For analysis of this point, see David Gwynn Morgan, *The Separation of Powers in the Irish Constitution* (Roundhall 1997); Mark de Blacam, 'Children, Constitutional Rights and the Separation of Powers' (2002) 37 Irish Jurist 115; Philip B Kurland, 'The Rise and Fall of the "Doctrine" of Separation of Powers' (1986) 85 Michigan Law Review 592; Bruce Ackerman, 'The New Separation of Powers' (2000) 113 Harvard Law Review 634.

Unlike the austere position taken in Ireland, it has been argued that a central feature of the doctrine is that its boundaries are flexible and undetermined,[302] with any stringent features mostly ameliorated by the 'checks and balances' system introduced.[303] The most common form of such checks and balances in action is the judicial review of executive and legislative decisions.[304]

[3–117] As the courts are the sole body with the power to administer justice,[305] they have determined that the supremacy of the Constitution trumps the separation of powers.[306] Thus, where the executive or legislature has exceeded its power, the court retains the ability to nullify the action. The issue with certain social and economic rights is the inaction of the state and whether the court has the power to compel action, rather than merely prohibit. To this end the court has categorically determined that issues involving distributive justice cannot be adjudicated upon, as this would breach the separation of powers. Arguably, by excluding an entire cache of rights from judicial review, it is giving sole power to one branch of state, creating the very situation that the doctrine of separation of powers was designed to avoid. Such an uncompromising application of the doctrine weakens judicial review to the 'point of futility'.[307]

[3–118] The argument that the court cannot engage in distributive justice shows a flawed understanding of the difference between distributive and commutative or corrective justice and the court has, in several cases, blurred the lines between the two, undermining the cogency of its reasoning.[308]

[3–119] The Supreme Court, in *Magee v Farrell,* considered the provision of civil legal aid[309] for representation at an inquest into a death in custody.[310] In the

---

[302] Cassels (n 261) 513.

[303] As initially introduced in American constitutional law. See Pieterse (n 196) 386. See also, Eoin Carolan, *The New Separation of Powers: A Theory for the Modern* State (Oxford University Press 2009).

[304] The Constitution provides for a tripartite split of executive, legislature and judiciary. However, the practicality of this is that the executive and the legislature have now merged and such division no longer exists. See David Gwynn Morgan, 'Judicial-o-centric: Separation of Powers on the Wane?' (2004) 1 Irish Jurist 142. The author argues that, technically, there are two: the judiciary and the 'political organs'.

[305] Article 34.1 states, 'Justice shall be administered in courts established by law by judges appointed in the manner prescribed by this Constitution, and, save in such special and limited circumstances as may be prescribed by law, shall be administered in public'.

[306] *Crotty v An Taoiseach* [1987] ILRM 400; *McKenna v An Taoiseach (No.2)* [2003] 2 IR 10; *McCrystal v Minister for Children and Youth Affairs* [2013] ILRM 217.

[307] TRS Allan, 'Human Rights and Judicial Review: A Critique of Due Deference' (2006) 65 Cambridge Law Journal 671, 677.

[308] Gerry Whyte, 'A Tale of Two Cases – Divergent Approaches of the Irish Supreme Court to Distributive Justice' (2010) 1 Dublin University Law Journal 365.

[309] [2009] IESC 60.

[310] This particular area was not covered in the Civil Legal Aid Act 1995 and, therefore, her claim was based on a constitutional right to legal aid.

High Court, Gilligan J found that the fair procedures guaranteed under the Constitution required the state to provide legal aid in these circumstances.[311] Prior to this, several cases had determined that the right extended only to the specific circumstances delineated in the Civil Legal Aid Act 1995.[312] The Supreme Court unanimously overturned the decision of the High Court, ending speculation over the advancement of legal aid for civil matters, and held that civil legal aid will only be available within the parameters of the legislation.[313]

Some three months later, a case relating to criminal legal aid came before the Supreme Court. The appellant in *Carmody v Minister for Justice, Equality and Law Reform* argued that the right to legal aid included an entitlement to be represented by a barrister in addition to a solicitor in a District Court case.[314] Under the Act,[315] a District Court judge had no power to appoint a barrister, save in the exceptional circumstances, where the accused is charged with murder.[316] The accused had been charged with 42 offences involving livestock in a relatively complex case, wherein the state was using a specialist barrister to prosecute. The appellant was unsuccessful in the High Court and appealed the decision to the Supreme Court. He contended that the offending provision was unconstitutional, as it precluded the District Court from appointing a barrister to a case, regardless of the seriousness or complexity of the issue. The court noted that the right to legal aid in criminal cases was a constitutional right, and the Act was merely a means of vindicating that right. Ultimately, the court held that criminal law had changed drastically since the enactment of the legislation and that the complexity of the case was something that should be considered. It also noted that, where the prosecution was represented by a barrister, this

[3–120]

---

[311] [2005] IEHC 388.

[312] For example, see *Grogan v Parole Board* [2008] IEHC 204; *McBrearty v Morris* [2003] IEHC 153; *Lawlor v Planning Tribunal* [2008] IEHC 282.

[313] Relying on the case of *O'Donoghue v Legal Aid Board* [1976] IR 325, the court held that the constitutional right was to have the Act administered in a fair way and not to infer a right to legal aid based on the unspecified right of access to the courts contained within Article 40.

[314] [2010] 1 ILRM 157.

[315] s 2(1)(b) of the Criminal Justice (Legal Aid) Act 1962 provides, "If it appears to the District Court … that by reason of the gravity of the charge or of exceptional circumstances it is essential in the interest of justice that [a person charged before it] should have legal aid in the preparation and conduct of his defence before it, the Court shall, on application being made to it in that behalf, grant in respect of him a certificate for free legal aid (in this Act referred to as a legal aid (District Court) certificate) and thereupon he shall be entitled to such aid and to have a solicitor and (where he is charged with murder and the Court thinks fit) Counsel assigned to him for that purpose in such manner as may be prescribed by regulations under S 10 of this Act".

[316] This exception was made redundant by the Criminal Justice Act 1999, which abolished the preliminary examination procedure in the District Court for murder charges. This was pointed out by Murray J in *Carmody v Minister for Justice, Equality and Law Reform* [2010] 1 ILRM 157, 161.

could be a relevant factor in determining the type of representation that was appropriate for the defendant.[317]

[3–121] The *Carmody* case illustrates that the courts have no issue in ordering what amounts to distributive justice, where they feel that the right in question is significant enough, and that is, in essence, what the Supreme Court did in this case. Arguments that resource implications are secondary in cases involving civil and political rights are misleading.[318] This ruling ensures that persons accused of criminal offences have the right to apply for the representation of a barrister in addition to a solicitor in District Court matters. Where this is granted, it will involve significant costs to the state. Even where legal aid is not granted in these circumstances, the application process and potential appeal against its refusal will have resource implications for the state. Thus, in terms of access to legal aid for criminal matters, the polycentric and distributive implications of assuring the right are not considered by the court. They are merely vindicating a fundamental right.

[3–122] Equally, the Supreme Court decision in *DPP v Gormley* determined that an accused has the right of access to a solicitor prior to being questioned by Gardaí.[319] Up to this point, an accused's right of access to a solicitor in Garda custody was defined as 'reasonable access',[320] and this was interpreted restrictively.[321] The extension of this right has clear resource implications. If an individual has the right to legal advice prior to questioning, and where that person cannot afford independent legal advice, it falls to the state to vindicate that right in the form of providing legal aid.

[3–123] Applying Hogan's argument (that resource implications are secondary when addressing civil and political rights) to the cases above shows the arbitrary and nonsensical nature of the distinction.[322] In assuring the right to a fair trial in criminal procedures, the court in *Carmody* declared that the complete exclusion of the ability to appoint a barrister was unconstitutional, while, in *Magee*, the complete exclusion of legal representation for inquests into death was not. Hogan might argue that the court in *Carmody* was not ordering the state to provide for a barrister in all cases in the District Court, but merely that the judge would have the ability to appoint one should the case require it. Resource implications would be secondary, as one would only be appointed where the seriousness of the case warranted it, and where existing criteria for the grant of legal aid had

---

[317] [2010] 1 ILRM 157, 181-182.
[318] Hogan (n 78) 181.
[319] [2014] IESC 17.
[320] *DPP v Healy* [1990] 2 IR 73.
[321] *DPP v Buck* [2002] 2 IR 268.
[322] Gerard Hogan, 'Judicial Review and Socio-Economic Rights' in Jeremy Sarkin and William Binchy (eds), *Human Rights, The Citizen and the State: South African and Irish Perspectives* (Clarus Press 2001) 1, 8.

been met. This could equally be applied to *Magee*. The resource implications would only arise in circumstances where existing criteria for the grant of legal aid had been met, and is not a blanket guarantee that all cases of this nature would be provided with state funded legal aid.

The strict interpretation of distributive justice as a bar to justiciability appears **[3–124]** to be losing some traction, in the High Court at least. In disagreeing with the state's contention that the court could not entertain claims of distributive justice, the court determined that where:

> State action results in a breach of human rights and where the only remedy is the expenditure of additional money, the Court, in my opinion, must be entitled to make an appropriate order, even if the consequence is that the State must spend money to meet the terms of that order.[323]

This appears to require some positive action on the part of the state in breaching **[3–125]** rights before such a remedy may be imposed, akin to the reasoning espoused in *AMCD v Minister for Education*.[324] As such, remedies could not be imposed for state inaction.

Equally, any arguments made against justiciability on the grounds of distributive **[3–126]** justice can only apply where the order sought imposes costly positive obligations on the state. Should a litigant seek a negative order restraining the state from action, such considerations become contestable. The stark inconsistencies, outlined above, undermine the court's position in relation to social and economic rights and distributive justice.

Conclusion

This chapter demonstrates that the restrictive interpretation of social and **[3–127]** economic rights has a significant and detrimental effect on their development. In order to succeed, a litigant must show that their claim falls within the vague and undefined 'exceptional circumstances' espoused by the Supreme Court. Such an excessively high threshold has, for the most part, deterred litigation. Despite ample opportunity to directly and indirectly constitutionalise these rights, the court has refused to do so. The other jurisdictions referenced herein may serve as persuasive authority in guiding the judiciary. Drawing primarily on the separation of powers doctrine in defence of this position, the Irish courts have remained steadfast. A number of flaws with this reasoning have been identified. First, the exclusion of an entire cache of rights from judicial review

---

[323] *CA and TA v Minister for Justice* [2014] IEHC 532 [12.6] (MacEochaidh J).
[324] [2013] IEHC 175.

is, in itself, an arguable breach of the separation of powers. Secondly, as is evident from Canadian jurisprudence, effective protection does not necessarily require expensive positive action, as many rights may be adequately vindicated by the imposition of negative obligations. Finally, the cogency of this reasoning is undermined by the court engaging in distributive justice when determining cases of civil and political rights.

[3–128]   Yet, despite this apparent shift towards constitutionalisation, Irish courts remain relatively insulated from this phenomenon due to Ireland's dualist nature, a concept discussed in the next chapter.

[3–129]   Given that the domestic approach is primarily opposed to the justiciability of these rights, the next chapters examine Ireland's international obligations. The state has signed up to many international treaties which may encompass certain social and economic rights, four of which are considered in the later chapters. These treaties, to varying degrees, require the state to protect and vindicate the rights contained therein. Ireland's record with each of these treaties is examined, in order to ascertain whether the domestic position is resulting in the state falling foul of its international obligations, and, further, whether any of these obligations could be used to enhance domestic judicial protection.

CHAPTER 4

The International Covenant on Economic Social and Cultural Rights

The ICESCR: An Introduction

In the aftermath of World War II and the utter failure the League of Nations to
achieve its objective of maintaining international peace, the Charter establishing
the United Nations (UN) entered into force on 24 October 1945.[1] Its purposes
were twofold: to maintain international peace and stability and to protect human
rights.[2] One of the first tasks assigned to the newly created organisation was to
draft an international human rights document. The Commission during its first
session established a Committee to undertake this task.[3] On 10 December 1948,
the Universal Declaration of Human Rights (UDHR) was adopted by the General
Assembly, a document which, for the first time, provided a comprehensive
catalogue of human rights. It speaks, in its preamble, of the dignity and worth
of the human person and states that human rights should be protected by the
rule of law.[4] Thus, the UDHR clearly envisioned a legalistic approach to the
protection of human rights, in recognition that, in order for human rights to be
effective, vindication in law was an essential prerequisite.

[4–01]

No distinction is made in the UDHR between civil and political rights on the one
hand, and social and economic rights on the other. Rather, it is a thorough account
of the rights which should be protected, suggesting that, at the commencement of
the modern human rights movement, social and economic rights were envisaged
as being equally as important as civil and political rights. Brodsky and Day use
this as their starting point to argue that international law does not, and never
has, supported a division of the rights and such division is based in national law
perspectives, which cling to a negative model of human rights.[5]

[4–02]

---

[1] United Nations, Charter of the United Nations (adopted 24 October 1945) 1 UNTS XVI.
[2] Article 1.
[3] Report of the Commission on Human Rights, New York, February 1947 E/259. Initially,
     this Committee consisted of Eleanor Roosevelt, Pen-Chung Chang and Charles Malik,
     with the assistance of the UN Secretariat. The following month, following a request from
     the Chairman of the Human Rights Commission, representatives from Australia, Chile,
     France, Russia (then the Soviet Union) and the UK were included in the drafting process.
[4] Full text of the Preamble is available at <www.un.org/en/documents/udhr/index.shtml>
     last accessed on 16
[5] February 2017.
     Gwen Brodsky and Shelagh Day, 'Beyond the Social and Economic Rights Debate:

[4–03] Unfortunately, the UDHR was not a legally binding document, but rather, an aspirational one. It was merely a guide to the rights to which states should have regard when implementing their national law provisions. It did not require that any of the rights contained therein actually be transposed into national law, nor could they be relied upon in national or international courts.

[4–04] Negotiations began in 1949 to transpose the rights contained within the UDHR into legally binding obligations, concluding in 1966. The divide between the categories of rights came to the fore during this transposition. Despite the official position that the two sets of rights are universal, interdependent, interrelated and indivisible,[6] there was profound disagreement regarding the proper status of social and economic rights, with both sides adopting extreme and discordant views.[7] Negotiations devolved into polemics, and, against this backdrop, attempts to transpose the UDHR into one legally binding document were abandoned.[8] Accordingly, it was agreed that two separate documents would be drafted, marking the initial and persistent divide in international law between the two sets of rights. The International Covenant on Civil and Political Rights (ICCPR)[9] (containing civil and political rights) and the International Covenant on Economic Social and Cultural Rights (ICESCR)[10] (consisting of social and economic rights) were adopted by the General Assembly and opened for signature, ratification and accession on 16 December 1966.[11]

[4–05] The effect of this compromise cannot be overstated. The two categories of rights were set on divergent paths, with different importance ascribed to each. Often described as a casualty of Cold War politics, social and economic rights were relegated to a subordinate status to civil and political rights.[12] This subordination created significant difficulties in the propagation of, and force accorded to, these rights in international, regional and domestic contexts.

[4–06] Perhaps due to prevailing ideas at the time that individuals would need protection from interference *by* the state rather than rights that could be asserted *against* the state, civil and political rights were framed in terms of negative, rather than

---

Substantive Equality Speaks to Poverty' (2002) 14 Canadian Journal of Women and the Law 185.

6   Vienna Declaration, Second World Conference on Human Rights 1993 [5].
7   Henry Steiner, Ryan Goodman and Philip Alston, *International Human Rights in Context; Law Politics Morals*, (3rd edn, Oxford University Press 2007) 263.
8   Primarily due to pressure from the Western-dominated Commission; UN Doc A2929 (1955) 7.
9   (adopted 16 December 1966, entered into force 23 March 1976) 999 UNTS 171 and 1057 UNTS 407.
10 (adopted 16 December 1966, entered into force 3 January 1976) 993 UNTS 3.
11 UN Resolution 2200A (XXI).
12 Daniel J Whelan and Jack Donnelly, 'The West, Economic and Social Rights, and the Global Human Rights Regime: Setting the Record Straight' (2007) 29 Human Rights Quarterly 908, 931.

positive obligations. The state had a clear obligation to refrain from or cease performing a particular act, and, where it failed to do so, would be required to have an adequate system of redress in place.

Social and economic rights, on the other hand, were to be realised progressively, subject to available resources,[13] a 'programmatic'[14] approach not applied to civil and political rights. The absence of immediate and concrete obligations in the ICESCR, coupled with the lack of any complaints mechanism,[15] were powerful factors contributing to continued violations,[16] compounding the inferior status of the rights on an international scale.[17] In contrast, the ICCPR contains more compulsory wording, such as, 'all peoples have the right', compelling states to 'ensure' these rights.[18] Additionally, the first optional protocol to the ICCPR accorded the right of individual and inter-state petition to the Human Rights Committee, a mechanism not afforded to the rights within the ICESCR. [4–07]

The state has three core obligations under the ICESCR: the duties to respect, protect and fulfil the rights contained therein.[19] The duty to respect is a passive obligation and requires the state to avoid interfering, by law or conduct, with the enjoyment of the rights contained within the Covenant. The duty to protect, [4–08]

---

[13] (n 10) Part II, Article 2(1) states, 'Each State Party to the present Covenant undertakes to take steps, individually and through international assistance and co-operation, especially economic and technical, to the maximum of its available resources, with a view to achieving progressively the full realization of the rights recognised in the present Covenant by all appropriate means, including particularly the adoption of legislative measures'.

[14] Steiner, Goodman and Alston (n 7) 284.

[15] In contrast to the ICESCR, the ICCPR contained, within its first optional protocol an individual complaints mechanism to the Human Rights Committee.

[16] Michael J Dennis and David P Stewart, 'Justiciability of Economic, Social and Cultural Rights: Should there be an International Complaints Mechanism to Adjudicate the Rights to Food, Water, Housing and Health?' (2004) 98 American Journal of International Law 462; Wouter Vandenhole, 'Completing the UN Complaint Mechanisms for Human Rights Violations Step by Step: Towards a Complaints Procedure Complementing the International Covenant on Economic Social and Cultural Rights' (2003) 21 Netherlands Quarterly of Human Rights 423.

[17] Catarina de Albuquerque, 'Chronicle of an Announced Birth: The Coming into Life of the Optional Protocol to the International Covenant on Economic Social and Cultural Rights – The Missing Piece of the International Bill of Human Rights' (2010) 32 Human Rights Quarterly 144.

[18] (n 9) Article 2(3) states, 'Each State Party to the present Covenant undertakes: (a) To ensure that any person whose rights or freedoms as herein recognised are violated shall have an effective remedy, notwithstanding that they violation has been committed by a person acting in an official capacity; (b) To ensure that any person claiming such a remedy shall have his right thereto determined by competent judicial, administrative, or legislative authorities, or by any other competent authority provided for by the legal system of the State and to develop the possibilities of judicial remedies; (c) To ensure that competent authorities shall enforce such remedies when granted.'

[19] Maastricht Guidelines on Violations of Economic, Social and Cultural Rights (26 January 1997) [6].

however, is more active in nature, requiring the state to take positive steps to protect against violations by third parties. This requires that the state put effective measures in place by way of legislation or policy to prevent abuses from more powerful actors against the individual, such as landlords or banks. The duty to fulfil is the most contentious, as it requires the state to provide social and economic rights for those who cannot support themselves, through ensuring access to existing services and providing services directly where access through existing structures is unavailable.[20]

[4–09] The Committee on Economic Social and Cultural Rights (CESCR) was established in 1985 to monitor state compliance with the Covenant.[21] Each state party is obliged to provide reports to the Committee at regular intervals, who, in turn, reports on the state's progress on implementation and fulfilment of social and economic rights. The Committee can issue recommendations, but has no power to compel compliance, as their concluding observations are non-binding in nature. The Committee has also been active in producing general comments, which clarify the content, scope and interpretation of rights contained within the ICESCR.[22] These general comments, again, are of a non-binding nature and do not create a legally enforceable right, Rather, they are merely an authoritative interpretation. They set out the obligations on the state and what steps should be taken in order to ensure that they respect, protect and fulfil the rights. However, given that the ICESCR is a treaty which contains rights which are to be progressively realised, the general comments are of limited use unless the right is contained elsewhere in a legally binding treaty.[23] They are published with a view to assisting the state in its implementation.

[4–10] The wording of the ICESCR has contributed to the continuing view that social and economic rights are lesser rights than their counterparts. The only obligation placed on states is that they take steps 'with a view to achieve progressively the full realisation of the rights' and thus leaves states with a wide margin of appreciation on how to implement the right.[24]

---

[20] Messenbet Assafa, 'Defining the Minimum Core Obligations – Conundrums in International Human Rights Law and Lessons from the Constitutional Court of South Africa' (2010) 1(1) Mekelle University Law Journal 1, 5.

[21] ECOSOC Resolution 1985/17 of 28 May 1985.

[22] To date, the Committee has released 23 General Comments. For the full text of each, see <tbinternet.ohchr.org/_layouts/treatybodyexternal/TBSearch.aspx?Lang=en&TreatyID=9&DocTypeID=11> last accessed 06 January 2017.

[23] For example, General Comment 8 on the Right to Water is strengthened by a number of other conventions aside from the ICESRC, including The Watercourse Convention 1997, The Convention on Biological Diversity 1992, The Convention on the Rights of the Child 1990 and The Convention on the Elimination of all forms of Discrimination against Women 1979.

[24] Article 2(1).

While the UN formally recognises the interdependent nature of the two sets of rights, the CESCR astutely observed that **[4–11]**

> ...the international community as a whole continue to tolerate all too often breaches of economic, social and cultural rights which, if they incurred in relation to civil and political rights, would provoke expressions of horror and outrage and would lead to concerted calls for immediate remedial action.[25]

When the Committee was established, it had three main objectives; to develop the normative content of the rights, to develop state benchmarks and to hold states accountable.[26] States are required to submit reports to the Committee every five years, detailing the steps taken to progressively realise the rights. A shadow report is also submitted to the Committee by an NGO, which provides an alternative view on the state's compliance with its obligations. Having considered both the state and shadow reports, the Committee then compiles a list of issues which it sends to the state and publishes on its website. The state then replies to these specific questions raised by the Committee and an updated shadow report is also submitted. Based on these renewed submissions, the Committee makes its concluding observations, which contain recommendations on further implementation. The Committee has no power to enforce any of its recommendations. **[4–12]**

States have a duty only to progressively realise these rights, and this obligation is not sufficiently clear to place any positive obligation thereon. Even where a state does not have a programme in place to progressively realise these rights, there is little that can be done about it. The only power that the Committee has is to 'name and shame' the violators through publishing their reports, but, without a clear international consensus as to the legal status of these rights, the reports do little to sway the position. Given that the international community has historically been dominated by Western powers, who opposed the inclusion of these rights from the beginning, it is unsurprising that the position has been slow to change. **[4–13]**

Progressive Realisation and Minimum Core Rights

The Maastricht Guidelines clarify that the state is in breach of its international obligations if it fails to allocate the maximum of its resources to the realisation **[4–14]**

---

[25] Committee Statement to the World Conference, UN Doc E/1993/22 [83].
[26] Economic and Social Council Resolution 1985/17 established the Committee to take over the monitoring functions of the ICESCR which had originally been ascribed to ECOSOS under part IV of the Covenant.

of human rights.[27] Following from this, the Committee in 2007 made a statement entitled 'An Evaluation of the Obligation to Take Steps to the Maximum of Available Resources under an Optional Protocol to the Covenant', which, regrettably, did not define what constitutes available resources.[28] The Committee has several indicators in assessing compliance, including comparing spending on social and economic rights with spending on non social and economic rights, comparing expenditure with other states of similar status and comparing with international indicators.[29]

[4–15]   The concept of progressive realisation introduces an element of flexibility, which imposes a continuing obligation on states to take concrete steps towards full realisation. There are three main elements to progressive realisation. First, there must be immediate and tangible progress towards realisation, thus, the element of flexibility does not mean that the state can postpone implementation.[30] The second element is that the state cannot pursue retrogressive measures, creating a strong presumption of impermissibility should the state deliberately introduce such. Where such measures have been taken, the Committee has emphasised that the state would need to fully justify itself.[31] Liebenberg postulates that a regressive measure may be justified where it can be demonstrated as necessary to achieve equity in the realisation of the right, or to create a more sustainable basis for realisation.[32] The state is likely to be held to a higher standard in relation to retrogressive measures and, when assessing such, the Committee will examine whether:

> (a) There was reasonable justification for the action (b) alternatives were comprehensively examined (c) there was genuine participation of affected groups in examining the proposed measures and alternatives (d) the measures were directly or indirectly discriminatory (e) the measures have a sustained impact on the realisation of the right …. and (f) whether there as an independent review of the measure at national level.[33]

---

27   Maastricht Guidelines on Violations of Economic, Social and Cultural Rights (26 January 1997).

28   UN Doc E/C.12/2007/1.

29   Centre for Women's Global Leadership, *Maximum Available Resources and Human Rights* (Rutgers University 2011) 3.

30   UN Commission on Human Rights, *Note verbale dated 5 December 1986 from the Permanent Mission of the Netherlands to the United Nations Office at Geneva Addressed to the centre for Human Rights* ("Limburg Principles") UN Doc E/CN.4/1987/17 [21].

31   UN Committee on Economic Social and Cultural Rights (CESCR), *General Comment No. 13: The Right to Education (Article 13 of the Covenant)* UN Doc E/C.12/1999/10 [45].

32   Sandra Liebenberg, *Socio-Economic Rights Adjudication under a Transformative Constitution* (Juta 2010) 190.

33   UN Committee on Economic Social and Cultural Rights (CESCR), *General Comment No. 19: The Right to Social Security (Article 9 of the Covenant)* UN Doc E/C.12/GC/19 [42].

However, the Committee has produced by way of little further guidance. At times, it will criticise a measure without identifying whether such has, in fact, breached the state's obligation, which is problematic particularly during straitened fiscal times.[34]   **[4–16]**

The third element for progressive realisation is that special measures must be implemented for particularly vulnerable and disadvantaged groups. This requires the state to take positive steps to reduce structural inequality and to give preferential treatment to these groups.[35]   **[4–17]**

The steps to be taken towards progressive realisation vary depending on the resources of the state.[36] The minimum core approach sets out that there is a minimum standard of living which the state must ensure. While the general application of the Convention is one of progressive realisation subject to state resources, the obligation to implement minimum core rights is an immediate one.   **[4–18]**

As noted above, one of the Committee's functions is to define the content and scope of rights through its general comments and it has been most taxed when tasked with articulating this in terms of a state's minimum core obligations. The importance of these minimum core obligations cannot be overstated. They seek to establish a minimum legal content, asserting that people are entitled to a minimum standard and that it is unacceptable for individuals to live in conditions of extreme poverty and deprivation which fall below that of the minimum standard.[37] The general comments, while useful in elaborating upon the content of the rights, fail to address adequately what the minimum core of each right is.[38] However, the Committee has given several examples, including the right not to be hungry,[39] basic primary education and equality of access   **[4–19]**

---

34 Colm O'Cinneide, 'Austerity and the Faded Dream of a Social Europe' in Aoife Nolan (ed), *Economic Social and Cultural Rights after the Global Financial Crisis* (Cambridge University Press 2014) 21.

35 Lillian Chenwi, 'Unpacking Progressive Realisation, its Relation to Resources, Minimum Core and Reasonableness and some Methodological Considerations for Assessing Compliance' (2013) 39 De Jure Law Journal 738, 746.

36 Resources in this context include both national and international assistance. See UN Commission on Human Rights, *Note verbale dated 5 December 1986 from the Permanent Mission of the Netherlands to the United Nations Office at Geneva Addressed to the centre for Human Rights* ("Limburg Principles") UN Doc E/CN.4/1987/17 [26].

37 Katharine G Young, 'The Minimum Core of Social and Economic Rights: A Concept in Search of Content' (2008) 33 Yale Journal of International Law 113.

38 Mesenbet Assefa, 'Defining Minimum Core Conundrums in International Human Rights Law and Lessons from the Constitutional Court of South Africa' (2010) 1 Mekelle University Law Journal 48, 50.

39 UN Committee on Economic Social and Cultural Rights (CESCR), *General Comment No. 12: The Right to Adequate Food (Article 11 of the Covenant)* UN Doc E/C.122/1999/5.

to education at other levels[40] and non-discriminatory access to and equitable distribution of healthcare services.[41]

[4–20]   General Comment No. 3 states that the state's responsibility is to provide

> … [a] minimum core obligation to ensure the satisfaction of, at the very least minimum essential levels of each of the rights is incumbent upon every state party. Thus, for example, a state party in which any significant number of individuals is deprived of essential food stuffs, of essential primary health care, of basic shelter and housing, or of the most basic forms of education is, prima facie, failing to discharge its obligations under the Covenant.[42]

[4–21]   However, this is somewhat qualified, as the Covenant goes on to provide a number of preconditions that must be met before a state can be said to have breached its minimum core obligations. First, there must be a significant number of people who are suffering from the particular deprivation. What constituted a significant number appeared impossible to quantify and the Committee subsequently clarified, in General Comment No. 15, that minimum core obligations apply as an individual right, thereby effectively obviating this initial requirement.[43] However, in the absence of an individual complaints mechanism, the practical result of this change is effectively moot. Secondly, 'any assessment as to whether a state has discharged its minimum core obligations must also take into account of resource constraints applying within the country concerned'.[44] It must be demonstrated that the resources available have been used to meet those minimum core obligations which may dilute the prima facie breach of rights considerably. Notwithstanding criticisms, this qualification in practice shifts the burden of proof to the state. The individual does not have to show that the state has failed, but rather, the state must show that it has used its resources in a manner compatible with its obligations under the Covenant.

[4–22]   As clear benchmarks for progressive realisation have not been precisely

---

[40] UN Committee on Economic Social and Cultural Rights (CESCR), *General Comment No. 13: The Right to Education (Article 13 of the Covenant)* UN Doc E/C.12/1999/10.

[41] UN Committee on Economic Social and Cultural Rights (CESCR), *General Comment No. 14: The Right to the Highest Attainable Standard of Health (Article 12 of the Covenant)* UN Doc E/C.12/2000/4.

[42] UN Committee on Economic Social and Cultural Rights (CESCR), *General Comment No. 3: The Nature of States Parties' Obligations (Article 1 Para 1 of the Covenant)* UN Doc E/1991/23 [10].

[43] UN Committee on Economic Social and Cultural Rights (CESCR), *General Comment No. 13: The Right to Education (Article 13 of the Covenant)* UN Doc E/C.12/1999/10 [44].

[44] UN Committee on Economic Social and Cultural Rights (CESCR), *General Comment No. 3* UN Doc E/1991/23 .

delineated, nor has the content of minimum core rights been catalogued, this has resulted in a more theoretical approach being taken. Katherine Young identifies three separate approaches to understanding the minimum core rights and obligations.[45] First, she explains, the essence approach, which seeks to establish the essential minimum of the right, stating, 'it is the absolute, inalienable and universal crux, an unrelinquishable nucleus that is the *raison d'etre* of the basic legal norm, essential to its definition'.[46] There is no definitive reason as to the rationale for each right and, resultantly, conflicting justifications for rights may emerge. Thus the core of the right to housing can arguably flow from a right to be protected from the elements[47] or, equally, from a right to have access to a place to wash and excrete, as they are prohibited in public places.[48] In this context, the minimum core is to satisfy the basic needs of the individual, interpreted by the Committee as the essentials to survival and life.[49] However, focusing on biological survival may also be problematic, as it deteriorates into an exercise determining the minimum requirements necessary for a human to survive.[50] Moving towards a value based approach, which looks further than what is strictly required to maintain life, and focussing instead on what it means to be human, provides an alternative. The inherent dignity of the human person is a concept which has flourished since the introduction of the UDHR and has been used to guide the interpretation of social and economic rights.[51] This approach equally creates difficulties in that dignity can be measured either objectively or subjectively and further hampers the development of a precise definition of the minimum core of the right.[52] Thus, Young suggests that this approach is not suitable for determining the normative content of the minimum core.[53]

The second approach identified by Young is the consensus approach, which **[4–23]** focuses on identifying where a consensus has been reached rather than on the

---

[45] Young (n 37).

[46] ibid 126.

[47] David Bilchitz, *Poverty and Fundamental Rights: The Justification and Enforcement of Socio-Economic Rights* (Oxford University Press 2007) 187.

[48] Jeremy Waldron, 'Homelessness and the Issue of Freedom' (1991) 39 UCLA Law Review 295

[49] UN Committee on Economic Social and Cultural Rights (CESCR), *General Comment No. 3* (n 42).

[50] Johan Galtung, 'Goals, Processes and Indicators of Development' (1978) 13 available at <www.transcend.org/galtung/papers/Goals%20and%20Processes%20of%20 Development-An%20Integrated%20View.pdf> last accessed 19 October 2016.

[51] For example, in *Khosa v Minister of Social Development* 2004 (6) SA 505 (CC), the South African Constitutional Court emphasised the connection between dignity and social assistance; *Social and Economic Rights Action Centre v Nigeria*, Comm No 155/96 2001-2002. The African Commission held that the right to food is inseparably linked to dignity.

[52] Oscar Schachter, 'Human Dignity as a Normative Concept' (1983) 77 American Journal of International Law 848.

[53] Young (n 37) 138.

normative content of the minimum core. The idea is that, through an examination of jurisprudence, evidence of a consensus would emerge which would, in turn, develop the normative content of the right. Despite the significant lack of justiciability in many national jurisdictions, the Committee has been able to ascertain a consensus (or an emerging one) from state reports. Arguably, the focus on a consensus in this approach adds to its legitimacy.[54]

[4–24] Finally, the minimum obligation approach focuses on the duties required to implement the minimum core right. While this approach is helpful in establishing the steps that states should take to implement the right, it does little in the way of establishing the normative content.

[4–25] Practically, the difficulty in determining the minimum core of a given right has been played out in the South African Constitutional Court. In *Grootboom*, the court felt that it was impossible to say what the minimum threshold was without identifying the need, which would vary depending on factors such as income, employment and availability of land and preferred to examine the case based on the reasonableness of the steps taken.[55] Similarly, in the *Treatment Action Campaign* case, the court rejected arguments that the minimum core right is not subject to resource constraints.[56] In contrast, the Columbian Supreme Court has expressly endorsed the minimum core approach, in a recent case reviewing 22 tutela claims[57] in relation to the right to health.[58] In this case, the court made a distinction between the minimum core rights which were immediately enforceable and other elements subject to progressive realisation. With this determination, the court ordered an overhaul of the health system, ordering a wide range of goods and services to be made available immediately.

[4–26] The concept of progressive realisation and minimum core rights have, to a large degree, curtailed the development of social and economic rights. The steps required by the state to realise the rights may be minimal and subject to the resource constraints of the state. While the Committee has been highly critical of regressive measures, the financial crisis in recent years has resulted in less available resources and austerity has impacted significantly on the enjoyment of rights protected. Further, the minimum core content of each right is not being met, largely due to its imprecise and contested nature. Given that the role of the

---

[54] Mesenbet Assefa, 'Defining Minimum Core Conundrums in International Human Rights Law and Lessons from the Constitutional Court of South Africa' (2010) 1 Mekelle University Law Journal 48, 58.

[55] 2000 (11) BCLR 1169 (CC).

[56] *Minister of Health v Treatment Action Campaign (TAC)* (2002) 5 SA 721 (CC).

[57] A tutela is a special constitutional writ of protection for human rights introduced by the Columbian Constitution, whereby a citizen can ask any judge in the country to protect their rights when they are being violated by the state and where no other legal action exists to prevent the continuation of the violation.

[58] Constitutional Court of Columbia, CC Decision T-760 (2008).

Committee has primarily, to date, been as a monitoring body, the introduction of the optional protocol to allow it to deliver opinions and decisions on particular cases may serve to clarify these areas.

The Optional Protocol to the ICESCR

In 1966, when the ICCPR opened for signature, so too did its first optional protocol. This protocol gave the Human Rights Committee the power to hear individual and inter-state complaints in relation to alleged violations of the rights contained therein. The omission of a comparable forum to adjudicate breaches of the rights contained within the ICESCR was a powerful factor that contributed to continuing violations.[59]

[4–27]

From 1990, the Committee began calling for the introduction of an optional protocol, which would establish an individual complaints mechanism.[60] In the absence of such a complaints mechanism, the Committee's primary method of ensuring compliance was through the periodic reporting procedure. With a complaints mechanism in place, the Committee would be empowered to offer more effective protection in instances of concrete abuse, issue more definitive guidance on the interpretation of rights, and increase the stature afforded to the Covenant.[61] The continuing opposition to the justiciability of social and economic rights was apparent at the outset of negotiations on the optional protocol.[62] Delegates argued that a complaints mechanism would be impractical, given the imprecise nature of the rights, and would undermine the democratic process in policy and budgetary matters.[63]

[4–28]

In June 2008, the protocol was approved by the Human Rights Council, adopted by the General Assembly and opened for signature in December 2008.[64] It

[4–29]

---

[59] Dennis and Stewart (n 16); Wouter Vandenhole, 'Completing the UN Complaint Mechanisms for Human Rights Violations Step by Step: Towards a Complaints Procedure Complementing the International Covenant on Economic Social and Cultural Rights' (2003) 21 Netherlands Quarterly of Human Rights 423.

[60] The first discussion on the optional protocol was initiated by the Committee UN Doc E/C.12/1991/2 [9].

[61] Tara Melish, 'Introductory Note to the Optional Protocol to the International Covenant on Economic Social and Cultural Rights' (2009) 48 International Legal Materials 256.

[62] For an overview of the main arguments used in negotiations, see Malcolm Langford, 'Closing the Gap? – An Introduction to the Optional Protocol to the International Covenant on Economic Social and Cultural Rights' (2009) 27 Nordic Journal of Human Rights 1, 9-18, which effectively echoes the objections examined herein.

[63] UN Economic and Social Council, *Report of First Session* UN Doc E/CN.4/2004/44 (Geneva 15 March 2004) 7; UN Economic and Social Council, *Report of Fourth Session* UN Doc A/HRC/6/8 (Geneva 30 August 2007) 5.

[64] Resolution of the Human Rights Council 8/2 of 18 June 2008; (adopted 10 December 2008) UNGA A/RES/63/11. For a detailed analysis of the background to the drafting of the optional protocol, see Claire Mahon, 'Progress at the front: The Draft Optional

entered into force on 5 May 2013[65] and, to date, 48 states have signed the protocol. However, only 22 have ratified it.[66]

[4–30]   As per the protocol, there are numerous admissibility criteria which must be met before a complaint can be addressed by the Committee.[67] These include the exhaustion of domestic remedies, a time limitation of one year and requiring that the claim must not be anonymous, vexatious or an abuse of the right to petition.[68] While the Committee does have the power to request interim measures to protect against on-going violations,[69] it only has the jurisdiction to hear claims where the breach occurred, or continued, after the protocol came into effect, confirming the principle of non-retrospectivity.[70]

[4–31]   The optional protocol has two main weaknesses. First, the wording of the treaty itself remains the same: overwhelmingly, the rights are to be realised progressively subject to resources, rather than by way of immediate obligation. Therefore, it may be a difficult task to show that a state has breached these obligations.[71]

[4–32]   There is currently no jurisprudence from the Committee as to how it will interpret state obligations or how influential the general comments will be in defining them.[72] It is anticipated that this ambiguity will decline once it begins to deliver its opinions. There are, at present, six cases pending. Three of these are against Spain, alleging discrimination in accessing pensions in prison,[73] the

---

Protocol to the International Covenant on Economic Social and Cultural Rights' (2008) 8 Human Rights Law Review 617; Melish (n 148); Scott Leckie, 'Another Step Towards Indivisibility: Identifying Key Features of Violations of Economic, Social and Cultural Rights' (1998) 20 Human Rights Quarterly 81.

[65]   Following Uruguay's ratification in February 2013.

[66]   Full list of countries available at <treaties.un.org/Pages/ViewDetails. aspx?src=TREATY&mtdsg_no=IV-3-a&chapter=4&lang=en> last accessed 06 January 2017.

[67]   Option Protocol ICESCR, Article 3; Claire Mahon, 'Progress at the front: The Draft Optional Protocol to the International Covenant on Economic Social and Cultural Rights' (2008) 8 Human Rights Law Review 617, 628.

[68]   Article 3(1) and (2).

[69]   Under Article 5, the Committee can request this where the victim may suffer irreparable damage due to exceptional circumstances.

[70]   Article 3(2)(b).

[71]   Claire-Michelle Smyth, 'The Optional Protocol to the International Covenant on Economic Social and Cultural Rights in Ireland; Will it make a difference?' (2013) 2 Socio Legal Studies Review 1.

[72]   Arne Vandenbogaerde and Wouter Vandenhole, 'The Optional Protocol to the International Covenant on Economic Social and Cultural Rights: An Ex Ante Assessment of its Effectiveness in Light of the Drafting Process' (2010) 10 Human Rights Law Review 207, 231.

[73]   Communication 1/2013.

denial of access to a court to protect the right to housing[74] and non-consensual medical treatment.[75] A further three cases are pending against Ecuador, relating to discrimination against minors,[76] access to compensation established by collective bargaining procedure[77] and the discrimination of women domestic workers.[78]

The weak wording of the optional protocol itself (which resulted from political, rather than legal considerations) is equally of concern.[79] The extensive admissibility criteria was inserted to assuage fears of opening the floodgates.[80] Further, it requires the Committee to take account of the 'reasonableness' of any steps which the state has taken.[81] The interpretation of reasonableness may have a considerable impact upon the efficacy of the optional protocol, which, in turn, could influence the interpretation in regional and domestic systems.[82]   [4–33]

The second issue relates to the enforcement and sanction powers of the Committee, which extend only as far as making recommendations; it has no authority to enforce the decisions or to impose sanctions on the offending state. The only requirement is that the state party gives due consideration to its views.[83]   [4–34]

Despite its inherent weaknesses, the introduction of the optional protocol is a significant step in approximating the treatment of all rights, regardless of derivation and classification.[84] It elevates social and economic rights to a level comparable to civil and political rights in international law,[85] providing a forum whereby violations of rights can be voiced and adjudicated upon, albeit in a   [4–35]

---

74 Communication 2/2014.
75 Communication 4/2014.
76 Communication 3/2014.
77 Communication 7/2015.
78 Communication 10/2015.
79 Vandenbogaerde and Vandenhole (n 72) 209.
80 ibid, 235.
81 Article 8(4) provides, 'when examining communications under the present Protocol, the Committee shall consider the reasonableness of the steps taken by the State Party in accordance with part II of the Covenant'. For an analysis of the drafting of this section, see Brian Griffey, 'The Reasonableness Test: Assessing Violations of State Obligations under the Optional Protocol to the International Covenant on Economic Social and Cultural Rights' (2011) 11 Human Rights Law Review 275, 291-304.
82 Bruce Porter, 'The Reasonableness of Article 8(4) – Adjudicating Claims from the Margin' (2009) 27 Nordic Journal of Human Rights 39, 40.
83 Article 9(2).
84 Statement by Louise Arbour, High Commissioner for Human Rights, to the Open Ended Working Group on OP-ICESCR, Fifth Session, 31 March 2008, which referred to it as being a 'high point in the gradual trend toward a greater recognition of the indivisibility and interrelatedness of all human rights', available at <www.ohchr.org/EN/NewsEvents/Pages/DisplayNews.aspx?NewsID=8688&LangID=E> last accessed 4 April 2015.
85 Lilian Chenwi, 'Correcting the Historical Asymmetry between Rights: The Optional Protocol to the International Covenant on Economic Social and Cultural Rights' (2009) 9 African Human Rights Law Journal 23.

non-enforceable manner.[86] This step marks a considerable advancement and categorically affirms their status as rights.

Ireland and the ICESCR

[4–36]   Ireland signed the ICESCR in 1973 and ratified it in 1989. It signed the Optional Protocol in February 2012, but has not yet ratified it, which means that individual complaints cannot be taken against Ireland to the Committee. In addition, due to Ireland's dualist nature, ICESCR rights cannot be litigated before domestic courts, and even in circumstances where the state ratified the optional protocol, a decision of the Committee could not be enforced in the domestic courts.

[4–37]   In the application of international law generally, a state may be either monist or dualist.[87] Under a monist regime, international treaties automatically form part of domestic law.[88] The Dutch Constitution, having been described as the 'only truly monist system in Europe',[89] provides an excellent example[90] where the state is obliged to promote the development of the international rule of law.[91] National legislation is not applied where it conflicts with international law.[92] However, courts have no power to nullify, or amend, offending national law, such power resting solely with the government.[93]

[4–38]   In contrast, dualism asserts that international law does not automatically form part of domestic law.[94] In order for it to be enforceable in national courts, a positive act by the legislator is required.[95]

---

[86]   Catarina de Albuquerque, 'Chronicle of an Announced Birth: The Coming into Life of the Optional Protocol to the International Covenant on Economic Social and Cultural Rights – The Missing Piece of the International Bill of Human Rights' (2010) 32 Human Rights Quarterly 144, 177.

[87]   Malcolm N Shaw, *International Law* (7th edn, Cambridge University Press 2014) 21.

[88]   Philip Alston and Ryan Goodman, *International Human Rights: The Successor to International Human Rights in Context* (Oxford University Press 2013) 1058.

[89]   Guiseppe Martinico, 'Is the European Convention Going to be Supreme? A Comparative Constitutional Overview of ECHR and EU Law before National Courts' (2012) 23 European Journal of International Law 414.

[90]   Germany also subscribes to the monist theory, albeit in a lesser form. Here, international treaties are treated the same as national legislation and take precedence over prior enacted national legislation. See Daniel Lovric, 'A Constitution Friendly to International Law: Germany and its Volkerrechtsfreundlichkeit' (2006) 25 Australian Yearbook of International Law 75.

[91]   Article 90 of the *Grondwet* (Basic Law).

[92]   Article 94, 'Statutory regulations in force within the Kingdom shall not be applicable if such application is in conflict with provisions of Treaties that are binding on all persons or of resolutions by international institutions'.

[93]   Jorg Polakiewicz and V Jacob-Foltzer, 'The European Human Rights Convention in Domestic Law' (1991) 12 Human Rights Law Journal 65, 125. See also Antonio Cassese, *International Law in a Divided World* (Clarendon Press 1992).

[94]   Alston and Goodman (n 88) 1058.

[95]   Andrew Byrnes and Catherine Renshaw, 'Within the State' in Daniel Meockli, Sangeeta

If the Netherlands is seen as a truly monist state, Ireland could be called 'ultra- **[4–39]**
dualist',[96] a position clearly intended by the Constitution.[97] While it accepts
international law 'as its rules of conduct in its relations with other states,'[98]
Ireland requires a positive act by the Oireachtas before any part of international
law can be effective domestically.[99] In general terms, the extent to which
unincorporated treaties can have an effect on national law is not entirely clear. In
Fakih v Minister for Justice,[100] three asylum seekers sought to have their claim
determined in line with the unincorporated 1951 Refugee Convention[101] and its
Protocol.[102] The applicants relied on a letter sent to the UN High Commissioner
for Refugees in 1985 confirming that applications would be considered in
line with the criteria set forth in the Refugee Convention.[103] In finding for the
applicants, Hanlon J found that this letter created a legitimate expectation, a
decision which was swiftly overruled.[104] In a comparable case in the Australian
High Court, a determination that an unincorporated treaty could give rise to a
legitimate expectation[105] was met with significant executive opposition,[106] and
also subsequently overruled.[107]

Shah and Sandesh Sivakumaran (eds), *International Human Rights Law* (Oxford
University Press 2014) 464.

[96] Gerard Hogan, 'The Constitution and the Convention' in Suzanne Egan, Liam Thornton
and Judy Walsh (eds), *Ireland and the ECHR: 60 Years and Beyond* (Bloomsbury 2014)
75.

[97] Article 29.6 'No international agreement shall be part of the domestic law of the State
save as may be determined by the Oireachtas'.

[98] Article 29.3.

[99] Article 15.2.1 states, 'The sole and exclusive power of making laws in the State is hereby
vested in the Oireachtas; No other legislative authority has power to make laws for the
State'.

[100] [1993] 2 IR 406.

[101] UN Convention Relating to the Status of Refugees (adopted 28 July 1951, entered into
force on 22 April 1954) 189 UNTS 137.

[102] UN Protocol Relating to the Status of Refugees (adopted 31 January 1967, entered into
force on 4 October 1967) 606 UNTS 267.

[103] Known as the Von Arnim Letter.

[104] *Gutrani v Minister for Justice* [1993] 2 IR 427, upheld again in *Anisimova v Minister for
Justice* [2001] IESC 202.

[105] *Minister of State for Immigration and Ethnic Affairs v Teoh* (1995) 183 CLR 273, 279
(Mason CJ). It was argued that deportation of aliens must be balanced with the rights
contained in Article 3 of the Convention on the Rights of the Child, which had been
signed, but not transposed into national law and provides that the best interests of the
child be a primary concern. For full facts of the case, see Anne Twomey, 'Minister of State
for Immigration and Ethnic Affairs v Teoh' (1995) 23 Federal Law Review 348; Wendy
Lacy, 'A Preclude to the Demise of *Teoh*: The High Court Decision in Re Minister for
Immigration and Multicultural Affairs; Ex Parte Lam' (2004) 26 Sydney Law Review
131.

[106] Ryszard Piotrowicz, 'Unincorporated Treaties in Australian Law' [1996] Public Law 190,
194. See also, Wendy Lacy, 'In the Wake of *Teoh*: Finding an Appropriate Government
Response' (2001) 29 Federal Law Review 219.

[107] *Re Minister for Immigration and Multicultural Affairs; Ex Parte Lam* (2003) 195 ALR
502. See also Glen Cranwell, 'Re Minister for Immigration and Multicultural Affairs; Ex

[4–40]   The most authoritative statement regarding the position of unincorporated international law is that of the Supreme Court judgment in *Kavanagh v The Governor of Mountjoy Prison and the Attorney General*, where the appellant was tried and convicted in the Special Criminal Court[108] of a variety of criminal offences.[109] When his application to have the matter judicially reviewed (on the grounds that he had been denied a trial by jury) was refused by the High Court[110] and the Supreme Court,[111] the applicant brought his case to the UN Human Rights Committee,[112] claiming that Article 26 of the ICCPR had been breached.[113] The Committee found in favour of the applicant, as the state did not demonstrate that the decision to use the Special Criminal Court was made on reasonable and objective grounds.[114]

[4–41]   Armed with this decision, the applicant returned to the Irish courts, seeking an order of *certiorari* and a declaration that s 47(2) of the Offences against the State Act 1939 was incompatible with the ICCPR.[115] In dismissing his application, the court clarified the effect of unincorporated international law, finding:

> The Constitution establishes an unmistakable distinction between domestic and international law. The government has the exclusive

---

Parte Lam' (2003) 10 Australian Journal of Administrative Law 208.

[108]   The Special Criminal Court was established under the Offences Against the State Act 1939 (which is empowered to hear cases where the ordinary courts are inadequate) in 1972, as a direct response to the situation with Northern Ireland. It has the power to hear certain 'scheduled' criminal offences. In this case, the possession of the firearm was a scheduled offence for the purpose of invoking the jurisdiction of the Special Criminal Court. See Shane Kilcommins and Barry Vaughan, 'A Perpetual State of Emergency: Subverting the Rule of Law in Ireland' (2004) 35 Cambrian Law Review 55; Elizabeth Campbell, 'Decline of Due Process in the Irish Justice System: Beyond the Culture of Control' (2006) 6 Hibernian Law Journal 125.

[109]   [2002] IESC 13 [6].

[110]   (HC, 6 October 1995).

[111]   (SC, 18 December 1996).

[112]   Communication No. 819/1998 (27 August 1998) CCPR/C/71/D/819/1998.

[113]   Article 26 ICCPR states, 'All persons are equal before the law and are entitled without any discrimination to the equal protection of the law. In respect of this, the law shall prohibit any discrimination and shall guarantee to all persons equal and effective protection against discrimination on any ground such as race, colour, sex, language, religion, political or other opinion, national or social origin, property, birth or other status'.

[114]   Communication No. 819/1998 (27 August 1998) CCPR/C/71/D/819/1998 [10.4].

[115]   s 7(2) allows for the AG (and latterly the DPP) to certify that the ordinary courts are inadequate to deal with the trial and have to the trial conducted in the Special Criminal Court. The DPP does not have to give specific reasons for this certification. For a more detailed examination of the procedure of the Special Criminal Court, see Tom O' Malley, *The Criminal Process* (Roundhall 2009); Denis Kennedy, 'Has Packer's "Crime Control Model" become the Dominant Force in Irish Criminal Justice?' (2013) 23 Irish Criminal Law Journal 76; Patrick McInerney, 'Do We Need a Jury? Composition and Function of the Jury and the Trend Away from Jury Trials in Serious Criminal Cases' (2009) 19 Irish Criminal Law Journal 9.

prerogative of entering into agreements with other states. It may accept obligations under such agreements which are binding in international law. The Oireachtas on the other hand has the exclusive function of making laws for the state. These two exclusive competencies are not incompatible. Where the government wishes a term of an international agreement to have effect in domestic law it may ask the Oireachtas to pass the necessary legislation.[116]

Conclusively, it was confirmed that the provisions of international law are binding on the state internationally, not domestically, until the instrument is transposed into Irish law by an Act of the Oireachtas.[117] Additionally, unincorporated international treaties cannot form the basis of claim for legitimate expectation. This leaves the provisions of international documents having little practical effect on the furtherance of human rights litigation in dualist systems. The ICESCR has been cited only once, indirectly, in the superior courts of Ireland, in *SI v Minister for Justice, Equality and Law Reform*.[118] Here, the applicant argued that she would face persecution should she be deported to Nigeria due to her HIV positive status. In finding that she formed part of a particular social group, Finlay Geoghegan J referred to the inter relationship between the ICESCR and the Refugee Convention, although she did not rely on the ICESCR in determining the core issues of the case.   [4–42]

The Irish position is not unique and the vast majority of common law states subscribe to the dualist approach. A modern restatement of international law in domestic systems is contained in the Bangalore Principles.[119] These principles affirm that, in dualist systems, while international law does not automatically form part of national law, it can be used as an interpretive tool where an issue of uncertainty or ambiguity arises in the application of national law.[120]   [4–43]

---

[116] [2002] IESC 13, 43.

[117] This decision was again appealed to the UN Human Rights Committee in Communication No. 1114/2002/Rev.1 (8 July 2002) CCPR/C/76/D/1114/2002/Rev.1, on the basis that he had been denied an effective remedy However, this claim was found to be inadmissible.

[118] [2007] IEHC 165.

[119] Report of Judicial Colloquium on the Domestic Application of International Human Rights Norms, Bangalore, India, reprinted in The Bangalore Principles on 'the Domestic Application of International Human Rights Norms' (1988) 14 Commonwealth Law Bulletin 1196. See also, Michael Kirby, 'International Law – The Impact on National Constitutions' (2006) 21 American University International Law Review 327; Michael Kirby, 'Judicial Colloquium on the Domestic Application of International Human Right Norms Harare, Zimbabwe, 19-22 April 1989 Implementing the Bangalore Principles on Human Rights Law' (1989) 58 Nordic Journal of International Law 206.

[120] See generally, Michael Kirby, 'Implementing the Bangalore Principles on Human Rights Law (1989) 106 South African Law Journal 484.

Compliance with ICESCR Obligations

[4–44]   To date, Ireland has had three reports considered by the CESCR, in 1999, 2002 and in 2015. Ireland was due to submit a report in 2007, which was submitted as a joint report in 2013 and does not consider issues post 2010. This section will address, article by article, Ireland's submission to the Committee, the shadow report submissions, any issues raised by the Committee and the state's subsequent response and the final concluding observations of the most recent examination in 2015, as the most up to date statement of how Ireland is complying with its obligations.

[4–45]   It is worth noting that, on all three occasion, the Committee has repeatedly expressed concern that Ireland has not yet incorporated the ICESCR into domestic law and about the lack of engagement by the judiciary with ICESCR rights.[121] In response to this, Ireland replied that the courts 'do not operate a rigid classification of rights which puts economic social and cultural rights beyond their reach' and that they are asserted and litigated in the courts with reference to the Constitution rather than the ICESCR.[122] This is quite clearly at odds with the reality of litigating social and economic rights as seen in Chapter 3. Further, consistent criticism related to the failure to adopt a rights-based approach in the areas of anti-poverty,[123] provisions of healthcare,[124] housing[125] and social welfare payments, have been levied.[126]

Article 2 – The Progressive Realisation of Rights

[4–46]   Ireland's initial report for its third periodic review under this article focused solely on foreign aid and its continuing commitment to providing international aid for developing countries.[127] The shadow report, prepared by the Free Legal Advice Clinic (FLAC), notices that the state does not mention how resources

---

[121] *Concluding Observations, Ireland* UN Doc E/C./12.1/Add.35 [9]; *Concluding Observations, Ireland* UN Doc E/C.12/1/Add.77 [12]; *Concluding Observations of the Third Periodic Report of Ireland* UN Doc E/C.12/IRL/CO/3 [7].

[122] *List of Issues in relation to the Third Periodic Report of Ireland, addendum, Replies of Ireland to the list of issues* UN Doc E/C.12/IRL/Q/3/Add.1 [2-3].

[123] *Concluding Observations, Ireland* UN Doc E/C./12.1/Add.35 [12]; *Concluding Observations, Ireland* UN Doc E/C.12/1/Add.77 [31]; *Concluding Observations of the Third Periodic Report of Ireland* (n 121) [24].

[124] *Concluding Observations, Ireland* UN Doc E/C.12/1/Add.77 [35]; *Concluding Observations of the Third Periodic Report of Ireland* (n 121) [27-29].

[125] *Concluding Observations, Ireland* UN Doc E/C./12.1/Add.35 [20]; *Concluding Observations, Ireland* UN Doc E/C.12/1/Add.77 [32-33]; *Concluding Observations of the Third Periodic Report of Ireland* (n 121) [32].

[126] *Concluding Observations, Ireland* UN Doc E/C./12.1/Add.35 [13]; *Concluding Observations, Ireland* UN Doc E/C.12/1/Add.77 [28]; *Concluding Observations of the Third Periodic Report of Ireland* (n 121) [20-24].

[127] *Third Periodic Reports of State Parties due in 2007, Ireland* UN Doc E/C.12/IRL/3 [31-33].

are being used for the progressive realisation of rights within the domestic context.[128] As the report by the state covers the period 2002-2010, it precedes the financial bailout programme and the subsequent austerity measures imposed. When this bailout was agreed, there was no human rights assessment undertaken of its impact on the most vulnerable sections of society. Further, FLAC observes that the cuts to the Irish Human Rights Commission and the Equality Authority funding is a retrogressive measure detrimental to the progressive realisation of rights.[129] In 2002, the Committee had urged Ireland to maintain the Combat Poverty Agency.[130] However, in 2009 it was abolished and subsumed by the Department of Social Protection. Additionally, cuts have been made to community projects, family support units and initiatives against drugs programmes.[131]

In its list of issues in relation to the third periodic report of Ireland, the Committee **[4–47]** then asks Ireland to indicate to what extent austerity measures under the National Recovery Plan 2011-2014 have affected the enjoyment of rights, particularly in relation to marginalised and disadvantaged groups. Further, it asked Ireland whether it intended to adopt comprehensive anti-discrimination legislation.[132] In response, the state asserted that its social assistance programmes have maintained their effectiveness and, in 2013, reduced the "at risk of poverty" category from 38.4% to 15.2% (excluding pensions).[133] However, the poverty line is calculated at 60 per cent of the median income and, if incomes are falling, changes in poverty rates will depend on income changes at different points. In other words, if income decreases are primarily concentrated on persons above the poverty line, then poverty is likely to decrease, despite an overall fall in income.[134] Significantly, those in poverty fared the worst, with those in the bottom decile suffering a 27.2% decrease after housing costs, against 15% on average.[135] Further, the updated shadow report criticises the lack of data provided by Ireland, making it impossible to identify the effects of budgetary measures on

---

[128] FLAC, 'Our Voice Our Rights: A Parallel Report in Response to Ireland's Third Report under the International Covenant on Economic Social and Cultural Rights' (November 2014) 17.

[129] ibid 20.

[130] The Combat Poverty Agency was a statutory agency established under the Combat Poverty Agency Act 1986 and had four general functions: policy advice, project support and innovation, research and public education on anti-poverty and social inclusion issues.

[131] FLAC 'Our Voice Our Rights' (n 128) 23.

[132] *List of Issues in Relation to the Third Periodic Report of Ireland* UN Doc E/C.12/IRL/Q/3 [3-4].

[133] *List of Issues in Relation to the Third Periodic Report of Ireland, addendum, Replies of Ireland to the List of Issues* (n 122) [9].

[134] Michael Savage, Tim Callan, Brian Nolan and Brian Colgan, 'The Great Recession, Austerity and Inequality: Evidence from Ireland' ESRI Working Paper No. 499 (April 2015) 4.

[135] ibid 9

particularly vulnerable groups.[136] In its concluding observations, the Committee observed that the state party's response to the crisis has been disproportionately focused on instituting cuts to public spending, without altering its tax regime. In addition, it noted that the austerity measures were adopted without proper assessment of their impact and that the steps taken had had a significant impact on the enjoyment of ESC rights of marginalised and vulnerable groups. The Committee urged Ireland to ensure that austerity measures are phased out and enhanced protection is given to ESC rights, to consider reviewing its tax regime and to institute human rights impact assessments in the policymaking process.[137]

[4–48]   Despite these recommendations, the state did not undertake a human rights assessment for Budgets 2015 and 2016 and the tax changes implemented disproportionately benefitted high earners (in 2015, a single unemployed person gained €95 per annum while a single person earning €75,000 gains €902 per annum).[138] In Budget 2017, there were slight improvements for those on lower incomes. The universal social charge was reduced slightly and social welfare payment was increased by €5 per week.[139]

Article 3–Equality Between Men and Women

[4–49]   In its report, the state points to a number of ways in which it ensures equality of men and women in Ireland. In particular, it points out that the Convention on the Elimination of Discrimination against Women (CEDAW) has impacted positively upon women's rights in Ireland. This is somewhat misleading because, as with all international treaties which have not been transposed into national law, CEDAW is not legally enforceable in domestic courts and women cannot assert the rights contained therein. The state refers to multiple legislative provisions which ensure equality, together with the establishment of the Equality Authority and the Equality Tribunal to monitor and enforce the legislation. It refers to 'significant' funding made to the National Women's Council of Ireland. However, in its shadow report, FLAC observes that funding to this organisation has almost halved since 2009.[140] Under the National Women's Strategy 2007-2016, a number of key areas are identified in the state report. In relation to women and poverty, the state identifies a number of conditional payments which can be made to those at risk of poverty. It is not clear, but it is assumed that these relate to discretionary payments which can be made by a Community Welfare

---

136 FLAC, 'Our Voice, Our Rights: An Update to the Civil Society Parallel Report in Response to Ireland's Third Report under the International Covenant on Economic, Social and Cultural Rights' (May 2015) 10.

137 *Concluding Observations of the Third Periodic Report of Ireland* (n 121) [11].

138 Social Justice Ireland, 'Budget 2016: Analysis and Critique' (2015) available at <www.socialjustice.ie/sites/default/files/attach/publication/4051/sjibudget2016analysis.pdf> last accessed 17 February 2017.

139 See <budget.gov.ie> last accessed 17 January 2017, for further details.

140 FLAC, 'Our Voice, Our Rights: An Update' (n 136) 25.

Officer often referred to as exceptional hardship payments. The state also refers to the increases in child benefit paid to mothers as of 2010. However, since 2010, this benefit has been cut year-on-year, with only a small increase in 2016. In relation to women in employment, the state refers to several initiatives aimed at improving women's access to the workplace, including education, training and childcare.[141] Despite these moves, one of the most regressive measures came in the Social Welfare Act 2012, which made changes to the One Parent Family Payment (OPFP). The recipients of this payment are overwhelmingly women, the 2011 census shows that 86.5% of lone parents were women.[142]

Previously, the OPFP was paid to recipients until the child reached the age of   **[4–50]** 18. The 2012 Act began the process of reducing this age limit to 7, meaning that, once the child reaches the age of 7 the parent must transfer to another social welfare payment, most likely the Jobseeker's Allowance. While there is no difference in monetary payment, the difference lies in the conditions attached. Those on Jobseeker's Allowance must be actively looking for work and must, if offered, attend unpaid training or internships or risk having their payment reduced or stopped. No additional payment or provision for childcare is made, often forcing primarily women into further poverty.[143] In addition, women primarily occupy part time and lower paid positions, with the gender pay gap increasing in 2014 to 14.4% from 12.6% in 2009.[144] In 2016, a study by Morgan McKinley found that the gender pay gap in Ireland stood at 20%, with a 50% gap in bonus pay.[145]

Omitted from the state's initial report and its reply to the list for issues, but   **[4–51]** contained within the shadow report, is the inconsistency of Article 40.1 of the Constitution with the enjoyment of equality. This article confirms that the state can 'have due regard to differences of capacity, physical and moral, and of social function'. Further, Article 41.2.1 perpetuates gendered stereotyping, stating, 'the state shall… endeavour to ensure that mothers shall not be obliged by economic necessity to engage in labour to the neglect of their duties in the home'. Despite a recommendation of the Constitutional Review Group in 2013 to amend both of these clauses, there has been no progressive action on the part

---

[141] *Third Periodic Reports of State Parties due in 2007, Ireland* (n 127) [51-71].

[142] Census 2011, 'Profile 5: Households and Families – Living Arrangements in Ireland' available at <www.cso.ie/en/census/census2011reports/census2011profile5householdsa ndfamilies-livingarrangementsinireland/> last accessed 21 February 2017.

[143] Claire-Michelle Smyth, 'Renewed Discrimination Against Non-Marital Children' *Human Rights in Ireland* (5 July 2012).

[144] European Commission, 'Tackling the Gender Pay Gap in the European Union' (2014) 12.

[145] Morgan McKinley, 'Gender Pay Gap: Ireland 2016', available at <www.morganmckinley. ie/sites/morganmckinley.ie/files/gender_pay_gap_in_ireland_2016.pdf> last accessed 07 January 2017.

of the state, resulting in the Committee recommending that they be amended to comply with their obligations under the ICESCR.[146]

[4–52]   Articles 4 and 5, relating to limitations on rights and restrictions or derogations on rights respectively, were not considered by any of the reports, as there had been no changes. In the initial report to the Committee in 1997, the state confirmed that, under Article 28.3.3 of the Constitution, there remains the power for the state to enact emergency legislation limiting the enjoyment of rights in times of national emergency.[147]

Article 6–The Right to Work

[4–53]   The state's initial report reiterates the legislative provisions designed to protect employment[148] and sets out the Back to Work Allowance scheme, which allows social welfare recipients to retain a portion of their benefit when re-entering the workforce.[149] While the rate of unemployment is decreasing, people with disabilities are 2.5 times more likely to be unemployed.[150] Further, recent case law suggests that the state is not fulfilling its obligations in respect of victims of forced labour. For example, in *P v Chief Superintendent Garda National Immigration Bureau, DPP, Ireland and the AG*, the High Court found that the high burden of proof required and the length of time required to identify victims of trafficking and forced labour, which resulted in a victim being imprisoned for 2.5 years, highlighted the 'fundamental difficulties'.[151] Since 2006, the Migrants Rights Centre Ireland has dealt with in excess of 230 cases involving trafficking and exploitation.[152] Further, in *NHV & FT v Minister for Justice and Equality*, the High Court found that the blanket prohibition of the right to work on asylum seekers in circumstances where their claim was being processed for 8 years did not breach the right to earn a livelihood.[153] While the right of asylum seekers to access employment was not addressed in the Committee's concluding observations, they did criticise the state for failing to provide data in relation to the disproportionate levels of unemployment among the Roma, members of the Travelling community and the disabled.[154]

---

146   *Concluding Observations of the Third Periodic Report of Ireland* (n 121)[15].
147   *Initial Report Submitted by Ireland* UN Doc E/1990/5/Add.34 [94].
148   The Employment Equality Acts 1998 – 2015.
149   *Third Periodic reports of State parties due in 2007, Ireland* (n 127) [99-110].
150   National Disability Authority, 'Disability and Work: The Picture we Learn from Official Statistics' (2015).
151   [2015] IEHC 222.
152   See Migrant Rights Centre Ireland, 'Forced Labour & Trafficking', available at <www.mrci.ie/our-work/forced-labour-trafficking/> last accessed 6 January 2017.
153   [2015] IEHC 246.
154   *Concluding Observations of the Third Periodic Report of Ireland* (n 121) [16].

Article 7–The Right to Just and Favourable Conditions of Work

The provision in legislation for the national minimum wage was welcomed by the Committee. However, 21.8% of workers are on low income[155] and, possibly spurred by the findings of the European Social Committee in January 2015 that the national minimum wage was insufficient to ensure a decent standard of living,[156] the Committee recommended that the level be reviewed.[157]The Committee also expressed concern over statutory exemptions to the minimum wage and urged the state to tackle zero-hours contracts.

[4–54]

Undocumented migrants have statutorily been exempt from legislative protection. However, the Supreme Court decision in *Hussein v Labour Court* allowed an individual employed without a valid permit to recover significant damages for breach of the Minimum Wage Act 2000.[158] Further, in March 2016, the Workplace Relations Committee made an award to an au pair for breach of the same legislation, confirming that au pairs must be paid the required minimum wage.[159] These cases appear to show a judicial trend towards an interpretation compatible with ICESCR obligations. However, it is clear that legislative change is also required.

[4–55]

Article 8–The Right to Form and Join Trade Unions

Particular emphasis in this section has been placed upon the issue of collective bargaining. In the case of *McGowan & Ors v Labour Court, Ireland & Anor,* the Supreme Court declared Part III of the Industrial Relations Act 1946 repugnant to the Constitution.[160] It came to this conclusion, as it determined that the power given to the representatives to make collective agreements registered by the Labour Court was a law making power contrary to Article 15.2.1. The effect of this ruling is twofold. First, all previously registered agreements have no effect beyond the parties subscribed to it and even to those parties, the terms are not enforceable in law. Secondly, any future collective bargaining mechanisms would require significant limitations.[161] The impact of this ruling was seen in 2014, when Dunnes Stores refused to comply with the Labour Court's

[4–56]

---

[155] Low Pay Commission, 'Recommendations for the National Minimum Wage' (July 2015) LPC No. 1 2015.

[156] European Committee of Social Rights, *Conclusions 2014 (Ireland)* (January 2015).

[157] *Concluding Observations of the Third Periodic Report of Ireland* (n 121) [17].

[158] [2015] IEHC 246.

[159] Elaine Edwards, 'Au pair awarded €9000 after couple broke employment laws' *The Irish Times* (8 March 2016).

[160] [2013] IESC 21.

[161] For a further analysis of this case, see John Hendy, 'McGowan and Collective Bargaining in Ireland' (Trinity College Dublin, 30 January 2014), available at <www.ictu.ie/download/ pdf/collective_bargaining_ireland_jan_30.pdf> last accessed 23 December 2016.

recommendation that it should engage with workers' representatives, as it had a 'constitutional right not to engage with trade unions'.[162]

[4–57] The Industrial Relations (Amendment) Act 2015 sought to clarify the area. In contrast to previous definitions of collective bargaining as being 'more than mere negotiation or consultation',[163] the new legislation defines them as 'voluntary engagements or negotiations'.[164] Further, unions cannot bring a claim under the new legislation where the employer has negotiated with a group of workers not as part of the union. In addition, the court can refuse to hear a claim where the number of workers affected is 'insignificant'.[165] The legislation allows unions or groups to have the dispute determined by the Labour Court, which must take into account the pay and conditions in comparable companies.[166] The Committee, in its concluding observations, recommended that the state remove the requirement to obtain collective bargaining licences.[167] However, the legislation does not address this matter, and, in its replies to the list of issues, the state confirms that it has no plans to change this licencing requirement.[168]

Article 9–The Right to Social Security

[4–58] The state, in its report, sets out the various payments and rates of payments available and, as identified above, it has been concluded that the rates of payment are insufficient for an adequate standard of living. Aside from rates of payment, the primary concern of the Committee has been the application of the habitual residence test. This test was introduced in 2004 and seeks to determine, as a matter of fact, whether the person habitually resided within the state. The five criteria required to establish habitual residence have been adopted from the CJEU case of *Robin Swaddling v Adjudication Officer*, being the length and continuity of the stay in the state, the length of and reasons for any absences from the state, the nature and pattern of employment, the main centre of interest and the future intentions of the person applying.[169] In addition to the right to reside test, which was introduced in 2009[170] there is also a legal test. If the claimant does not have a lawful right to reside, they cannot claim

---

[162] *Dunnes Stores v Mandate Trade Union* Labour Court Determination No LCR20874.

[163] *Ashford Castle Ltd v SIPTU* Labour Court Decision No DECP032.

[164] See Michael Doherty, 'Engagements, Unions and the Law: The Re-Boot of Collective Bargaining in Ireland' *Human Rights in Ireland* (18 May 2015).

[165] s 28(b)

[166] s 30(2).

[167] *Concluding Observations of the Third Periodic Report of Ireland* (n 121) [19].

[168] *List of Issues in relation to the Third Periodic Report of Ireland, addendum, Replies of Ireland to the list of issues* (n 122) [45].

[169] Case C-90/97 *Robin Swaddling v Adjudication Officer* [1999] ECR I-1075.

[170] Social Welfare and Pensions (No.2) Act 2009, s 15.

social welfare payments. The state has confirmed that it has no current plans to revise or review the tests.[171]

In this, the Committee expressed signs of disapprobation in relation access to social welfare for victims of domestic abuse where their legal status in the state derived solely from that of their spouse. Guidelines confirm that status will be given to 'genuine' victims of domestic abuse, which necessarily means providing evidence such as court orders, medical records, police reports.[172] The combination of these two tests have resulted in a situation whereby certain people fleeing domestic violence have no right to work and no right to social assistance, leaving them at a disproportionate risk of destitution. **[4–59]**

Article 10 – The Protection of the Family

Significant inroads have been made in relation to the protection of the family within Irish Law. The Children and Families Relationship Act 2015 modernises the law and regulates for families of divorce, same sex couples and children who have been born through IVF. The Supreme Court in 2015 rejected a challenge to re-run the constitutional amendment on children's rights, paving the way for a new Article 42A in the Constitution, which places the best interest of the child at the centre of any legal proceedings or decisions being made in relation to that child.[173] **[4–60]**

Of concern to the committee under this article was the high cost of childcare. While the Committee welcomed the introduction of the free childcare place during the pre-school year, the fact that this scheme is only available for three hours per day between September and June does little to ameliorate the high burden of childcare costs, particularly for those on low income.[174] **[4–61]**

Article 11 – The Right to an Adequate Standard of Living

This right includes the right to adequate food, clothing, housing and living conditions. In 2013, approximately 15% of the population lived below the poverty line.[175] This figure shows an increase of child poverty, up from 8.8% in 2010 to 11.7% in 2013.[176] In its reply to the list of issues, the government stated **[4–62]**

---

[171] *List of Issues in relation to the Third Periodic Report of Ireland, addendum, Replies of Ireland to the list of issues* (n 122) [54].
[172] Irish Naturalisation and Immigration Service, 'Immigration Guidelines on Victims of Domestic Violence' (2012).
[173] *Jordan v Minister for Children and Youth Affairs* [2015] IESC 33.
[174] *Concluding Observations of the Third Periodic Report of Ireland* (n 121) [23].
[175] Central Statistics Office, 'Survey on Income and Living Conditions: 2013 Results' (21 January 2015).
[176] Department of Social Protection, 'Social Inclusion Monitor 2013' (2015).

that social welfare was effective in decreasing child poverty.[177] However, in 2013 the largest group living in poverty were children, accounting for 25.7%.[178] In addition, the number of lone parents living in poverty has more than doubled, from 9.3% in 2010 to 23% in 2013.[179] This has resulted in the Committee recommending that Ireland increase its efforts to reduce poverty and to implement a human rights-based approach to poverty reduction programmes.[180]

[4–63] The Committee, in its list of issues, raised concern at the increase in food insecurity and malnutrition, particularly among disadvantaged groups and single parents. [181] Ireland, in its response, did little more than state that it was currently reviewing plans under the suspended National Food and Nutrition Policy. As the shadow report points out, while there are five departments with responsibilities for food provision within schools, there is no one supervisory body ensuring that policy is being implemented.[182] Ireland was urged in the concluding observations to expedite a national action plan on food security, which, at the time of writing, had not yet come to fruition.

[4–64] The issue of housing was also of deep concern for the Committee, though some of that has been ameliorated by the Housing (Miscellaneous) Act 2015, allowing for the District Court to determine the merits of an eviction application. When asked about the living conditions of asylum seekers, the state responded simply that there is no obligation on asylum seekers to avail of the direct provision system.[183] Direct provision is a means of housing those who are waiting to have their asylum claim processed or, having been refused asylum, have their appeal heard. It was established in 2000 and is coordinated by the Reception and Integration Agency (RIA). There are currently 34 direct provision centres in Ireland, only 7 of which are state owned. The remainder are owned by private, for profit companies. Within these centres adults receive an allowance of €19.10 per week plus €9.60 per child. Accommodation, food, heating, laundry and medical costs are provided.[184] While this seems like it may be a good deal, there are numerous serious problems with the system. Firstly, it was established as being a short term solution while claims were being processed. At the end of December

---

177 *List of Issues in relation to the Third Periodic Report of Ireland, addendum, Replies of Ireland to the list of issues* (n 122) [63].
178 Social Justice Ireland, 'Towards a Fairer Future' (2015) Socio-Economic Review 42.
179 Central Statistics Office, 'Survey on Income and Living Conditions: 2013 Results' (21 January 2015).
180 *Concluding Observations of the Third Periodic Report of Ireland* (n 121) [24].
181 *List of Issues in Relation to the Third Periodic Report of Ireland* (n 133) [18].
182 FLAC, 'Our Voice, Our Rights: An Update' (n 136) 35.
183 *List of Issues in Relation to the Third Periodic Report of Ireland, addendum, Replies of Ireland to the list of issues* (n 122) [78].
184 See Reception and Integration Agency, 'Reception, Dispersal & Accommodation' <www.ria.gov.ie/en/RIA/Pages/Reception_Dispersal_Accommodation> last accessed 22 February 2017 for a full list of entitlements.

2016 there were 4665 people residing in direct provision centres, however 11.4% or 509 people had been resident in these centres for over 7 years.[185] The house rules in these centres are stringent, residents cannot have visitors, they cannot prepare their own food, they do not have their own bathrooms in many instances, many families live in one room with no play area for children. The state is technically correct when it says that there is no absolute requirement for an asylum seeker to remain in these centres. However, the asylum seeker has no right to work until their claim has been decided and should they leave these centres they are not entitled to any state allowances. Therefore, those with limited means have in reality no option but to remain in direct provision. In 2013 the issue of the direct provision system in Ireland was brought before the court in Northern Ireland.[186] The applicants had unsuccessfully applied for asylum which failed, and then applied for subsidiary protection. While this application was pending the applicants entered Northern Ireland and claimed asylum there. The authorities sought to return the applicants under the Dublin II Regulation and the applicants argued that a return to Ireland meant a return to direct provision which would violate their rights under the Charter of Fundamental Rights of the European Union.[187] Stephens J did not consider whether the direct provision system breached human rights, stating 'it is not for the court in this jurisdiction to determine whether the evidence of conditions in direct provision amounts to a breach'.[188] Notwithstanding this the applicants were successful with Stephens J making his determination on the best interests of the child. While he would not cast aspersions directly against the system in making his decision he noted that communal living with the inability to make ones own meals was not in the best interest of the child. Further he commented on the significant physical and mental health issues suffered by asylum seekers by virtue of the amount of time that they have to spend in direct provision.[189]

A challenge to the system was heard in the Irish courts in *CA and TA v Minister for Justice*.[190] Mac Eochaidh J determined that many of the house rules employed by direct provision centres were a breach of human rights however given the disputed evidence in the case did not make any determination as to whether the length of stay in a direct provision centre constituted a breach.[191] Following   **[4–65]**

---

[185] Reception and Integration Agency, 'Interim Figures–December 2016', available at <www.ria.gov.ie/en/RIA/RIA%20Interim%20figures%20December%202016.pdf/Files/RIA%20Interim%20figures%20December%202016.pdf> last accessed 22 February 2017.

[186] *In the matter of an Application for Judicial Review by AJL and A, B and C* [2013] NIQB 88.

[187] Specifically, under Article 4 (the prohibition on torture, inhuman and degrading treatment) and Article 7 (respect for private and family life).

[188] [2013] NIQB 88 [84].

[189] ibid [102]-[103]; See Liam Thornton, 'Direct Provision and the Rights of the Child in Ireland' (2014) 17(3) Irish Journal of Family Law 68.

[190] [2014] IEHC 532.

[191] For full analysis of the case, see Liam Thornton, 'C.A and T.A: The Direct Provision

on from this case (and the vast criticism of the system[192]) a working group was established to examine the system. The report was delivered in 2015 which recommended, inter alia, an improvement in living conditions and a reduction in the length of stay.[193]

Article 12 – The Right to the Highest Attainable Standard of Health

[4–66]   In its list of issues to Ireland, the UN Committee was concerned about a number of things which it asked the state to clarify. First, it was concerned with the shortage of hospital beds, in particular, mental health units and Traveller health units, and it asked the state to clarify what measures were being taken to address this. Secondly, it was concerned with the shortage of mental health facilities for children and alcohol abuse. Finally, it expressed deep concern on relation to the grounds on which a woman can obtain a lawful abortion in Ireland, particularly requesting to know whether the state would revise its stance on the criminalisation of women.[194] In its responses, the state acknowledged that, during the period 2008-2011, €1.5 billion was taken from the health budget and, while there was a modest increase in 2015, it remains relatively flat.[195] The updated shadow report draws the Committee's attention to the fact that access to medical services in Ireland remains costly and difficult for most and that Ireland is the only European country that does not offer some form of universal subsidised access to primary care.[196] Appearing to accept the state's responses in this matter, the concluding observations refer to the necessity to remove children from adult psychiatric units and to ensure adequate secure facilities for children. It is worth noting here that this is, in effect, what the *TD* case centred on–the needs of children with serious challenging behaviour that

---

Case' (2014) 17(4) Irish Journal of Family Law 116.

[192] For example see Claire Breen, 'The Policy of Direct Provision in Ireland: A Violation of an Asylum Seekers Right to an Adequate Standard of Housing' (2008) 20(4) International Journal of Refugee Law 611; Samantha Arnold, 'State Sanctioned Child Poverty and Exclusion: The Case of Children in State Accommodation for Asylum Seekers' (2012) Irish Refugee Council, available at <www.irishrefugeecouncil.ie/wp-content/uploads/2012/09/State-sanctioned-child-poverty-and-exclusion.pdf>; Liam Thornton, 'The Rights of Others: Asylum Seekers and Direct Provision in Ireland' (2014) 3(2) Irish Community Development Law Journal 22.

[193] See Working Group to Report to Government on Improvements to the Protection Process, including Direct Provision and Supports to Asylum Seekers, Final Report–June 2015' (2015) available at <www.justice.ie/en/JELR/Report%20to%20Government%20on%20Improvements%20to%20the%20Protection%20Process,%20including%20Direct%20Provision%20and%20Supports%20to%20Asylum%20Seekers.pdf/Files/Report%20to%20Government%20on%20Improvements%20to%20the%20Protection%20Process,%20including%20Direct%20Provision%20and%20Supports%20to%20Asylum%20Seekers.pdf> last accessed 22 February 2017.

[194] *List of Issues in Relation to the Third Periodic Report of Ireland* (n 133) [20-23].

[195] *List of Issues in Relation to the Third Periodic Report of Ireland, addendum, Replies of Ireland to the list of issues* (n 122) [94].

[196] FLAC, 'Our Voice, Our Rights: An Update' (n 136) 44.

required secure care. In the aftermath of this case, there has been inertia on the part of the state, with no mandatory obligation being placed upon them. In certain cases, children requiring immediate secure psychiatric care have been placed in adult institutions wholly inappropriate to their health and well-being. Despite this recommendation, the practice is still ongoing. In 2015, there were 95 children admitted to adult psychiatric wards in Ireland.[197]

In relation to the abortion question, the state responds, rather simply, that the legislation was enacted to give effect to the Supreme Court ruling in *AG v X*. It goes on to say that the state will provide information on services available outside of the state, provide aftercare where a termination is performed outside of the state and give proper consideration to any claim being made under the legislation.[198] The shadow report does not respond to this question. The legislation, the Protection of Life During Pregnancy Act 2014, was enacted primarily as a result of the death of Mrs Savita Halappanavar in a Galway hospital in December 2012. The *X* case was decided in the Supreme Court in 1992[199] and was the first time that the court had to determine the parameters of the right to life of the unborn in the constitution.[200] The court found that, where there was a real and substantial risk to the life of the mother, including by way of suicide, then, in those circumstances, the right to life of the mother outweighed that of the unborn. It set the precedent that only in circumstances where the physical life of the mother was in real and substantial danger could a pregnancy be terminated. **[4–67]**

In the intervening years, the legislature did not intervene and the position remained the same. In 2010, the European Court of Human Rights found that Ireland was in breach of Article 8 for failing to legislate on foot of the Supreme Court judgement.[201] In essence, the breach was founded on the fact that the state did not have a framework in place, under which the applicant could determine whether she qualified for a lawful abortion. Despite these two rulings, nothing really changed until the death of Mrs Halappanavar. She was not seeking a termination, rather she was admitted to hospital in the process of suffering a slow miscarriage. Nothing could be done to save the foetus and she requested that a termination be carried out to speed up the process. This was refused. Over the course of a number of days, her health deteriorated drastically, until she eventually succumbed to sepsis. The Coronor's report seems to suggest that, **[4–68]**

---

[197] Mental Health Commission, *Annual Report 2015* (MHC 2016) 8, available at <www.mhcirl.ie/File/2015-Annual-Report-inc-Report-OIMS.pdf> last accessed 07 January 2017.

[198] *List of Issues in Relation to the Third Periodic Report of Ireland, addendum, Replies of Ireland to the list of issues* (n 122) [119-129].

[199] *AG v X* [1992] 1 IR 1.

[200] Article 40.3.3 states 'The State acknowledges the right to life of the unborn, and with due regard to the equal right to life of the mother, guarantees in its laws to respect, and as far as practicable by its laws, to defend and vindicate that right'.

[201] *A, B and C v Ireland* [2010] ECHR 2032.

had a termination been carried out when it was requested, her fate would have been different.[202] It was her death that resulted in worldwide vigils and protests at Ireland's abortion regime. Within months of her death, draft legislation was published, which effectively codified the ruling in the *X* case. Three cases since the introduction of this legislation show that it is insufficient and that, while the Committee recommend expanding the legislation to include further grounds and clarity,[203] the reality is that they should be recommending that the Eighth Amendment be repealed.

[4–69]   The first case to really test the bounds of the legislation was that of Miss Y. Miss Y entered Ireland as an asylum seeker and discovered that she was pregnant as a result of rape in her home country. What happened after is the subject of debate, however, there are a number of facts which are indisputable. She did not wish to be pregnant and she said that she would rather kill herself than go ahead with the pregnancy. She tried to leave Ireland to obtain a termination in the UK, but she was turned around by immigration at Liverpool and sent back to Ireland. She was informed of the provisions of the legislation and sought to have a termination on the grounds of her life being at risk from suicide. Delays, the reasons for which were unclear, resulted in her not being assessed under the Act until she was 20 weeks pregnant. At the assessment, it was agreed that there was a substantial risk to her life, however, the team did not sanction a termination as, at this stage, the foetus was viable. On hearing this news, Miss Y's condition deteriorated rapidly, she reiterated that she did not want to live and began to refuse food and water. The medical team responded by obtaining a High Court order to forcibly hydrate her in order that the foetus be kept alive. At 24 weeks, she underwent a caesarean section, where a baby boy was delivered and placed in state care. It is not clear whether she freely consented to this procedure or whether it was under the threat of another court order forcing her to comply.[204] There is an ongoing investigation into the treatment of Miss Y in this case. However, it is clear that, even with the legislation in place, the unborn is of paramount concern, not the woman.

[4–70]   Another area for which the legislation does not account is that of fatal foetal abnormality. In 2011, Amanda Mellet discovered that the foetus she was carrying had congenital heart defect, known as Trisomy 18, and even though this would be fatal, it would not entitle her to a legal termination in Ireland. She was advised to contact a family planning organisation, who could give her details about travelling to obtain a termination. She travelled with her husband to Liverpool and underwent an abortion. She travelled back to Dublin 12 hours after the

---

[202] For full facts of this case, see Kitty Holland, *Savita: The Tragedy that Shook a Nation* (Transworld 2013).
[203] *Concluding Observations of the Third Periodic Report of Ireland* (n 121) [29].
[204] For full details of the case, see Fiona de Londras, 'Constitutionalizing Fetal Rights: A Salutary Tale from Ireland' (2015) 22 Michigan Journal of Gender and Law 243.

procedure, as they could not afford to stay any longer and no financial support is offered in these circumstances. On her return, she was not given any follow up care or counselling. The hospital offers counselling for those who miscarry, but not for those who have a termination. Mrs Mellet alleged that this system of forcing women to travel abroad, coupled with the lack of support on their return, amounted to inhumane and degrading treatment, contrary to Article 7 of the ICCPR, a contention with which the Human Rights Committee agreed in its judgment delivered in 2016.[205]

A final case to consider, and one not relating to abortion, is that of *PP v HSE*.[206]   **[4–71]**
In *PP*, the claimant was the father of a woman referred to in the court documents as NP, who, at 26 years of age, was pregnant with her third child. She was admitted to hospital for nausea and headaches and, while in hospital care, slipped and fell. At 15 weeks' pregnant, her medical team determined that she was brain dead. However, as there was still a foetal heartbeat, she was kept on life support in order to sustain the life of the foetus. The case arose as her father, PP, wanted the life support to be switched off and the hospital was unsure of its obligations. Article 40.3.3 states that the life of the unborn has equal regard to that of the mother. The life of the mother here no longer existed, so, without that consideration, to what lengths should the hospital go in order to preserve the life of the foetus? The High Court did agree with the claimant and allowed for the life support to be switched off. However, what is of concern in this ruling is that the judge appeared to place considerable emphasis on whether the foetus was likely to survive. Given the early gestational stage and the multiple infections from which the mother was suffering as a result of being kept artificially alive, it was highly unlikely that the foetus would last to a viable stage. It appears that if this were more of a possibility, he would have allowed her to remain on life support to protect the life of the unborn, relegating the mother to no more than an incubator with no right to any dignity in death.[207]

Thus, it is clear that this legislation and position is breaching human rights   **[4–72]**
in Ireland and the Committee could take a firmer stance in relation to Article 40.3.3, which needs to be repealed for meaningful protection of women's rights in this regard.

Articles 13-14–The Right to Education

Within this article, the Committee raised questions in relation to Traveller   **[4–73]**
education and special needs education.[208] The state has responded that it is

---

[205] *Amanda Jane Mellet v Ireland* CCPR/C/116/D/2324/2013.
[206] [2014] IEHC 622.
[207] For a full summary of this case and its implications, see Clara Hurley, 'Case Note: PP v Health Service Executive' (2015) 18 Trinity College Law Review 205.
[208] *List of Issues in Relation to the Third Periodic Report of Ireland* (n 133) [24-26].

making efforts based on the need of an individual rather than their cultural background and steps have been taken to enhance participation and retention.[209] However, the shadow report observes that more needs to be done in relation to children with special needs, stating that only 4% go on to third level education.[210]

[4–74]   The matter of discriminatory admission practices came before the Supreme Court in 2015.[211] Mary Stokes, a member of the Traveller community, claimed that the admission policy for the CBS secondary school in Clonmel was discriminatory, in that one of the three conditions required that the father had attended the school. Mrs Stokes adduced evidence of the discrimination stating that, during the 1980s, less than half of members of the Travelling community attended a secondary school. The Equality Tribunal and the Circuit Court agreed with Mrs Stokes. However, this was overturned in the High Court, where the judge found that there was insufficient evidence to come to a conclusion of discrimination. The appeal of this decision to the Supreme Court was subsequently dismissed.

[4–75]   As a result, the Committee, in its concluding observations, expressed concern in relation to discriminatory admission policies, including those affecting inter alia members of the Traveller community.[212]

Article 15 – Cultural Rights

[4–76]   In relation to this category of rights, the Committee posed two questions to Ireland, one centring on the recognition of Travellers as an ethnic minority and the other referring to affordable access to the internet for marginalised groups and rural areas.[213] This status was granted by the Taoiseach in March 2017. In relation to the latter question, the state responded that it has been investing in infrastructure to ensure that broadband be delivered to rural areas and that, by the end of 2016, an additional 700,000 premises in rural Ireland would have access to this. This seems to be falling short, as a report published in 2016 shows that one fifth of all those in rural Ireland have no access to the internet, while a quarter of those who do have access say it is too slow.[214] The Committee recommends that Ireland intensify its efforts to bring broadband to rural areas.[215]

---

[209] *List of Issues in relation to the Third Periodic Report of Ireland, addendum, Replies of Ireland to the list of issues* (n 122) [130-135].
[210] FLAC, 'Our Voice, Our Rights: An Update (n 136) 55.
[211] *Stokes v CBS Clonmel* [2015] IESC 13.
[212] *Concluding Observations of the Third Periodic Report of Ireland* (n 121) [30].
[213] *List of Issues in Relation to the Third Periodic Report of Ireland* (n 133) [27-28].
[214] Vodafone, 'Connected Futures: Bridging Ireland's Urban-Rural Divide', available at <www.vodafone.ie/connected-futures/> last accessed 07 January 2017.
[215] *Concluding Observations of the Third Periodic Report of Ireland* (n 121) [33].

Conclusion

It seems apparent that there are considerable areas where Ireland is falling short **[4–77]** of meeting its obligations under the ICESCR. Undoubtedly, there are areas of progress, particularly in respect of the legal regulation of family and child rights. However, areas which are solely left to policy, with no judicial review, appear to fare worst. Consistently the Committee has expressed concern in relation to the lack of justiciability and consistently this has been ignored. A number of instances highlighted show that certain situations, in fact, worsened following a recommendation of the Committee, showing a lack of regard for these reviews, coupled with the fact that Ireland has not yet ratified the optional protocol, resulting in a situation where no matter can be brought before the Committee.

It can be argued that the ICESCR and the periodic review process is nothing **[4–78]** more than a non-binding overview, which creates no legal obligations or sanction for failing to meet basic minimum standards. The reports of the Committee have served to highlight certain areas where state policy is failing to protect and vindicate social and economic rights, but no more. There is no obligation on the state, or the court for that matter, to act in order to ameliorate the breach.

Should the optional protocol be ratified, it is worth noting that Ireland does **[4–79]** have a good record of responding when a decision is made against it. Having categorical determinations of breaches of fundamental rights against it does little to elevate Ireland's status among its peers in the international community. For example, when the UNHRC found in favour of Amanda Mellet, the state did respond with an offer of compensation for a breach of her rights. This does little to change the situation as it stands for the women who are forced to endure the same scenario as Mrs Mellet and, arguably, means that every woman who has done so is entitled to compensation, illustrating the polycentric nature and cost implications of vindicating civil and political rights. Equally, a failure to address the underlying reason for the claims will undoubtedly result in future cases being taken to international tribunals. Therefore, it is likely that, should a determination be made against Ireland by the CESCR, a response would be forthcoming (albeit probably in line with its response to Mrs Mellet). However, this would pave the way for future challenges and the ultimate justiciability of the rights.

CHAPTER 5

The European Social Charter

The ESC: An Introduction

The European Social Charter (ESC), which entered into force in 1965, is a **[5–01]** regional instrument, which, like the Covenant on Economic Social and Cultural Rights, protects only social and economic rights. It is a creation of the Council of Europe and was designed as a counterpart to the European Convention on Human Rights (ECHR). The Council, like the UN, in a post war era found it impossible to create one Treaty encompassing both sets of rights, and consequently, the regional human rights system within Europe suffered from the same division of rights. The ECHR, which entered into force in 1953, encompasses civil and political rights and is overseen and enforced by the European Court of Human Rights in Strasbourg, while the Charter took a further 12 years to enter into force and is overseen by a committee (again, like the CESCR) and not a court.

Initially, there was hostility towards the ESC, with the priority of many states **[5–02]** focusing on civil and political rights, which, in their view, would safeguard democracy. Thus, the ECHR was prioritised in terms of its enforcement and stance, while the ESC relied solely on a reporting/supervisory system, akin to that in place for the ICESCR. Several revisions to the Charter have occurred, culminating in the Revised Social Charter of 1996, which came into force in July 1998.[1] Of the 47 Council of Europe states, 33 have ratified the revised Charter, with a further 10 having ratified the original 1961 Charter. However, of these, only 15 have accepted the collective complaints mechanism.[2] Arguably, this collective complaints mechanism is the most important aspect of the revitalisation of the Charter, which was adopted in 1995. Ireland signed and ratified the Charter in November 2000 and accepted the collective complaints procedure.

This chapter provides an overview of the basic principles of the ESC, together **[5–03]** with the role of the Committee and the collective complaints mechanism, before examining Ireland's record of compliance with it.

---

[1]   Additional Optional Protocols were annexed to the Charter in 1988, 1991 and 1995. European Social Charter (revised) E.T.S No 163, Strasbourg, 1996.

[2]   Full details of Charter ratifications are available at <www.coe.int/t/dghl/monitoring/socialcharter/Presentation/Overview_en.asp> last accessed July 2016.

The Principles of the European Social Charter

[5–04]   The rights in Part I of the Charter have been grouped into several pillars, covering housing, health, education, employment, legal and social protection, movement of persons and non-discrimination. Part I lists the rights in the form of objectives, while Part II establishes the corresponding obligations which the state must fulfil in order to meet these objectives. The Committee does not see the ESC as a mere statement of rights. Rather, its aim is to 'protect rights not merely theoretically, but also in fact'.[3]

[5–05]   Unlike other international Charters or Conventions, where the state must enter an express reservation or derogation to an article to avoid being bound by it, here, it can choose its obligations, to a significant extent. Article 20 of the ESC establishes that the state must accept a minimum of 6 of the 9 core obligations. These are the right to work,[4] the right to organise,[5] the right to collectively bargain,[6] the right of children and young persons to protection,[7] the right to social security,[8] the right to social and medical assistance,[9] the right of the family to social, legal and economic protection,[10] the right of migrant workers and their families to protection and assistance[11] and the right to equal opportunity and equal treatment in matters of employment without discrimination on the grounds of sex.[12] All other provisions are not deemed to be core. However, the state must choose an additional 16 articles to which it will bind itself. Thus, when signing up, the state can, to a substantial degree, pick and choose which of the social and economic rights it will be bound by, thereby retaining ultimate control.

[5–06]   This was, no doubt, included as another concession to those arguing against the legal protection for this class of rights and it once again undermines the status of social and economic rights when compared to their civil and political

---

3   *International Commission of Jurists v Portugal,* Complaint No 1/1998 Decision on the Merits (9 September 1999).
4   Article 1 provides, 'Everyone shall have the opportunity to earn his living in an occupation freely entered into'.
5   Article 5 provides, 'All workers and employers have the right to freedom of association in national or international organisations for the protection of their economic and social interests'.
6   Article 6 provides, 'All workers and employers have the right to bargain collectively'.
7   Article 7 provides, 'Children and young persons have the right to special protection against the physical and moral hazards to which they are exposed'.
8   Article 12 provides, 'All workers and their dependants have the right to social security'.
9   Article 13 provides, 'Anyone without adequate resources has the right to social and medical assistance'.
10   Article 16 provides, 'The family as a fundamental unit of society has the right to appropriate social, legal and economic protection to ensure its full development'.
11   Article 19 provides, 'Migrant workers who are nationals of a Party and their family have the right to protection and assistance in the territory of another Party'.
12   Article 20 provides, 'All workers have the right to equal opportunities and equal treatment in matters of employment and occupation without discrimination on the grounds of sex'.

counterparts. For example, its sister Treaty, the ECHR, has strict rules in relation to derogation. Article 15 of the Convention allows states to derogate only during 'a time of war or other public emergency threatening the life of the nation'. However, under no circumstances can a state derogate from Articles 2 (the right to life), 3 (freedom from torture and from inhuman and degrading treatment) and 4 (prohibition of slavery) of the Convention. Further, there can be no derogation from Protocol 6, Article 1 and Protocol 13, Article 1 (abolishing the death penalty). All other derogations must be temporary and limited to a particular space.[13]

The difference in application of these documents illustrates the divide and promulgates the idea that social and economic rights are of lesser importance than their civil and political counterparts. Choosing which provisions it will be bound by offers a level of flexibility not available to the state with other human rights treaties. Further, there is a considerable level of discretion as to how it will implement the chosen articles. This may vary depending on the economic circumstances, political ideology and democratic institution. While it may allow the state to feel more in control and does not impose excessive burdens, it also has the effect of failing to establish the minimum core of each right or a basic standard to which each person is entitled. Again, this demonstrates the divide between the two sets of rights, where social and economic rights protection can vary from state to state without establishing a basic threshold below which a violation can be imposed. **[5–07]**

Another significant difference between the ECHR and the ESC is the matter of who can assert and rely on the rights contained therein. The ECHR sets out, in Article 1, that the rights contained therein apply to everyone in the jurisdiction of the contracting state.[14] This has had two practical effects. The first is that it has extended state responsibility to jurisdictions wherein that state has effective **[5–08]**

---

[13] Frederick Cowell, 'Sovereignty and the Question of Derogation: An Analysis of Article 15 of the ECHR and the Absence of a Derogation Clause in the ACHPR' (2013) 1 Birkbeck Law Review 135.

[14] Article 1 provides, 'The High Contracting Parties shall secure to everyone within their jurisdiction the rights and freedoms defined in Section 1 of this Convention'.

control.[15] The second is that protection is not contingent upon citizenship.[16] By contrast, the ESC only applies to 'foreigners ... insofar as they are nationals of other parties lawfully resident or working regularly with the territory of the party concerned',[17] meaning that only citizens and lawful residents can invoke ESC rights. Irregular migrants, victims of trafficking and asylum seekers are all excluded from its remit.

The Committee of the European Social Charter

[5–09] The European Committee on Social Rights (previously called the Committee of Independent Experts) oversees the enforcement of the ESC and engages in legal interpretation of its provisions, reviewing large volumes of materials to determine whether a state is in compliance with the articles to which it has bound itself.[18] It is made up of 15 independent and impartial members, who hold their post for 6 years. The Council of Europe's Parliamentary Assembly has previously called for an enhancement of the Committee and recommended that a court akin to the European Court of Human Rights be established.[19] This new court would be solely concerned with social and economic rights, making the rights within the ESC enforceable in the same manner as those protected by the ECHR. This recommendation has not been met with rapturous enthusiasm and, to date, the Committee's role remains primarily that of a supervisory body who issues recommendations.

---

[15] For analysis of this aspect, see the cases of *Bankovic and others v Belgium* (2007) 44 EHRR SE 5 and *Al-Skeini v UK* (2011) 53 EHRR 18, and Marko Milanovic, 'Al-Skeini and Al-Jedda in Strasbourg' (2012) 23 European Journal of International Law 121; Samantha Besson, 'The Extraterritoriality of the European Convention on Human Rights; Why Human Rights Depend on Jurisdiction and What Jurisdiction Amounts to' (2012) 25 Leiden Journal of International Law 857; Sarah Miller, 'Revisiting Extraterritorial Jurisdiction: A Territorial Justification for Extraterritorial Jurisdiction under the European Convention' (2010) 20 European Journal of International Law 1223; Matthew Happold, 'Bankovic v Belgium and the Territorial Scope of the European Convention on Human Rights' (2003) 3 Human Rights Law Review 77; Joanne Williams, 'Al Skeini: A Flawed Interpretation of Bankovic' (2005) 23 Wisconsin International Law Journal 687; Tariq Abdel-Monem, Patrick JD Kennedy and Ekaterina Apostolova, 'R (on the Application of Al Skeini) v Secretary of Defence: A Look at the United Kingdom's Extraterritorial Obligations in Iraq and Beyond' (2005) 17 Florida Journal of International Law 345.

[16] Colin Harvey and Stephen Livingstone, 'Protecting the Marginalised: The Role of The European Convention on Human Rights' (2000) 51 Northern Ireland Legal Quarterly 445. As the authors point out, human rights refer to personhood and not citizenship and, as such, at least in Convention terms, are not restricted on the basis of citizenship.

[17] European Social Charter (revised) (n 1) Appendix [1].

[18] Holly Cullen, 'The Collective Complaints System of the European Social Charter: Interpretative Methods of the European Committee on Social Rights' (2009) 9(1) Human Rights Law Review 61, 64.

[19] Recommendation 1354 of 28 January 1998.

In order to fulfil this supervisory role, states have an obligation to report on the implementation of the ESC rights that they have agreed to be bound by, every two years in respect of core rights and every four years for all other provisions. The Committee then issues compliance reports based upon its investigations of these submissions.[20] Nedelka argues that this supervision is unsatisfactory, in that it, like the reporting structure for the ICESCR, relies solely on the subjective view of the state and submits that an independent assessment would be better.[21] This criticism is well founded, particularly as there is no consensus between states as to an appropriate level of protection for social and economic rights. [5–10]

The Committee is also tasked with enhancing state knowledge of the provisions and, in that respect, it hosts information seminars which are primarily aimed at newer state parties. [5–11]

The Collective Complaints Procedure

The collective complaints procedure was introduced as part of the revitalisation of the Charter, which began in 1990. In 1991 the Committee established a working party to create proposals for a collective complaints mechanism. Following consultation with the Assembly, the text of the Protocol was approved in June 1995 and opened for signature in November of that same year. The Protocol required five ratifications before it could enter into force and this was met in July 1998.[22] The explanatory report to the Protocol explains that it is 'designed to increase the efficiency of the supervisory machinery based solely on the submission of government reports'.[23] This, according to Cullen, demonstrates that it was intended to compliment this reporting regime.[24] However, unlike the reporting system which is compulsory for all member states, acceptance of the collective complaints mechanism is optional.[25] [5–12]

Significantly, the revised ESC established the first forum in Europe where breaches of social and economic rights could be presented and adjudicated upon. This affirms that the purpose of the ESC was to go beyond a mere statement of principles and that it would impose obligations on the ratifying states. The enforcement mechanism for breaches of the ESC is not judicial like the European [5–13]

---

[20] David Harris and John Darcy, *The European Social Charter* (2nd edn, Transnational Publishers 2001) 310.

[21] Martin Nedelka, 'Forty Years of the European Charter; Celebration or Commiseration' (2001) 1 University College Dublin Law Review 67.

[22] Article 14(1) of the Protocol.

[23] Council of Europe, Explanatory Report on the Collective Complaints Protocol [1995] COETSER 3 (9 November 1995) [1-8].

[24] Cullen (n 18) 64.

[25] To date, 15 of the 47 state parties have accepted the protocol. See <www.coe.int/en/web/turin-european-social-charter/signature-ratifications> last accessed 31 July 2016.

Court and sanctions cannot be imposed on states. The recommendations and decisions are not legally binding and, thus, a violation may continue for years before any changes are made. It relies mainly on political pressure to ensure that obligations are fulfilled. Operating on a 'name and shame' basis, the Committee publishes its reports and declares whether a state is in conformity or not with its obligations. In contrast to the complaints procedure in the ECHR, there is no avenue for individuals to bring a complaint. As the name suggests, the complaint must be made collectively.

[5–14]   The ESC identifies four groups which are permitted to bring a complaint: (1) international organisations of employers and trade unions; (2) NGOs which have consultative status with the Council of Europe; (3) national organisations of employers or trade unions within the jurisdiction of the state against whom they have lodged a complaint; and (4) (for states that have accepted) other NGOs with particular competence in the matter complained of.[26] To date, Finland is the only member state which has authorised national NGOs to take collective complaints. These groups can instigate a claim that there has been 'unsatisfactory application' of rights, as opposed to a 'violation of rights', which can be claimed in relation to the rights contained in the ECHR.[27] In this manner, it has been asserted that the ESC again reaffirms the inferior status of social and economic rights.[28]

[5–15]   As established under the Rules of Procedure, a qualified complainant must make a submission in writing to the Secretary of the Committee, alleging that a state has not satisfactorily applied a provision of the Charter.[29] Failure to have this complaint signed by an authorised member of the organisation can result in the claim being deemed inadmissible.[30] Article 66 states that the complainant must indicate how the state has not satisfactorily implemented the Charter. The level of evidence required to show this is not explicitly stated in the Charter, although it appears not to be overly onerous or excessive.

[5–16]   Once a complaint has been submitted, the Committee must then decide whether it is admissible. Churchill and Khaliq observe that, unlike other human rights treaties, the ESC does not contain a comprehensive list of conditions and comment that, to date, the Committee has taken a rather relaxed attitude to

---

[26]   Additional Protocol to the European Social Charter Providing for a System of Collective Complaints, Strasbourg, 9 XI 1996 ETS No 158.

[27]   Article 34.

[28]   Tonio Novitz, 'Are Social Rights Necessarily Collective Rights? A Critical Analysis of the Collective Complaints Protocol to the European Social Charter (2002) European Human Rights Law Review 50, 53.

[29]   Rule 23, revised during 207th Session, May 2005.

[30]   See *Frente Comum de Sindicatos da Administracao v Portugal* Complaint No. 36/2006 (December 2006) [4].

admissibility.[31] Once a decision on admissibility is made, the state is then requested to submit its views on the merits of the complaint and to write a response. It may also invite the complainant to submit further information. The Committee may then decide to hold a hearing, although it is not required to do so and can make its determination on the basis of the written submissions alone. The Committee then gives its opinion and also sets out any recommendations. If it adopts a recommendation, the state must do everything in its power to bring the area into compliance. In contrast, if it adopts a resolution, it is merely taking note of the decision and does not require any action on the part of the state. It has no power to award damages or costs to the complainant if it finds that the state has not complied with its obligations. On the rare occasion that it has asked for a financial contribution to be paid to the claimant, such a request has been denied.

Cullen identifies that the main weaknesses of the Charter are the lack of **[5–17]** an individual complaints mechanism and the inability to award remedies.[32] The failure to allow individual complaints may, in turn, have an effect on its perceived effectiveness, as individuals may not see the rights as being directly relevant or applicable to them. The classification of social and economic rights as collective rather than individual is noteworthy. Often called a contradiction in terms,[33] many modern jurisprudential scholars conclude that collective rights should not take precedence over the individual.[34] The definition of a collective right proffered by Raz is that the right will arise where there is an aggregate interest in a public good, which together creates a duty, where alone it would not.[35] An example of this might perhaps be clean public parks, a right that one could not hold individually, but which would, instead, be a collective right of the community. Thus, by this definition, in order for social and economic rights to be collective rights, they must not be capable of being individually enforced, which promulgates the inferior status of social and economic rights and, again, brings up another significant difference between the ECHR and the ESC. The ESC refers to classes of persons such as 'workers' or 'employed women', while the ECHR simply refers to the individual. This stance is equally at odds with the ICESCR interpretation, which has abandoned the requirement for an appreciable

---

[31] Churchill Robin and Khaliq Urfan, 'Violations of Economic Social and Cultural Rights. The Current Use and Future Potential of the Collective Complaints Mechanism of the European Social Charter' in Baderin Mashood and McCorquodale (eds), *Economic, Social and Cultural Rights in Action* (Oxford University Press 2007).

[32] Cullen (n 18) 67.

[33] M Galenkamp, 'Collective Rights' Studie-en Informaticcentrum, Netherlands Institute of Human Rights Report Commissioned by the Advisory Committee on Human Rights and Foreign Policy in the Netherlands, Utrecht, 1995.

[34] For example, see Ronald Dworkin, *Taking Rights Seriously* (Harvard University Press 1977); Jeremy Waldron (ed), *Nonsense on Stilts: Bentham, Burke and Marx on the Rights of Man* (Routledge 1987).

[35] Joseph Raz, *The Morality of Freedom* (Oxford University Press 1996) 208.

amount of persons to be compromised by a violation and confirmed that the minimum core rights contained therein are self-executing.[36]

[5–18]   The Committee must strictly adhere to its powers and cannot award compensation.[37] In the limited cases where the Committee has requested that the Committee of Ministers make a contribution to the costs of the complainant, such requests have been denied.[38] This, again, undermines the status of social and economic rights when compared with the European Convention, where the court can order 'just satisfaction', which is legally binding on the state concerned.

[5–19]   Despite the ESC being binding on states (at least, in respect of the obligations to which they have signed up), the recommendations made by the Committee are not legally binding on the state.[39] The sole obligation is to include in its next report the measures that it has taken to alleviate the breach.

[5–20]   Nedelka recommends the introduction of a number of novel measures which would make it more effective in the face of continued neglect by some member states. He recommends that states should be forced to sign up to all the provisions of the Charter, that compliance should be monitored by independent assessors, that decisions should become binding and that sanctions should attach for ongoing breaches.[40] Given that the Charter, at present, relies on the cooperation of states, it is unlikely that any of these measures will, in fact, be implemented.

Links with the European Convention on Human Rights

[5–21]   The link between the ESC and the ECHR has always been close, with the Charter being developed as a counterpart to the Convention. In recent years, each has had recourse to the jurisprudence of the other in assisting with their determinations. The Committee has utilised the rulings of the ECHR numerous times in interpreting breaches of the ESC. In complaints made by the World Organisation against Torture,[41] the Committee cited the judgements in *Tyrer v UK*[42] and *A v UK*,[43] in holding that there had been breaches of the ESC. While this is significant to show that there is a clear link and consistency between the two, as the Committee has limited enforcement mechanisms, the impact of the

---

[36]   UN Committee on Economic Social and Cultural Rights, General Comment No. 15: The Right to Water (Arts 11 and 12 of the Covenant) UN Doc E/C 12/2002/11.

[37]   *Confederation Francaise de lEncadrement v France* Complaint No 9/2000.

[38]   For example, see *European Roma Rights Centre v France* Complaint No 15/2003.

[39]   Council of Europe, *Social Charter of the 21ˢᵗ Century: Colloquy organised by the Secretariat of the Council of Europe, 14-16 May 1997* (Council of Europe 1998) 108.

[40]   Nedelka (n 21).

[41]   Complaints Nos 17/2003, 18/2003, 19/2003, 20/2003, 21/2003 and 34/2006.

[42]   (1979) 2 EHRR 1.

[43]   (1998) 27 EHRR 611.

Committee adopting the Convention interpretation is limited. More significant, however, is the European Court adopting and utilising the recommendations and deliberations of the Committee. In *Wilson v UK,* the European Court relied heavily on the fact that the Committee had found the UK to be in violation of the ESC in determining that it had also breached Article 11 of the ECHR.[44]

Further, in the *ASLEF* case,[45] the European Court, once again, had regard to the European Commission's jurisprudence in *Cheall v United Kingdom*, in determining whether refusal to allow the applicant join a trade union due to his political affiliation breached Article 11 of the ECHR.[46]   **[5–22]**

Notable is how the Committee has expanded the reach of the ESC beyond the existing textual rights by identifying and enunciating the values that underpin it. Identifying dignity as a foundational concept is also ensuring that an individualist aspect to a collective complaint is relevant. The Committee has stated, 'Human dignity is the fundamental value and indeed the core of positive European human rights law… whether under the ESC or under the European Convention'.[47] The Committee was also clear that dignity is relevant to civil and political rights and not just to social and economic rights violations. This aspect has been particularly relevant when dealing with cases relating to housing and eviction. While those dealt with through the European Court centre on procedural safeguards[48] the Committee has proposed that the dignity of the person must be protected when evictions are proposed.[49] Over a number of years, it has built up a body of jurisprudence dealing with housing rights and, in particular, housing rights of the Roma community.[50]   **[5–23]**

The very recent decision of *COHRE v Italy* adds considerably to the jurisprudence on the area.[51] The complaint was brought by the *COHRE*, following mass expulsions of non-Italian Roma and Sinti and a marked decrease in the conditions of living standards experienced by these groups. In its complaint, it alleged breaches of Articles 16 (family rights to social legal and economic protection), 19(1), 19(4)(c), 19(8) (the rights of migrant workers and their families to protection and assistance), 30 (the right to protection against poverty and social exclusion), 31(1) and 31(3) (the right to housing).   **[5–24]**

---

[44]   (2002) 35 EHRR 523.
[45]   *Associated Society of Locomotive Engineers and Firemen v UK* [2007] ECHR 184.
[46]   (1986) 8 EHRR CD74.
[47]   Complaint No 19/2003 [31].
[48]   See, for example, *Connors v UK* (2004) 40 EHRR 189.
[49]   *European Roma Rights Centre v Italy* Complaint No 27/2004. The Committee stated that evictions must be conducted in a manner which respects the dignity of the persons affected in order to be compliant with the Charter obligations.
[50]   For example, see *COHRE v Croatia* Complaint No 52/2008 and *INTERIGHTS v Greece* Complaint No 49/2008.
[51]   Complaint No 58/2009.

[5–25]   A number of significant issues arise from this case. First, the issue of admissibility in relation to repeat complaints is firmly solidified. The Committee had previously had an opportunity to examine the status of the Roma in the earlier case of *European Roma Rights Centre v Italy* and this case centred on almost identical facts.

[5–26]   Whether a repeat claim would be admissible was first established in *International Centre for the legal Protection of Human Rights (INTERIGHTS) v Greece,* where the Committee stated that the fact that it had already examined this situation does not itself imply inadmissibility. Moreover, the fact that the particular section of the Charter had already been the subject of a previous complaint of the same nature also does not, in itself, render the complaint inadmissible.[52] This position was firmly established in *COHRE v Italy*, where it was stated:

> The present complaint indeed not only alleges that Italian Authorities have not ensured proper follow up to the decision on the merits… It also more specifically raises new issues linked to the adoption by the Italian authorities of allegedly regressive measures that would have worsened the situation assessed by the Committee.[53]

[5–27]   Nolan observes that this is a significant step for the Social Charter, as international complaints mechanisms will generally deem a complaint to be inadmissible if it is something with which the court has already dealt.[54] This case further established what is known as an aggravated violation of rights, which sends a clear message of zero tolerance to the state commission of, state failure to address and state collusion in, discrimination suffered by vulnerable groups. The Committee, again, deliberately aligned itself with the jurisprudence of the European Court and, further, saw it taking account of General Comment 4 regarding the interpretation and application of housing under the ICESCR.

[5–28]   Notwithstanding the Committee's clear commitment and enthusiasm, the fact remains that its decisions are not binding, which significantly weakens the impact that it can have. As Nolan observes, 'If the Committee's findings in relation to Charter rights are consistently ignored, then the utility of the mechanism other than as a largely symbolic standard setting exercise will be limited'.[55] Churchill and Khaliq warned that, without change, the practical effect of the collective

---

[52]   Complaint No 49/2008.
[53]   ibid [24].
[54]   Aoife Nolan, 'Aggravated Violations, Roma Housing Rights and Forced Expulsions in Italy, recent Developments under the European Social Charter Collective Complaints System' (2011) 11(2) Human Rights Law Review 343.
[55]   ibid.

complaints procedure would be significantly diminished and that seems now
to be the reality.[56]

The general consensus is that the ESC falls down in three distinct areas. First, **[5–29]**
in that there is only a mechanism for collective complaints and no mechanism
for individual complaints to take place. As the collective complains mechanism
does not require the claimants to exhaust domestic remedies prior to application,
it may provide a speedier avenue than other international forums. However, as
this is a collective complaint, if an approved organisation refuses to bring the
complaint, the individual may be left with little remedy.[57]

The second issue is that the state need not sign up to all of the rights and, further, **[5–30]**
it does not have to accept the collective complaints procedure at all. Therefore,
the state is only agreeing to be 'bound' by the obligations which it has signed up
to, and if it breaches other rights, then there is no recourse, regardless of whether
or not it has accepted the collective complaints mechanism. As Nedelka suggests,
the general impression is that it would be strengthened by ensuring that states
must sign up to all of the rights contained within the ESC and express specific
derogations to certain articles.[58] This would ensure that, if a state wanted to be
excluded, it would have to expressly opt out, rather than opt in.

The final area where the ESC fails is in the remit of remedies. The position is **[5–31]**
little different from that established by the optional Protocol to the ICESCR,
whereby recommendations are made. The Committee has no power to enforce
any decision and the state can (and does) routinely ignore the recommendations
made. This is becoming somewhat mitigated now with the overlapping of the
ESC and the ECHR. The latter, which does hear cases of individual petition,
have utilised decisions of the Committee in order to find violations of individual
rights.[59] Therefore, where the Committee has determined that the state has
breached the rights, if an individual can link this right to an existing textual
right of the ECHR, they may be able to get a more effective remedy from the
European Court of Human Rights, though this may be a lengthy, onerous and
expensive avenue to pursue.

Ireland and the European Social Charter

As previously observed, Ireland is a dualist nation and international law **[5–32]**

---

[56] Robin Churchill and Urfan Khaliq, 'The Collective Complaints System of the European
Social Charter: An Effective Mechanism for Ensuring Compliance with Economic and
Social Rights' (2004) 15(3) European Journal of International Law 417.
[57] Aoife Nolan, 'Litigating Housing Rights: Experiences and Issues' (2006) 28 Dublin
University Law Journal 145.
[58] Nedelka (n 21).
[59] See *Wilson v UK* [2002] ECHR 552.

(including regional treaties) is not binding domestically, unless and until it has been transposed into national law by an act of the Oireachtas. This is equally true of regional documents and, as the ESC has not been incorporated into Irish law, its provisions cannot be relied upon in national courts. It binds the state internationally only. This is a wholly unsatisfactory situation, whereby the state can be taken to task in the international tribunals, but the successful litigants have no way of enforcing any favourable judgement.

[5–33]   Ireland ratified the Revised ESC on 4 November 2000 and accepted 92 of the 98 provisions. The provisions to which Ireland did not agree were the introduction of specific leave entitlements for nursing mothers,[60] the right to information and consultation for workers,[61] ensuring equality and non-discrimination for workers with families,[62] and all provisions in relation to the right to housing.[63] Ireland has also accepted the collective complaints mechanism, although NGOs are not currently permitted to bring complaints under the procedure.

The Reports

[5–34]   The reports submitted to the Committee are compiled thematically. The Committee does not require that the state report on all 98 provisions. Rather, it sets a thematic approach, requiring that a select amount of these provisions be considered in each reporting session. The Committee has created four thematic groups, upon which the state reports, sequentially, every four years.[64] Between 1966 and 2015, Ireland has submitted a total of 34 reports to the Committee. In December 2015, Ireland submitted its report on provisions relating to Thematic Group 1, entitled 'Employment, Training and Equal Opportunities'. The conclusions are expected to be published in 2017. The state last reported on this theme in 2011 and, in its conclusions, the Committee outlined a number of concerns. It found that the upper limits on compensation for discrimination cases and the exclusion of army personnel from legislative protection in employment may be in breach of Article 1.2.[65] Under Article 1.4, it found that the length of residence clause, which prohibited many from accessing vocational training,

---

[60]   Article 8.3.
[61]   Article 21.
[62]   Article 27.1.
[63]   Article 31.
[64]   Decision of the Committee of Ministers, 963rd Meeting (3 May 2006) (CM (2006)53).
[65]   Conclusions 2012 on Article 1 (right to work), Article 9 (right to vocational guidance) Article 10 (vocational training) Article 18 (gainful employment in the territory of another state party) and Article 24 (protection in cases of dismissal).

amounted to indirect discrimination.[66] Finally, it found that the restrictions applied by the Unfair Dismissals Act 1996 go beyond what is permitted.[67]

Under Thematic Group 2, entitled 'Health Social Security and Social Protection', [5–35] the Committee issued conclusions in 2013 and in 2015 and, again, was critical of many aspects. It found that there was no strategy in place to develop occupational health services for all workers, nor was there a strategy in place to prevent or reduce accidents in the workplace.[68] Echoing a previous conclusion in 2006, it found that levels of social welfare benefits were inadequate.[69] It further expressed concern over access of migrants to social welfare and emergency medical care, particularly in respect of the habitual residence clause.[70]

The Committee published its last conclusions on Thematic Group 3, entitled [5–36] 'Labour Rights', in 2014. Amongst its concerns were that the national minimum wage was not sufficient to maintain a decent standard of living,[71] that the notice periods for termination of employment were inadequate,[72] in addition to restrictions in relation to collective bargaining and certain trade union activities.[73] This report was primarily concerned with those in employment and the rights attaching to that employment.

The conclusions of the final Thematic Group, entitled 'Children, Families [5–37] and Migrants', were published in 2011. Within this context, the Committee overwhelmingly focused on the rights of migrant workers, leaving the population of unemployed migrants outside of its net. It again considers women's rights, but only in the context of employment and maternity benefit. The ESC and the Committee therefore omits a rather large section of the public from its scope and furthers the proposition that this is, in fact, a labour or employment charter, rather than one that protects social and economic rights generally, a contention bolstered by the narrow list of those who can bring a collective complaint.

---

[66] This concern was reiterated in terms of Article 9 (right to vocational training) and Article 10 (promotion of vocational and technical training, retraining of adult workers and full use of facilities available).

[67] This was a breach of Article 24 (right to protection in case of dismissal).

[68] Conclusions 2015 on Articles 3.4 (right to safe and healthy working conditions) and 11.3 (prevention of diseases and accidents) respectively.

[69] Conclusions 2012 on Article 12.1 (right to social security).

[70] Conclusions 2012 on Articles 12.4 (right to social security of people moving between states), 13 (right to social and medical assistance) and 14.2 (right to benefit from social services).

[71] Article 4.1 (right to decent remuneration).

[72] Article 4.4 (right to reasonable notice).

[73] Articles 6.4 (right to bargain collectively), 5 (right to organise) and 6.2 (negotiation procedures).

The Jurisprudence

[5–38]   In total, there have been nine collective complaints lodged against Ireland, four of which are currently under consideration. Of the five decided cases, two have found no violation. The first of those cases, *International Federation of Human Rights Leagues v Ireland*, alleged that Ireland was discriminating against those in receipt of the contributory pension not permanently residing within the state, in that it refused to issue them with a free travel pass for use when they returned.[74] The travel scheme, being non-statutory in nature, was operated by the Department of Social Protection, offering free travel on public transport to those over the age of 66 permanently residing within the jurisdiction.[75] This case contended that the permanent residency clause violated Article 23, which provides that every elderly person has the right to social protection. The Committee determined that the restriction imposed therein was reasonable and 'did not constitute a denial of the core entitlements of elderly persons to essential social protection'.[76] As such, they found no rights violation

[5–39]   The second and more recent unsuccessful case was the *Federation of Catholic Family Associations in Europe (FAFCE) v Ireland*.[77] The complainant in the case asked the Committee to find that the rights of children who have been the victims of trafficking have not been respected, in violation of Article 17.1, a claim which the government rejected in its entirety. In its initial objections, Ireland argued that, as the claimant had incorrectly alleged a breach of Article 17.1 rather than Article 7.10, the entire case should be dismissed, but this was rejected by the Committee, which reaffirmed the principle that the ESC is to be read as a whole and watertight divisions between rights cannot be maintained.[78] As such, it continued to determine the case on the basis of the correct article, evidencing the fluvial nature of the admissibility criteria. On the substantive merits of the case, however, while reiterating the positive obligations placed on the state, it determined that the legislative framework in place was sufficient and no violation was found. While the Committee did have regard to reports which concluded that the situation in Ireland needed to be improved,[79] it found that the complaint was not 'sufficiently grounded in evidence' to establish a violation.

[5–40]   There have been four successful collective complaints taken against Ireland. The first, *World Organisation against Torture (OMCT) v Ireland*, argued that

---

74   Complaint No 42/2007 Decision on the Merits (3 June 2008).
75   This scheme is also available to persons in receipt of other social welfare payment provided that they meet additional criteria.
76   (n 74) [19].
77   Complaint No 89/2013 Decision on the Merits (12 September 2014).
78   A principle espoused in *Mental Disability Advocacy Centre (MDAC) v Bulgaria* Complaint No 41/2007 Decision on Admissibility (26 June 2007).
79   Such as OSCE, 'Special Representative and Coordinator for Combatting Trafficking in Human Beings' (2013) SEC.GAL\246/12.

permitting corporal punishment of children in the home, foster care and by certain child minders breached Article 17 of the Charter.[80] Ireland, in its defence, contended that the complaint was unfounded and that the law adequately protects children. It argued that the common law defence of reasonable chastisement (which was codified in the Children Act 1908) is proportionate and does not fall foul of its obligations. In particular, it placed reliance on the Children Act 2001, which criminalises physical punishment beyond reasonable chastisement. The OMCT countered that this defence ought to be removed from law, as it sends a clear message to parents and certain caregivers that physical punishment is permissible. It relied extensively on the concluding observations of Ireland's first report under the Convention on the Rights of the Child, wherein the Committee expressed considerable concern that there was no legislative framework prohibiting corporal punishment within the home,[81] a concern which they reiterated in their second report.[82]

In arriving at its conclusion, the Committee had regard to provisions of the UNCRC, jurisprudence of the European Court of Human Rights and recommendations of the Parliamentary Assembly.[83] In referring to these provisions, the Committee 'recalls that the Charter is a living instrument and must be interpreted in light of developments in the national law of member states... as well as international instruments'.[84] While acknowledging that the criminal law prohibits forms of more serious violence, ill treatment and neglect against children, it concluded that the defence of reasonable chastisement permitted some violence and that this breached Article 17 of the Charter. **[5–41]**

This precise issue was the subject matter of another successful complaint against Ireland, which came before the Committee in 2015. The case, *Association for the Protection of all Children (APROACH) v Ireland,* once again alleged that the failure to legislatively prohibit corporal punishment within the home and repeal the defence of reasonable chastisement amounted to a violation of Article 17 of the Charter.[85] While the Committee had regard to provisions enacted since its previous determination, which enhance generally the protection of children, nothing specific was undertaken to remove the defence of reasonable chastisement which remains in law and thus found the second breach of Article 17 against Ireland. Supporting this second finding are the concluding observations of the Committee which, in its reports in 2003, 2005 **[5–42]**

---

[80] Complaint No 18/2003 Decision on the Merits (7 December 2004).

[81] *Concluding Observations of the Committee on the Rights of the Child* CRC/C/15/Add.85 [16].

[82] *Concluding Observations of the Committee on the Rights of the Child* CRC/C/IRL/CO/2 [39].

[83] Social, Health and Family Affairs Committee, 'Europe-wide ban on Corporal Punishment of Children', Doc No 10199 (4 June 2004).

[84] Complaint No 18/2003 Decision on the Merits (7 December 2004) [35].

[85] Complaint No 93/2013 Decision on the Merits (2 December 2015).

and 2011, cautioned that the defence of reasonable chastisement did not meet the requirements under the ESC.

[5–43] The Children First Act 2015 repeals the defence of reasonable chastisement, bringing Ireland in line with its international obligations. However, this case clearly shows the status of the ESC in Irish law. Given that the Committee is not a court, its decisions are not legally binding and the state need only take them into account. There is no legal requirement to amend the law, nor does the ESC have any power to enforce its decision, nor can it be relied upon in courts to challenge the offending legislation, resulting in an 11-year delay to remedy the situation. Cousins argues that an avenue may open through the ECHR. This Convention has been transposed into Irish law by way of the European Convention on Human Rights Act 2003 and can be used to in the Irish courts. As there is a clear link between them (as outlined above), Cousins opines that national courts could use the ESC jurisprudence to interpret articles of the ECHR.[86] However, as will be seen in the next chapter, Ireland has taken a rather restrictive approach to interpreting the ECHR and existing jurisprudence of the European Court within the domestic system and, given this position, it is unlikely that Cousins' proposition would succeed.

[5–44] The third violation by Ireland to date was the subject of the case of *European Confederation of Police (EuroCOP) v Ireland*, alleging that Articles 5, 8 and 21 of the Charter were breached, as national police representative associations did not enjoy full trade association rights.[87] They claimed that national police are prohibited from establishing trade unions, denied access to pay negotiations, the Labour Relations Commission and the ability to take collective action. Ireland argued that it had not accepted Article 21 and was, therefore, not bound by its provisions, a contention accepted by the Committee. Further, it argued that, while there is no requirement to exhaust domestic remedies, the fact that, in this case, all domestic remedies had not been exhausted, is something that should be persuasive to the Committee, a proposition which was rejected. Finally, Ireland raised the issue that this was not a matter addressed by the Committee in any of its previous reports to the state. In response, the Committee affirmed that this was not a necessary precursor for a case to be heard.[88] It found breaches of Article 5, due to the prohibition on joining a national employees' organisation, and of Article 6, due to the prohibition on collective bargaining. The restrictions on collective bargaining generally were an issue raised by CESCR, where it

---

[86] Mel Cousins, 'Corporal Punishment in Ireland and the European Committee on Social Rights' (2015) 20(4) Bar Review 78.
[87] Complaint No 83/2012 Decision on the Merits (2 December 2013).
[88] ibid [44].

urged Ireland to enhance the rights of trade unions in this regard.[89] Further, it found that the prohibition on the right to strike breached Article 6 of the ESC.

The most recent decision against Ireland was released in May 2016 in the case of *European Roma Rights Centre (ERRC) v Ireland*, which contended that the housing conditions and evictions of traveller families, in particular traveller children, breach Articles 16, 17 and 30.[90]   **[5–45]**

As Ireland has not accepted Article 31 in relation to housing rights, the complaint was framed in terms of children's rights and the freedom from poverty and discrimination. In this way, the complaint relied on the case of *ERRC v Bulgaria*, where the Committee found that housing rights can be encompassed by other articles.[91] In summary, the complaint requested that the Committee find a breach of: Article 16 in respect of evictions, in relation to the inadequacy of national legislation, arbitrary use of the legislation and forced evictions of travellers; Articles 16 and 30, in that existing sites are inadequate and have resulted in insufficient living conditions; and Article 17, in that evictions and inadequate living conditions negatively affect the schooling and health of the children involved.[92]   **[5–46]**

The Committee unanimously found a breach of Article 16 in relation to insufficient provision of accommodation, inadequate conditions of accommodation and insufficient safeguards from eviction. They found that there were no violations of Articles 17 and 30.   **[5–47]**

At present, there are three complaints pending against Ireland. The first, *International Federation for Human Rights v Ireland*, alleges breaches of Articles 11, 16, 17 and 30 and relates specifically to housing conditions of residents in the Dolphins Barn area of Dublin.[93] This complex, built in the 1950s, has a plumbing and sewage system which is unable to cope with modern technology. As a result, over the last 20 years, the complex has been riddled with problems arising from mould, damp and raw sewage. Significant health implications for residents have been identified as arising from these conditions, particularly for children.[94]   **[5–48]**

---

[89] *Concluding Observations on the Third Periodic Report of Ireland* UN Doc E/C.12/IRL/CO/3 [19].

[90] Complaint No 100/2013 Decision on the Merits (16 May 2016).

[91] Complaint No 31/2005 Decision on the Merits (18 October 2006).

[92] For full background to the case, see the ERRC's Response to the Government's Observations (30 June 2014), available at <www.errc.org/cms/upload/file/ireland-observations-on-the-governments-submission-on-merits-19-august-2014.pdf> last accessed 31 January 2017.

[93] Complaint No 110/2014 Decision on Admissibility (17 March 2015).

[94] For full details, see Rialto Rights in Action Project, 'Report on the First Monitoring of Housing Conditions in Dolphin House Rialto' (5 October 2010).

[5–49] The Committee, in its decision on admissibility, observed that Ireland had not accepted Article 31 dealing with housing rights and, as such, the complaint frames the issues under the right to health, family rights to social, legal and economic protection and the right to be free from poverty and social exclusion. Since this case was initiated, regeneration works have begun on certain sections of the complex. It remains to be seen whether the Committee will find these measures sufficient, given that residents have been subjected to such conditions for in excess of 20 years.

[5–50] The further case pending against Ireland is the *Organisation of Military Associations (EuroMil) v Ireland*, which alleges breaches of Articles 5 and 6.[95] This case is almost identical to *EuroCOP v Ireland*, save that this pending case relates to the prohibition imposed on the Defence Forces, rather than the police force, in joining national employee unions, collective bargaining in relation to pay and conditions and taking collective action. A final complaint pending is the *Irish Congress of Trade Unions v Ireland*[96] which argues that the prohibition of certain workers deemed self employed from entering into collective agreements in relation to pay and conditions is a breach of article 6 of the ESC.

Conclusion

[5–51] Despite the Committee consistently reiterating that the rights contained within the ESC are to have a practical, not just a theoretical, impact, it can be said with a significant degree of certainty that it has not yet had any real impact on the furtherance of social and economic rights within Ireland.

[5–52] Its flexible admissibility criteria, coupled with the Committee's enthusiasm to read the ESC as a living instrument capable of evolving interpretation based on changing societal norms and in conjunction with other international documents, is to be welcomed. However, this is overwhelmingly undermined by the lack of an individual complaints mechanism and the non-existent enforceability of the Committee's decisions. These decisions are not legally binding and, as the Committee has no power to impose sanctions on the state, they are routinely ignored.

[5–53] It is clear that what is necessary for social and economic rights to be furthered within the domestic setting is an international body establishing legal and enforceable obligations on the state. In that regard, the next two chapters focus on the Charter of Fundamental Rights of the European Union and the ECHR, both of which are overseen by court systems that have legally enforceable sanction powers which are binding on the state concerned.

---

[95] Complaint No 112/2014 Decision on Admissibility (30 June 2015).
[96] Case No. 123/2016.

CHAPTER 6

The European Convention on Human Rights

The ECHR: An Introduction

As we have seen, the ICESCR and the ESC, which protect social and economic rights are, for a variety of reasons, relatively unhelpful to the furtherance of domestic justiciability and enforcement. Whether this is due to the lack of legal enforceability or the non-transposition into domestic law is arguable.   [6–01]

The European Convention on Human Rights (ECHR)[1] is unique among human rights treaties in its relationship with Irish domestic law. It has been transposed into national law by way of the European Convention on Human Rights Act 2003,[2] which places particular obligations on the court. Notable is the requirement to interpret Irish law in a manner compatible with the ECHR[3], and further the obligation to have cognisance of the jurisprudence of the European Court of Human Rights.[4]   [6–02]

Given the particular status of the ECHR in Irish law, coupled with the fact that it is overseen by the European Court of Human Rights, which delivers legally binding judgments and has the power to award remedies to an applicant, the position taken by this court in relation to social and economic rights could be of pivotal importance. The ECHR textually protects civil and political rights, with its sister treaty, the European Social Charter, having been created as its   [6–03]

---

[1] Convention for the Protection of Human Rights and Fundamental Freedoms (4 October 1950, CETS 005), entered into force on 3 September 1953.

[2] Adopted on 30 June 2003 and entered into force on 31 December 2003.

[3] s 2.1 states, 'In interpreting and applying any statutory provision or rule of law, a court shall, insofar as is possible, subject to the rules of law relating to such interpretation and application, do so in a manner compatible with the State's obligations under the Convention provisions'.

[4] s 4 states, 'Judicial notice shall be taken of the Convention provisions and of – (a) Any declaration, decision or advisory opinion or judgment of the European Court of Human Rights established under the Convention on any question in respect of which that Court has jurisdiction, (b) Any decision or opinion of the European Commission of Human Rights so established on any question in respect of which it had jurisdiction, (c) Any decision of the Committee of Ministers established under the Statute of the Council of Europe on any question on which it has jurisdiction–And a court shall, when interpreting and applying the Convention provisions, take due account of the principles laid down by those declarations, decisions, advisory opinions and judgments'.

counterpart to encompass social and economic rights. However, since its earliest cases the European Court has consistently opined that there is no clear division between categories of rights and that all rights are indivisible.[5] This interpretation has paved the way for the court to indirectly incorporate social and economic rights as integral components of certain civil and political rights

[6–04] The ECHR, proposed by the Council of Europe[6] and adopted in 1950, was drafted in the wake of the Second World War. The European Court of Human Rights[7] was established, which was empowered to hear both individual[8] and inter-state complaints.[9] It entered into force in 1953 and has been ratified by all 47 members of the Council of Europe.

[6–05] The ECHR was intended to provide a statement of the unifying principles of Western nations against the spectre of the communist advance.[10] As a consequence, this document protected the civil and political rights 'essential to a western democratic way of life',[11] As debates regarding the status of social and economic rights flared during the negotiations to transform the UDHR into a legally binding treaty, so, too, did they arise in the drafting of the European Convention. Arguing for their inclusion, socialist members feared that an undemocratic state could destroy individual freedoms through a complete

---

[5] See *Airey v Ireland* (1979) 2 EHRR 305 [26].

[6] Established in 1949 under the Statute of the Council of Europe (ETS 001), a top priority for the newly created institution was to develop a Charter of Human Rights and a court to enforce the rights contained therein. See Ed Bates, *The Evolution of the European Convention on Human Rights: From its Inception to the Creation of a Permanent Court of Human Rights* (Oxford University Press 2010) ch 1 and Alistair Mowbray, *Cases Materials and Commentary on the European Convention of Human Rights* (3rd edn, Oxford University Press 2012) 1-2.

[7] Initially, the Convention established two part-time institutions; the European Commission of Human Rights acted as a court of first instance that would, in certain circumstances, refer cases to the European Court. Protocol 11 (CETS 155) replaced these with a permanent court.

[8] Article 34 states, 'The Court may receive applications from any person, nongovernmental organisation or group of individuals claiming to be the victim of a violation by one of the High Contracting Parties of the rights set forth in the Convention or the Protocols thereto. The High Contracting Parties undertake not to hinder in any way the effective exercise of this right'.

[9] Article 33 states, 'Any High Contracting Party may refer to the Court any alleged breach of the provisions of the Convention and the Protocols thereto by another high contracting party'.

[10] David Harris, Michael O'Boyle, Ed Bates and Carla Buckley, *Harris O'Boyle and Warbrick; Law of the European Convention on Human Rights* (3rd edn, Oxford University Press 2014) 3. Conor Gearty, *On fantasy Island: Britain, Europe and Human Rights* (Oxford University Press 2016) 59.

[11] Michael O'Boyle, 'Practice and Procedure under the European Convention on Human Rights' (1980) 20 Santa Clara Law Review 697, 698. See also, Bernadette Rainey, Elizabeth Wicks and Clare Ovey, *Jacobs, White and Ovey, The European Convention on Human Rights* (6th edn, Oxford University Press 2014); Mowbray (n 6).

disregard for social and economic rights.[12] In the face of considerable opposition to this proposal, and in the interests of ensuring completion in a timely manner, only the rights which could be expressly agreed upon by all were included, thus omitting social and economic rights. Subsequent additional protocols to the Convention integrated supplemental fundamental rights and enhanced procedural efficacy. However, with the exception of education, neither the text of the Convention nor its protocols incorporate social and economic rights. [13]

Determining whether a case is admissible to the court essentially involves the consideration of nine questions.[14] Cases which satisfy this initial test[15] are then sent forward to be decided on their merits by a seven-judge Chamber, whereas cases of particular difficulty or importance may be heard by a Grand Chamber of seventeen judges.[16] While not strictly an appeals court, the Grand Chamber may decide to hear a case which has been referred to it following a judgment of the Chamber.[17] Protocol 16 will allow the Grand Chamber to provide non-binding advisory opinions on the interpretation and application of the ECHR.[18]   **[6–06]**

The Committee of Ministers is the body tasked with monitoring the implementation of the decisions of the court.[19] This body meets once a year and is comprised of the Minister for Foreign Affairs for each state party. At this meeting, it examines a select few cases from the court, in order to ensure that the decision of the court is being complied with. It is this body that can expel a state from the ECHR for failure to comply with its obligations.   **[6–07]**

The textual rights can be divided into two categories: unqualified and qualified rights. These unqualified or absolute rights are those from which the state cannot   **[6–08]**

---

[12] Gordon L Weil, 'The Evolution of the European Convention on Human Rights' (1963) 57 American Journal of International Law 804, 806-808.

[13] Protocol 1 (20 March 1952, CETS 9) incorporates the right to education and protection of private property; Protocol 4 (16 September 1963, CETS 46) prohibits imprisonment for contractual debt; Protocol 7 (22 October 1984, CETS 117) provides protection in relation to expulsion of aliens and compensation for wrongful conviction; Protocols 6 (28 April 1983, CETS 144) and 13 (3 May 2002, CETS 187) abolish the death penalty and Protocol 12 (4 November 2000, CETS 177) incorporates a general prohibition on discrimination.

[14] Rainey, Wicks and Ovey (n 11) 30-41 summarise the admissibility questions: (1) Is the applicant a victim of a violation of a Convention right?; (2) Is the respondent a state party?; (3) Have domestic remedies been exhausted?; (4) Is the application filed within the 6 month time limit?; (5) Is the application signed?; (6) Has the application been brought before?; (7) Is it compatible with the Convention?; (8) Is the application manifestly ill-founded?; and (9) Has there been an abuse of the right of petition?

[15] Protocol 14 (13 May 2004, CETS 194) allows one judge to determine admissibility.

[16] Articles 30 and 43.

[17] Article 31.

[18] (2 October 2013, CETS 214).

[19] The functions of the Committee are set out in Chapter 5 of the Statute, including the duty to conclude new treaties and the adoption of policies.

derogate.[20] Article 15 allows the state to derogate from their obligations in times of emergency, save for Articles 2 (the right to life), 3 (freedom from torture, inhuman and degrading treatment), 4 (prohibition on slavery), 7 (freedom from retrospective criminalisation) and Protocols 6, 7 and 13, dealing with the death penalty.[21]

[6–09]   Given that the textual rights are categorised as civil and political, the court's interpretation of those rights has been pivotal. It seeks to interpret the rights so as to give effect to the intention of the drafters (the protection of human rights) and, to accomplish this, may go beyond the text.[22] For example, in *Airey v Ireland*, the court held that the failure to provide legal aid effectively breached Article 6(1),[23] considering that the applicant, if acting on her own behalf, would not realistically be able to conduct her case effectively.[24] This interpretation ensures that the ECHR is practically effective. Further, it recognises that effective protection of fundamental rights necessarily entails moving beyond the traditional paradigm of imposing negative obligations, to include positive duties in certain circumstances.

[6–10]   Importantly, any particular interpretation of a right is not fixed. The evolutive, or dynamic interpretation was introduced in *Tyrer v UK*.[25] This is the notion that the ECHR is not stagnant and is to be interpreted in the context of contemporary societal conditions. This approach was approved in *Sigurjonsson v Iceland*, where the court reiterated that 'the Convention is a living instrument which must be interpreted in the light of present day conditions'.[26] This is a recognition that, as society evolves, so too do concepts of fundamental rights protection, which is essential if it is to maintain its effectiveness.[27]

---

[20]   See R St J McDonald, 'Derogations under Article 15 of the European Convention on Human Rights' (1998) 36 Columbia Journal of Transnational Law 225.

[21]   See Dimitris Xenos, *The Positive Obligations of the State under the European Convention on Human Rights* (Routledge 2012); Alistair Mowbray, *The Development of Positive Obligations under the European Convention on Human Rights by the European Court of Human Rights* (Hart 2004).

[22]   JG Merrills, *The Development of International Law by the European Court of Human Rights* (Manchester University Press 1988).

[23]   Article 6(1) provides, 'In determination of his civil rights and obligations or of any criminal charge against him, everyone is entitled to a fair and public hearing within a reasonable time by an independent and impartial tribunal established by law....'.

[24]   (1979) 2 EHRR 305.

[25]   (1978) 2 EHRR 1. The court had previously found that birching did not breach Article 3 and, in overruling its previous decision, confirmed that the instrument would be interpreted in light of societal changes within the member states.

[26]   (1993) 16 EHRR 462 [35].

[27]   Luzius Wildhaber, 'European Court of Human Rights' (2002) 40 Canadian Yearbook of International Law 310. See also George Letsas, *A Theory of Interpretation of the European Convention on Human Rights* (Oxford University Press 2009); Marton Varju, 'Transition as a Concept of European Human Rights Law' (2009) 2 European Human Rights Law Review 170.

The court relies primarily on a consensus among member states (or, at least, **[6–11]** an emerging consensus) in order to develop the scope of an article. However, a state may be able to offer reasonable justification for departing from such an accord. The court then balances the consensus (or an emerging one) with the 'margin of appreciation' afforded to each state in the application of rights. The term 'margin of appreciation' is a creation of the court which will placed on a textual basis by Protocol 15 to the Convention when it enters into force.[28]

This margin can be used to determine whether restrictions imposed on qualified **[6–12]** rights are justified, in assessing whether the state has complied with a positive obligation,[29] and in deciding whether a state response is legitimate.[30] The level of discretion allowed under the margin will differ depending on the context of the case.[31] A wide margin is given to the state when the subject matter relates to national security,[32] the protection of public morals,[33] and in circumstances where there is no consensus between member states.

The margin of appreciation, like the rights themselves, are not subject to a fixed **[6–13]** interpretation, as the situation relating to the legal recognition of post-operative transsexuals shows. In *Rees v UK*, the court found that the issue fell entirely within the margin of appreciation of the state.[34] One of the key factors in the court reaching this conclusion was that there was a considerably disparity in how state parties afforded recognition and legal rights to post-operative transsexuals. However, the opposite conclusion was reached in the similar case of *Goodwin v UK*, where the court found that, given the increase and importance of issues such as those raised by Ms Goodwin, the matter no longer fell within the margin of appreciation.[35] In coming to this decision, notice was taken of intervening cases,[36] and the emerging consensus among member states to grant legal recognition to post-operative transsexuals.[37] Thus, it is not bound by its previous decisions and where society has evolved its concepts regarding the protection of fundamental rights, so too will the court.

---

[28] (24 June 2013, CETS 213).
[29] See *Keegan v Ireland* (1994) 18 EHRR 342.
[30] See *Ireland v UK* (1978) 2 EHRR 25.
[31] Harris, O'Boyle, Bates and Buckley (n 10) 15.
[32] *Leander v Sweden* (1987) 9 EHRR 433.
[33] *Muller and Ors v Switzerland* (1991) 13 EHRR 212, *Wingrove v UK* (1997) 24 EHRR 1; *Open Door Counselling Ltd and Dublin Well Women Centre Ltd v Ireland* (1992) 15 EHRR 244.
[34] (1986) 9 EHRR 56.
[35] (1996) 22 EHRR 123, 93.
[36] In particular, the domestic case of *Bellinger v Bellinger* [2003] UKHL 21, where the House of Lords found that the non-recognition of a change of gender for the purpose of marriage was incompatible with the Convention.
[37] (1996) 22 EHRR 123, 84.

The Incorporation of Social and Economic Rights

[6–14]   Although the ECHR textually protects civil and political rights, the court has assiduously promoted the fact that they cannot exist in isolation from social and economic rights. It affirmed the existence of such an overlap between the two sets of rights in *Airey v Ireland*—a view that has been consistently upheld in subsequent decisions:

> Whilst the Convention sets forth what are essentially civil and political rights many of them have implications of a social or economic nature. The Court therefore considers, like the Commission, that the mere fact that an interpretation of the Convention may extend to the sphere of social and economic rights should not be a decisive factor against such interpretation. There is no watertight division separating that sphere from the field covered by the Convention.[38]

[6–15]   Indirect inclusion of social and economic rights is not unique to the European Court. The Inter-American Court of Human Rights has taken a similar approach. Despite the embodiment of social and economic rights in the American Declaration of the Rights and Duties of Man 1948[39] (such as the right to health,[40] education,[41] rest and leisure[42] and the right to social security[43]), these were not integrated into the judicially enforceable American Convention on Human Rights.[44] In the absence of specified protection, the Inter-American Court has

---

[38]   (1979) 2 EHRR 305.

[39]   OEA/Ser.L./V.II.23, doc.21,rev.6, adopted by the Ninth International Conference of American States, Bogota, 1948. Like the Universal Declaration of Human Rights, this was not a legally binding document, but rather an aspirational statement of principles. See Philip Alston and Ryan Goodman, *International Human Rights: The Successor to International Human Rights in Context* (Oxford University Press 2013) 978.

[40]   Article XI states, 'Every person has the right to the preservation of his health through sanitary and social measures relating to food, clothing, housing and medical care to the extent permitted by public and community resources'.

[41]   Article XII states, 'Every person has the right to an education which should be based on the principles of liberty, morality and human solidarity. Likewise every person has the right to an education that will prepare him to attain a decent life, to raise his standard of living and to be a useful member of society. The right to an education includes the right to equality of opportunity in every case, in accordance with natural talents, merit and the desire to utilise the resources that the state or the community is in a position to provide. Every person has the right to receive, at lease, free primary education'.

[42]   Article XV states, 'Every person has the right to leisure time, to wholesome recreation, and to the opportunity for advantageous use of his free time to his spiritual, cultural and physical benefit'.

[43]   Article XVI states, 'Every person has the right to social security which will protect him from the consequences of unemployment, old age, and any disabilities arising from causes beyond his control that makes it physically or mentally impossible for him to earn a livelihood'.

[44]   Organisation of American States (OAS), American Convention on Human Rights (Pact of San Jose) (Entered into force on 22 November 1969) OAS Treaty Series No 36. Full

interpreted civil and political rights in a manner that renders social and economic rights justiciable through the right to life.[45] One of the first cases that dealt with social and economic rights, known as the *Street Children*[46] case, involved the plight of children living on the streets of Guatemala, wherein it was reasoned that the right to live a dignified existence was implicit in the right to life.[47]

By applying the Convention in a manner harmoniously with its additional Protocol (commonly referred to as the Protocol of San Salvador),[48] this notion of a decent and dignified life came to encompass social and economic rights, particularly the right to health.[49] This Protocol specifically and solely encompasses social and economic rights.[50] It calls for the progressive realisation of rights, akin to the wording of the ICESCR, and, with the exception of education, cannot be enforced by the court.[51] This integrated approach to interpreting the Convention–not as a stand-alone document, but rather as an integral part of a system of human rights documents–has made social and economic rights justiciable. **[6–16]**

The imposition of positive obligations was affirmed in *Juan Humberto Sanches v Honduras*, where it was determined that the state must 'take all appropriate measures to protect and preserve the right to life'.[52] This case involved arbitrary detention and death in custody and, having found the state in breach of several rights under the Convention, the court made its orders. It awarded substantial damages to the family of the deceased and placed a positive obligation on the state to comprehensively record the detention, including details of arrest and detention, identification, details of admission and the arrest warrant.[53] This required legislative action on the part of the state to comply. This 'evolutionary **[6–17]**

---

text of the treaty is available at <www.oas.org/dil/treaties_B-32_American_Convention_on_Human_Rights.htm> last accessed 13 April 2015.

[45] For a full discussion, see Tara Melish, *Protecting Economic Social and Cultural Rights in the Inter American Human Rights System* (New Haven 2002).

[46] *Villagran Morales et al case*, Inter-Am Ct. H.R (ser C) No. 63 192 (19 November 1999).

[47] Monica Feria Tinta, 'Justiciability of Economic, Social and Cultural Rights in the Inter-American System of Protection of Human Rights: Beyond Traditional Paradigms and Notions' (2007) 29 Human Rights Quarterly 431, 446.

[48] Organisation of American States (OAS), Additional Protocol to the American Convention on Human Rights in the Area of Economic Social and Cultural Rights (Protocol of San Salvador) (Entered into force on 16 November 1999) OAS Treaty Series No 69.

[49] Advisory Opinion on Juridical Condition and Human Rights of the Child, Int-Am Ct H.R., Series A: No 17 Advisory Opinion OC-17/2002 (28 August 2002).

[50] Like the European Social Charter, this additional protocol is dedicated solely to the protection of social and economic rights.

[51] Oswalso R Ruiz-Chiriboga, 'The American Convention and the Protocol of San Salvador: Two Intertwined Treaties – Non-Enforceability of Economic Social and Cultural Rights in the Inter-American System' (2013) 31 Netherlands Quarterly of Human Rights 156.

[52] Int-Am Ct H.R Series C No 99 (7 June 2003) 110.

[53] ibid [210].

interpretation'[54] formed the backdrop for the case of *Comunidad Yakye Axa v Paraguay,*[55] and later, the case of *Sawhoyamaxa Indigenous Community v Paraguay.*[56] Both cases involved indigenous groups displaced from their lands, living in makeshift settlements, the unsanitary conditions of which resulted in malnutrition, anaemia, parasitism, and high infant mortality as a result of the lack of clean water, sanitation and access to medical treatment. The previous interpretation of the right to life was explicitly endorsed and the state was found in violation. In 2010, the court, in *Kákmok Kásek Indigenous Community v Paraguay,* expanded the right to a dignified existence under the right to life and established a two-part test in determining state liability.[57] This test first requires a determination of whether the state had knowledge of the conditions which present a real danger to life and, secondly, an analysis of whether reasonable measures were taken to ameliorate this risk.[58] The court here did not state precisely what these reasonable measures would be. However, it determined that the measures taken in this particular case did not meet the reasonableness requirement. This 'result-based standard' appears contrary to the court's insistence that a disproportionate burden should not be placed on state resources.[59]

[6–18]   Not only is the manner in which the Inter-American Court has embraced social and economic rights jurisprudence important in this context, but so too are the remedies which it has awarded. This court does not confine itself to the award of damages where the breach has occurred. Rather, it has developed a practice of ordering positive obligations at the interim stage. The court has ordered immediate measures to prevent violations of rights, rather than waiting for the violation to occur and acting in a reactionary manner.[60] Thus far, these measures have primarily involved ordering medical treatment and living conditions to those under the care or control of the state.[61] However, the potential to extend this precedent to those dependent on state resources has not been excluded.

---

54   Steven R Keener and Javier Vasquez, 'A Life Worth Living: Enforcement of the Right to Health Through the Right to Life in the Inter-American Court of Human Rights' (2009) 40 Columbia Human Rights Law Review 595, 607.
55   Int-Am Ct H.R Series C No 125 (17 June 2005).
56   Int-Am Ct H.R Series C No 146 (29 March 2006).
57   Int-Am Ct H.R Series C No 214 (24 August 2010).
58   ibid [188].
59   Tara Melish 'The Inter-American Court of Human Rights: Beyond Progressivity' in Malcolm Langford (ed) *Social Rights Jurisprudence: Emerging Trends in International and Comparative Law* (Cambridge University Press 2008) 376.
60   ibid 377.
61   *Cesti Hurtado Case* Int-Am Ct H.R Series E (21 January 1997). The court ordered the provision of proper medical treatment for a detainee with heart disease and in the *Mendoza Prison Case* Int-Am Ct H.R Series E (22 November 2004) and *Febem'Prison Case* Int-Am Ct H.R Series E (30 November 2005) the court made orders in relation to overcrowding, sanitation and nutrition to ensure conditions for detainees and workers compatible with their dignity.

Thus the Inter-American Court has indirectly given effect to social and **[6–19]**
economic rights through an expansive interpretation of existing civil and
political rights contained within the Convention, confirming the indivisibility
and interdependence of the two sets of rights in a manner which was 'always
intuitive'.[62] This is an approach which the European Court is now mirroring.

Margin of Appreciation and Social and Economic Rights

In matters relating to social and economic policies, states are generally afforded **[6–20]**
a wide margin of appreciation.[63] Established in *James v UK* it was found 'natural
that the margin of appreciation available to the legislature on implementing
social and economic policies should be a wide one'.[64] This was consistent with
the prevailing view at the time that social and economic rights were generally
to be relegated to the political sphere and should remain non-justiciable.

The margin will be narrowed where intervention is required to give effect to a **[6–21]**
textual right of the Convention. In *Airey,* the court found that Ireland breached
Article 6 for failing to establish a system of civil legal aid.[65] While this in
practice involved the distribution of resources, it was necessary in order to give
effect to the right to a fair trial. The power of the court to vindicate the rights
of individuals persists and it will act to resolve a controversy irrespective of
resource implications. The emerging international consensus (that the social
and economic rights should be judicially protected) and the court's intention to
treat the ECHR as a dynamic instrument, which must evolve and adapt to meet
the needs of evolving societies, has contributed significantly to its continued
development.[66]

Expansive Interpretation and Indirect Protection

While not conceptually restricted to reading social and economic rights into any **[6–22]**
particular article of the ECHR, the court has primarily applied Articles 2 (the
right to life), 3 (the freedom from torture, inhuman and degrading treatment) and

---

[62] Keener and Vasquez (n 54) 624; See also Colm O'Cinneide, 'The Constitutionalization of
Social and Economic Rights' in Helena Alviar Garcia, Karl Klare and Lucy A Williams
(eds), *Social and Economic Rights in Theory and in Practice: Critical Enquiries*
(Routledge 2014) 268.
[63] For discussion of the criteria used by the court to determine whether the margin of
appreciation afforded is wide or narrow, and an explanation of these terms, see Janneke
Gerards, 'Pluralism, Deference and the Margin of Appreciation Doctrine' (2011) 17
European Law Journal 80.
[64] (1986) 8 EHRR 123 [46].
[65] (1979) 2 EHRR 305.
[66] Ellie Palmer, 'Protecting Socio-Economic Rights Through the European Convention
on Human Rights; Trends and Developments in the European Court of Human Rights'
(2009) 2(4) Erasmus Law Review 397.

8 (respect for private and family life, home and correspondence), as the basis upon which it raises such considerations.[67] Article 6[68] has also been employed in cases which involve distributive justice, and it has been used, alongside Article 14, to ensure procedural equality in social entitlements and benefits, even where these are discretionary.

[6–23] Article 14 has been used in conjunction with Article 1, Protocol 1,[69] to ground claims of discriminatory treatment in respect of social welfare benefits. Having determined that non-contributory social welfare benefits constitute a property right, and, as such, must be administered in a non-discriminatory manner,[70] the court in *Koua Poirrez v France* found differential treatment of social benefits between French and foreign nationals, in breach of Article 14 in conjunction with Article 1, Protocol 1.[71]

[6–24] The right to education was included by virtue of Article 2 of Protocol 1 and it is worth briefly outlining the court's approach.[72] At first blush, the structure of this article comprises two separate, yet interdependent, rights, which do not textually allow for any limitation. In *Kjeldsen, Busk Madsen and Pedersen v Denmark*, it was explained that the first section obliges states to accord a right of access indiscriminately to individuals within their jurisdiction, whereas the second section introduces an adjunct right, recognising that the primary responsibility towards children rests with their parents, and requiring the state to respect that position.[73]

[6–25] The leading case on the right to education is known as the *Belgian Linguistics* case, where the central consideration, in determining the right to education, was

---

67 Referred to as the 'three gateways' by Colm O'Cinneide, 'A Modest Proposal: Destitution, State Responsibility and the European Convention on Human Rights' (2008) 5 European Human Rights Law Review 583.

68 Article 6 protects the right to a fair trial and, in ensuring the effective protection of this right, the court has required the state to provide legal aid in order to comply with its Convention obligations. See *Airey v Ireland* (n 5).

69 Article 1 states, 'Every natural or legal person is entitled to the peaceful enjoyment of his possessions. No one shall be deprived of his possessions except in the public interest and subject to the conditions provided for by law and by the general principles of international law. The preceding provision shall not however, in any way impair the right of a State to enforce such laws as it deems necessary to control the use of private property in accordance with general interest or to secure the payment of taxes or other contributions or penalties'.

70 *Stec v UK* (2005) 41 EHRR 295.

71 (2005) 40 EHRR 34.

72 First Protocol to the Convention for the Protection of Human Rights and Fundamental Freedoms, Paris, 20 March 1952, 'No one shall be denied the right to education. In the exercise of any functions which it assumes in relation to education and to teaching that state shall respect the right of the parents to ensure such education and teaching in conformity with their own religions and philosophical convictions'.

73 (1976) 1 EHRR 711.

one of minimum provision and access, rather than a positive duty to 'establish at their own expense or to subsidise education of any particular type of education at any level'.[74] What this guarantees is a right to access existing educational systems and structures, while, by the same operation, a wide margin of appreciation is afforded in terms of resourcing the education system.[75]

In application, there is no positive obligation upon the state to provide selective [6–26] education,[76] religious schools,[77] single sex schools,[78] or schools providing for those with special needs.[79]

The ruling in the *Belgian Linguistics* case does imply that there is a certain [6–27] minimum standard that the state must provide, thus imposing a positive obligation.[80] This minimum level requires, inter alia, that children of migrant parents with no right to reside be provided with basic education, in a non-discriminatory manner.[81] The court has dealt with a number of cases involving the educational discrimination against Roma children and have consistently confirmed that, where there appears to be a prima facie case of discrimination, it falls to the state to convince the court otherwise.[82]

In interpreting the right to education, the court has incorporated restrictions [6–28] which are not textually present. It has confirmed that the obligation is to provide a minimum core, the precise parameters of which remain undefined beyond unimpeded access and non-discrimination. There is no positive duty on the state to provide for any particular nature or form of education. Rather, the state retains the right to determine these.

Given this relatively restrictive approach by the court to the textual right to [6–29]

---

[74] *Case relating to certain aspects of the laws on the use of languages in Belgium* (1968) 1 EHRR 241. See also, J Lonbay, 'Rights in Education Under the European Convention on Human Rights' (1983) 46 Modern Law Review 345.
[75] Rainey, Wicks and Ovey (n 6) 508.
[76] *W & DM and M & HI v UK* (1984) 37 DR 96.
[77] *X v UK* (1977) 16 DR 101.
[78] *W & DM and M & HI v UK* (1984) 37 DR 96.
[79] *Graeme v UK* (1990) 64 DR 158; *Simpson v UK* (1989) 64 DR 188. The court is mindful of the staffing and resource issues and gives a wide margin of appreciation. Harris, O'Boyle, Bates and Buckley (n 10) 911.
[80] It does not go on to discuss what that minimum is, as it noted that all state parties had domestic systems in place providing for education. Ide Elisabeth Koch, 'The Right to Education for Roma Children under the European Convention on Human Rights' (2011) On-Line Festschrift in honour of Katerina Tomasevski available at <rwi.lu.se/wp-content/uploads/2012/04/Right-to-Education-for-Roma-Koch.pdf> last accessed 05 January 2017.
[81] *Timishev v Russia* (2005) 44 EHRR 776.
[82] *DH and Ors v Czech Republic* (GC, 2008) 47 EHRR 3. See also *Sampani and Others v Greece* App No 32526/05 (ECtHR, 5 June 2008); *Orsus and Ors v Croatia* [2010] ECHR 337; *Horvath and Kiss* Hungary [2013] ECHR 208 and *Lavida and Ors v Greece* [2013] ECHR 163.

education, it is somewhat surprising that it has chosen to follow a more dynamic and expansive interpretation of the Convention to incorporate indirectly a plethora of social and economic rights.

Social and Economic Rights and the Right to Life

[6–30]   The right to life under Article 2 has been invoked in numerous cases involving social and economic rights, primarily in relation to the provision of emergency medical care. For example, the court has imposed the obligation to remove the causes of disease and to 'make regulations compelling hospitals, whether public or private, to adopt appropriate measures for the protection of their patients' lives'.[83] Early jurisprudence linking the right to health with the right to life considered the procedural aspects in relation to the sufficiency of safeguards and systems in place to deal with complaints, investigations, and remedies.[84] While the court in *Pentiacova v Moldova*[85] refused to establish a right of free health care, there has been tentative recognition that, in certain limited circumstances, acts or omissions on the part of the state, which expose impoverished persons to a threat to their life, may engage Article 2.[86] In *Cyprus v Turkey*, it was acknowledged that Article 2 may require a minimum level of protection on the right to health.[87]

[6–31]   In *Nitecki v Poland,* it was accepted that Article 2 could be invoked where the state put an individual's life at risk through the denial of health care. However, this case was ultimately found to be inadmissible.[88]

[6–32]   A trend is emerging towards reasoning more in line with that of the Indian Supreme Court, particularly in relation to emergency medical care. In *Mehmet*

---

[83] *Calvelli and Ciglio v Italy* App No 32967/96 (ECtHR, 17 January 2002) [49].

[84] For example, see *Silih v Slovenia* (2009) 49 EHRR 37, where the Court found a violation of Article 2 on account of the inefficiency of the judicial system in establishing the cause of, and liability for, the death.

[85] (2005) 40 EHRR 209.

[86] For example, see *Powell v UK* (2000) 30 EHRR 362, where the court determined that there were positive obligations to make regulations which would compel hospitals to adopt measures and procedures aimed at the protection of patient life.

[87] (2002) 35 EHRR 731. See also Loukis G Loucaides, 'The Judgment of the European Court of Human Rights in the case of Cyprus v Turkey' (2002) 15 Leiden Journal of International Law 225.

[88] App No 65653/01 (ECtHR, 21 March 2002). In this case the applicant was required to pay 30% of medication costs with the state covering 70%. The court found that the refusal to cover this remaining 30% did not engage Article 2 as the state was covering the greater part of the cost. Potentially this could be interpreted to mean that where the state provides for the lower percentage, or no medical care at all, Article 2 could be engaged. Hanna I Hyry, Jonathan CP Roos, Jeremy Manuel and Timothy M Cox, 'The Legal Imperative for Treating Rare Disorders' (2013) 8 Orphanet Journal of Rare Diseases 134, 139.

Senturk and Bekir Senturk v Turkey,[89] which parallels that of *Laxmi Mandal v Deen Dayal Haringar Hospital & Ors* in India,[90] the applicant's wife, at eight months pregnant, had been admitted to hospital with severe abdominal pain. She was informed that the foetus was deceased and that surgery would be required to remove it. She was transferred due to her inability to pay a deposit for surgery and died in transit, without receiving any medical treatment. Here, the court found violations of Article 2, for failure to provide emergency medical care, and further, for refusal to hold medical staff involved to account.[91]

Again, in *Asiye Genc v Turkey*, the court found a violation in circumstances   **[6–33]** where a prematurely born baby suffering from respiratory illness died in an ambulance, having been refused admission to two hospitals on the grounds of insufficient space and equipment.[92] Instrumental to the decision was the state's lack of an appropriate response by way of investigation.

The *Oyal v Turkey* case is significant, not only for its finding of a violation of   **[6–34]** Article 2 where a newborn baby was infected with HIV as a result of a blood transfusion, but also in the remedial steps that it took.[93] In determining that an award of damages was insufficient, it ordered that the state provide the applicant with free medical care for the remainder of his life.[94]

Thus, in relation to Article 2, the court has begun to place positive obligations on   **[6–35]** the state, most notably the duty to provide emergency medical care. The decision in *Nitecki*, while ultimately inadmissible, recognises that the denial of medical care could potentially amount to a breach. This is an important development, as it extends the obligation, at least in principle, beyond access to emergency care. Of additional significance is *Oyal*, wherein the court confirmed that its remedial powers were not restricted to the award of damages. By ordering what amounts to mandatory injunctive relief, the court has entrenched its ability to enforce positive obligations to remedy significant breaches.

---

[89]   App No 13423/09 (ECtHR, 9 April 2013).
[90]   WP(c) No 8853 of 2008.
[91]   Joseph Dute, 'Selected Legislation and Jurisprudence, European Court of Human Rights' (2013) 20 European Journal of Health Law 423, 429.
[92]   App No 24109/07 (ECtHR, 27 January 2015).
[93]   App No 4864/05 (ECtHR, 23 March 2010). This ruling extends relief under the right to life to a life-threatening illness and does not require immediate death for vindication. See Rianka Rijnhout and Jessy M Emaus, 'Damages in Wrongful Death Cases in the Light of European Human Rights Law: Towards a Rights Based Approach to the Law of Damages' (2014) 10 Utrecht Law Review 91, 95.
[94]   App No 4864/05 (ECtHR, 23 March 2010) 102. See also Ingrid Nifosi-Sutton, 'Power of the European Court of Human Rights to Order Specific Non-Monetary Relief: A Critical Appraisal from a Right to Health Perspective' (2010) 23 Harvard Human Rights Journal 51.

Social and Economic Rights and the Freedom from Torture, Inhuman and Degrading Treatment

[6–36]   Article 3 provides that a person has the right to be free from torture, as well as inhuman and degrading treatment or punishment. There is a positive obligation on the state to ensure conditions which do not breach Article 3.[95] Therefore, in order to bring social and economic rights within this rubric, the question must be asked whether poverty-stricken conditions deteriorate to a level sufficient to invoke this protection, and whether there is any state responsibility for such.

[6–37]   Early cases primarily centred on treatment and conditions directly administered by the state, particularly within detention facilities. In *Dougoz v Greece*, the court held that prison overcrowding without adequate food and exercise breached Article 3.[96] In *Price v UK*, it further noted that if a detainee was disabled then there was an obligation on the state to provide accommodating facilities.[97] In *Nevmerzhitsky v Ukraine,* the court accepted the applicant's contention that conditions of his detention, including bed bugs and lice which caused him to develop an acute skin disease, breached Article 3.[98] In *Poltoratskiy v Ukraine*[99] and *Kalashnikov v Russia,*[100] it was found that there is an obligation to provide reasonable protection for the health of detainees,[101] a decision described as incorporating detainees' health rights into the normative content of Article 3.[102] In *McGlinchey v UK*, the Court found a breach where the officers of the prison service failed to respond to a deteriorating condition from which death ultimately resulted.[103] *Keenan v UK* extended this principle to encompass psychiatric issues, where the prisoner ultimately committed suicide as a result of improper mental health support within the prison system,[104] and *Sarban v Moldova* extended the obligation to prisoners on remand.[105]

[6–38]   The first steps in recognising the wider application of Article 3 to circumstances beyond treatment directly and/or intentionally inflicted by the state came in

---

[95] Molly Kos, 'The Protection of the Right to Health under the ECHR: Is Imposing Positive Obligations the Way to Go?' (2014) 1 Queen Mary Human Rights Review 119, 132.
[96] (2001) 34 EHRR 1480.
[97] (2001) 34 EHRR 1285.
[98] (2005) 43 EHRR 251.
[99] (2004) 39 EHRR 43.
[100] (2003) 36 EHRR 34.
[101] Andra le Roux-Kemp, 'Overcrowding in Prisons: A Health Risk in Need of (Re) Consideration' (2013) 21 Health Law Review 33, 35.
[102] Nifosi-Sutton (94) 61.
[103] (2003) 37 EHRR 41.
[104] (2001) 33 EHRR 38. Further, in *Dybeku v Albania* App No 41153/06 (ECtHR, 18 December 2007), insufficient detention facilities and care for a detainee suffering from schizophrenia violated Article 3. For an overview of cases involving mental health issues and detainees, see Martin Curtice, 'The European Convention on Human Rights: An Update on Article 3 Case Law' (2010) 16 Advances in Psychiatric Treatment 199.
[105] App No 3456/05 (ECtHR, 4 January 2006).

Ireland v UK.[106] Later cases have extended this principle beyond applying to those in state care or custody.[107] For example, in *Z v UK*, the Court held that the state's failure to prevent children being abused in the home amounted to a breach of Article 3.[108]

The court has also considered the provision of medical treatment under Article **[6–39]** 3. In *D v UK*, the UK sought to deport an AIDS sufferer to a state where he argued that he would receive minimal treatment of a substandard quality in comparison to that available in the UK. Here, the court found that his condition would be exacerbated by the action of the state and the deportation amounted to inhuman and degrading treatment.[109] The impact of this ruling was diminished in *N v UK*,[110] where the court found that the state did not have a duty to provide free medical care to all aliens without leave to stay in their jurisdiction. Notwithstanding the fact that the treatment required was of limited availability in Uganda, where she would face death within a short period of time,[111] the court did not find that this reached the minimum level of severity to invoke Article 3. The case of *SJ v Belgium*, where the applicant, who was HIV positive, contended that her deportation to Nigeria would breach Article 3, due to the lack of available and accessible treatment, has been struck from the Grand Chamber list following a friendly settlement.[112] In a powerful dissenting opinion, Pinto De Albuquerque J felt that this case could have been used to overrule the *N* case, which, in his opinion, downplays 'the importance of social and economic implications of the protection of civil and political rights'.[113] A chance for the court to re-examine the issue arose in *Paposhvili v Belgium*.[114] Mr Paposhvili was a Georgian national living in Belgium, who was seriously ill with several illnesses, including leukaemia and hepatitis C. He contended that his expulsion to Georgia amounted to a breach of Article 3, by virtue of inhuman treatment and an earlier death due to the withdrawal of medical treatment. Mr Paposhvili succumbed to his illness in June 2016. However, the Grand Chamber did not strike the case from its list, instead finding that there were special circumstances present and took the opportunity to revisit the restrictive criteria that it had previously established in *N*. The court found

---

[106] (1978) 2 EHRR 25.

[107] Palmer (n 66) 410; O'Cinneide (n 67); Antonio Cassese, 'Can the Notion of Inhuman and Degrading Treatment be Applied to Socio-Economic Conditions?' (1991) 2 European Journal of International Law 141.

[108] (2002) 34 EHRR 97.

[109] (1997) 24 EHRR 423.

[110] (2008) 47 EHRR 885.

[111] And ultimately, as observed in App No 70055/10 (ECtHR, 19 March 2015) [2] (Pinto De Albuquerque J, dissenting), did die shortly after her expulsion.

[112] App No 70055/10 (ECtHR, 19 March 2015). The Chamber found that there would be no breach of Article 3.

[113] ibid [10] (Pinto De Albuquerque J, dissenting).

[114] App No 41738/10 (GC, 13 December 2016).

that there would have been a violation of Article 3 had he been expelled from Belgium, without assessing whether appropriate treatment would be available. Further, the Grand Chamber found that there would have been a breach of Article 8 if he was expelled without the authorities carrying out an assessment in to the impact that his removal would have on his family life in light of the state of his health, including whether it could be reasonably expected that the family would follow him to Georgia. This overturned the decision of the Chamber, which found that his condition was stable and 'his life is therefore not in imminent danger and he is able to travel'.[115] In widening the scope of the exception in *N* of 'very exceptional cases', here, the court found that those who are seriously ill can also benefit from the provision:

> That the 'other very exceptional cases' within the meaning of the judgment in N v United Kingdom which may raise an issue under Article 3 should be understood to refer to situations involving the removal of a seriously ill person in which substantial grounds have been shown for believing that he or she, although not at imminent risk of dying, would face a real risk, on account of the absence of proper treatment in the receiving country or the lack of access to such treatment, of being exposed to a *serious, rapid and irreversible decline* in his or her state of health resulting in *intense suffering or to a significant reduction in life expectancy.*[116]

[6–40]   First, the court relaxed the strict criteria espoused in *N*, meaning that a person need no longer show that they will face imminent death, but only that their life expectancy will be shortened as a result of insufficient care. Further, it places a positive obligation on the state to carry out an assessment into the services that are available and the impact that removal would have on the family life of the applicant. This case affirms the importance of the right to health and medical treatment, and that actions on the part of the state to deny essential treatment which would result in a significantly reduced life expectancy and suffering can amount to a breach of Article 3. This case is clearly related to the expulsion of a person from the jurisdiction where he is receiving treatment. However, its principles could potentially be extrapolated to embrace circumstances where a state withdraws treatment, having the same implications.

[6–41]   It seems that circumstances of extreme poverty can only invoke the protection of Article 3 where they result in inhuman or degrading treatment, which is caused, contributed to or exacerbated by the state or its agents.[117] Accordingly, O'Cinneide observes:

---

[115] ibid (17 April 2014) [120].
[116] ibid (GC, 13 December 2016) [183].
[117] *X v Hounslow LBC* [2008] EWHC 1168.

If state responsibility can be triggered in respect of failures to protect children against abuse by third parties and in respect of deportees where there would be a denial of essential health care in receiving countries, then there would appear to be no intrinsic reason why state responsibility for degrading treatment that stems from poverty could not exist in some circumstances.[118]

To this point, the court appears to have accepted such a possibility. In *Van Volsem v Belgium*, the deprivation at issue was not of sufficient gravity to render the state liable, although the potential for deprivation to engage the protection of Article 3 was affirmed.[119] This decision has been criticised for its vagueness, failing to define precisely what level of deprivation is required before it becomes inhuman and degrading, thereby engaging Article 3.[120] In *Larioshina v Russia*, while, again, accepting that a claim could fall within Article 3, the court found, in this instance, that the pension in question (653 rubles per month, equating to €23.78),[121] was not so inadequate as to amount to inhuman and degrading treatment.[122] Thus, it would appear that, once the state is providing some benefit, the amount of that benefit will fall within the margin of appreciation.[123] **[6–42]**

The obligation to provide social housing has also been considered under Article 3. While reiterating that the ECHR does not provide a general right to be housed when homeless,[124] judicial attention has been given to the actions of state authorities surrounding the causes of homelessness.[125] In *Moldovan v Romania*, 13 homes were destroyed, leaving the applicants living in extremely cramped and unsanitary conditions.[126] Allegations of state involvement in the destruction of their homes were accepted by the court and, as a result, it had a positive duty to restore their previous living conditions.[127] However, the exact parameters of this obligation remain unclear.[128] This lack of clarity may be **[6–43]**

---

[118] O'Cinneide (n 87) 589.

[119] Application No 14641/89 Decision of the Commission (9 May 1990).

[120] For example, see Cassese (n 107).

[121] Exchange rate for 2002 sourced from <www.payeanytime.ie/en/customs/businesses/importing/exchange-rates/archive/eurcon1_apr02.html> last accessed 8 January 2017.

[122] App No 56869/00 (ECtHR, 23 April 2002).

[123] App No 65653/01 (ECtHR, 21 March 2002).

[124] See *Chapman v UK* (2001) 33 EHRR 399 and *Codona v UK* App No 485/05 (ECtHR, 7 February 2006).

[125] Kyra Olds, 'The Role of the Courts in Making the Right to Housing a Reality Throughout Europe: Lessons from France and the Netherlands' (2011) 28 Wisconsin International Law Journal 170, 179.

[126] (2005) 44 EHRR 302.

[127] Miltiadis Sarigiannidid and Ionna Pervou, 'Adequate Housing: Seeking Justiciability Through the Right to Property' (2013) 1 International Journal of Human Rights and Constitutional Studies 27, 35.

[128] Padraic Kenna, 'Housing Rights: Positive Duties and Enforceable Rights at the European Court of Human Rights' (2008) 2 European Human Rights Law Review 193.

positive, as it allows the court to 'develop the interests protected to take into account changing circumstances and understandings without being confined by an established theoretical framework'.[129]

[6–44] The court has also had regard to the conduct of the applicant in determining whether the state has complied with its obligations. In *O'Rourke v UK*, a period of homelessness following eviction from temporary accommodation did not reach a requisite level of severity to engage Article 3.[130] A mitigating factor in this case was that the applicant had refused several alternative temporary accommodations. Accordingly, it determined that he was the author of his own misfortune and 'largely responsible for his own deterioration following his eviction'.[131]

[6–45] The living conditions of asylum seekers are a relatively new expansion of the court's jurisprudence. Rights derived from the ECHR are not dependent on citizenship and apply to all within the jurisdiction of a given state. The case of *MSS v Belgium and Greece*[132] involved a challenge by an Afghan asylum seeker, who was, under the Dublin Regulation, removed from Belgium to Greece to have his asylum claim determined by the Greek authorities.[133] The court examined the practice of detaining asylum seekers in Greece 'from a few days to a few months' in conditions of:

> Overcrowding, dirt, lack of space, lack of ventilation, little or no possibility of taking a walk, no place to relax, insufficient mattresses, dirty mattresses, no free access to toilets, inadequate sanitary facilities, no privacy, limited access to care.[134]

[6–46] Taking into account the lack of suitable accommodation, and the failure to

---

129 David Harris, Michael O'Boyle, Ed Bates and Carla Buckley, *Harris, O'Boyle and Warbrick, Law of the European Convention on Human Rights* (2nd edn, Oxford University Press 2009) 353.

130 App No 39022/97 (ECtHR, 26 June 2001).

131 App No 39022/97 (ECtHR, 26 June 2001) [62].

132 (2011) 53 EHRR 2.

133 The Dublin Regulations, comprised of Regulation (EC) No 1560/2003, Regulation (EU) No 603/2013 and Regulation (EU) No 118/2014, govern asylum applications in the EU and seek to ensure an effective process. This system establishes criteria for determining which EU state is responsible for determining the asylum claim, on the basis of family links, the state first entered or the state responsible for entry. See Jan-Paul Brekke and Grete Brochman, 'Stuck in Transit: Secondary Migration of Asylum Seekers in Europe, National Differences and the Dublin Regulation' (2014) 10 Journal of Refugee Studies 1; Anna Lube, ''Systematic Flaws' and Dublin Transfers: Incompatible tests before the CJUE and ECtHR' (2015) International Journal of Refugee Law 1; Gina Clayton, 'Asylum Seekers in Europe: MSS v Belgium and Greece' (2011) 11 Human Rights Law Review 758.

134 (2011) 53 EHRR 2 [162].

provide for the essential needs of the applicant, it was found that his living conditions amounted to inhuman and degrading treatment and a breach of Article 3.[135]

While this judgment confirms that positive obligations may be placed on the state in cases of extreme poverty, it is somewhat limited. First, the fact that Greek law itself imposed this obligation to provide accommodation and assistance to asylum seekers effectively means that the court was simply enforcing domestic law. Secondly, in finding a breach of Article 3, the court reiterated the principle that this provision may be engaged where a person who is in state custody, or is dependent solely on the state, is living in conditions of extreme poverty.[136] Sajo J explains further, that where the state affords asylum seekers a genuine opportunity to take care of themselves, this releases it from responsibility.[137]   **[6–47]**

Therefore, the position has not significantly changed from the determination in *O'Rourke*.[138] Extreme poverty alone cannot impose positive obligations on the state. Instead, it must be coupled with acute individual need, which imposes a particular duty on the state.[139] A case currently pending, *Gjutaj and Ors v France*, centres on an assertion that emergency accommodation provided by the state (in tents) breaches their Article 3 rights.[140]   **[6–48]**

The jurisprudence of the court in relation to Article 3 has expanded significantly. As such, a distinct position is emerging, in that:

> Suffering which flows from naturally occurring illness, physical or mental, may be covered by Article 3 where it is or risks being exacerbated by treatment, whether flowing from conditions of detention, expulsion or other measure, for which the authorities can be held responsible.[141]

Moving beyond its traditional purview, it now imposes positive obligations to ensure that those in state care, and vulnerable persons are provided with medical care and shelter. Further, the court has accepted, in principle at least, that this article may be invoked to place positive obligations on the state in circumstances of extreme poverty, although the precise parameters of this obligation are yet to be defined.   **[6–49]**

---

[135] ibid [263].
[136] *Budina v Russia* App No 45603/05 (ECtHR, 18 June 2009).
[137] (2011) 53 EHRR 2 (Sajo J, partly dissenting, partly concurring).
[138] *O'Rourke v UK* App No 39022/97 (ECtHR, 26 June 2001).
[139] Ellie Palmer, 'Beyond Arbitrary Interference: The Right to a Home? Developing Socio-Economic Duties in the European Convention on Human Rights' (2010) 61(3) Northern Ireland Legal Quarterly 225, 231.
[140] App No 63141/13.
[141] *Pretty v UK* (2002) 35 EHRR 1 [52].

Social and Economic Rights and the Right to Respect for Private and Family Life

[6–50] Article 8 has also served as a means to indirectly incorporate social and economic rights. Unlike Articles 2 and 3, previously discussed, Article 8 is a qualified, not an absolute, right. State interference may be reasonable where it is pursuing a legitimate aim, is necessary in a democratic society and is proportionate.[142]

[6–51] In addressing health rights, the court has focused on information, access and non-discrimination in order to detect a violation of Article 8, rather than imposing a positive obligation to provide medical care. In *Roche v UK*[143] and *Vilnes & Ors v Norway*,[144] violations were determined on the basis that information had not been made available in relation to possible adverse effects to health. Similarly, a plethora of cases involving sterilisation of Roma women without their consent turned on the lack of information furnished[145] and the failure to include the applicant in the decision-making process, together with non-disclosure of risks.[146]

[6–52] While this Article has yet to be used to determine specific positive obligations to provide particular health care services, it is clear that health rights are encompassed within its parameters. The state is not required to provide any particular service (although a complete denial of services may result in a breach of Articles 2 or 3 as discussed above), this Article focuses on ensuring access to such services.

[6–53] In terms of housing rights, Article 8 has advanced the law in relation to evictions by state authorities. While the essential object of Article 8 is to protect the individual against arbitrary interference by public authorities, there may be positive obligations inherent in effective respect for private or family life.

[6–54] Therefore, the obligation on the state is not to provide homes for all, rather, the court postulated, there may be certain circumstances in which the obligation

---

[142] Kos (n 95) 133.
[143] (2005) 42 EHRR 30.
[144] App No 52806/09 and 22703/10 (ECtHR, 5 December 2013).
[145] See *KH & Ors v Slovakia* App No 32881/04 (ECtHR, 28 April 2009); *VC v Slovakia* App No 18968/07 (ECtHR, 8 February 2012); *NB v Slovakia* App No 29518/10 (ECtHR, 12 September 2012); and *IG & Ors v Slovakia* App No 15966/04 (ECtHR, 29 April 2013). See also, Elizabeth K Tomasovic, 'Robbed of Reproductive Justice: The Necessity of a Global Initiative to Provide Redress to Roma Women Coercively Sterilised in Eastern Europe' (2010) 41 Columbia Human Rights Law Review 765; Ronli Sifris, 'Conceptualising Involuntary Sterilisation as Severe Pain or Suffering for the Purpose of Torture Discourse' (2010) 28 Netherlands Quarterly of Human Rights 523; Lindsay Hoyle, 'V.C v Solvakia: A Reproductive Rights Victory Misses the Mark' (2014) 36 Boston College International and Comparative Law Review 17.
[146] *Csoma v Romania* App No 8795/05 (ECtHR, 15 January 2013).

arises in relation to a particular individual.[147] This approach was endorsed in *Marzari v Italy*, where the court held that the failure to assist those living with an illness or disability may result in a violation of Article 8.[148]

Jurisprudence in this area initially gave greater deference to the state. In the cases of *Chapman v UK*[149] and *Beard v UK*,[150] the court found that refusal of planning permission and subsequent eviction for 'environmental' reasons were legitimate causes and that there had been no breach of Article 8. **[6–55]**

In assessing whether there has been a violation, the court first establishes whether the property can be classed as a home. Arising from the case of *Gillow v UK*,[151] the court requires that there be sufficient continuing links between the person(s) and the property in question.[152] Having established this, the court then determines whether interference with this right is justified. **[6–56]**

In *Connors v UK*, the court found a violation in relation to the eviction procedures adopted by the state.[153] The parties were agreed that the provisions of Article 8 were engaged, thus, it fell to the court to determine whether the action taken was proportionate and justifiable. The court affirmed the general principle, that a restriction would be justified if (a) it is pursuing a legitimate aim (b) is proportionate, and (c) that the state will be given a margin of appreciation, as it is best placed to evaluate local needs.[154] However, it emphasised that eviction is an interference of such a magnitude that it may only be justified by weighty reasons of public interest. Significant to its finding was the lack of procedural safeguards.[155] **[6–57]**

McCann v UK heralded an expansion of the protections required for the eviction of council tenants,[156] specifically requiring procedural safeguards whereby the tenant could challenge such decisions.[157] The court rejected the state's assertion that the *Connors* case should be confined to its facts and that such safeguards should only be available to members of the gypsy community. The court stated: **[6–58]**

---

[147] Kenna (n 128) 202.
[148] (1999) 28 EHRR CD 175.
[149] (2001) 33 EHRR 399.
[150] (2001) 33 EHRR 18.
[151] (1986) 11 EHRR 335.
[152] Antoine Buyse, 'Strings Attached: The Concept of 'Home' in the Case Law of the European Court of Human Rights' (2006) 3 European Human Rights Law Review 294, 297.
[153] (2004) 40 EHRR 189.
[154] ibid [81–82].
[155] ibid [94].
[156] (2008) 47 EHRR 913.
[157] Martin Davis and David Hughes, 'Gateways or Barriers? Joint Tenants, possession claims and Article 8' (2010) Conveyancer and Property Lawyer 57, 59.

The loss of one's home is the most extreme form of interference with the right to respect for the home. Any person at risk of an interference of this magnitude should in principle be able to have the proportionality of the measure determined by an independent tribunal in light of the relevant principles under Article 8 of the Convention, notwithstanding that, under domestic law, his right of occupation has come to an end.[158]

[6–59]   While these cases are of considerable significance, they do not impose substantive, positive obligations on the state. They do, however, progress the recognition of social and economic rights by placing safeguards in the form of negative obligations, much in the same manner as the Canadian Courts have. However, in reality, these obligations necessarily entail the imposition of positive duties. For example, the establishment of an independent impartial tribunal to determine the proportionality of an eviction will have resource implications for the state.

[6–60]   In *Yordanova and Ors v Bulgaria*, the court had to determine the legitimacy of a lawful eviction of a Roma camp, which had been in existence since the 1960s.[159] Having accepted that the camp was 'home', and that the enforcement of the order would result in interference, the court then turned to the justification by the state. It identified two legitimate aims: seeking to regain land unlawfully possessed and the protection of health and the rights of others due to the unsanitary conditions of the camp. It determined that the existence of an impartial tribunal to determine the proportionality of an eviction was essential and that evictions cannot be premised on the unlawfulness of possession alone.[160] In holding that there had been a violation of Article 8, the court found that the state was under a positive obligation to assist particularly vulnerable groups and that in this case would have been required to provide assistance to find alternative housing.[161]

[6–61]   While previous cases were confined to procedural safeguards, this judgment goes further to consider more substantive issues. It considered alternative accommodation as a crucial element in determining proportionality, while, paradoxically, reaffirming that there is no general right to be provided with a home.[162]

[6–62]   The case of *Bjedov v Croatia*[163] examines this issue further. Notwithstanding the fact that the eviction was lawful under national law, the court held that the

---

[158] (2008) 47 EHRR 913 [50]. Affirmed in *Kay and Others v UK* (2010) 54 EHRR 1056.
[159] App No 25546/06 (ECtHR, 24 April 2012).
[160] Adelaide Remiche, 'Yordanova and Others v Bulgaria: The Influence of the Social Right to Adequate Housing on the Interpretation of the Civil Right to Respect for One's Home' (2012) 12 Human Rights Law Review 787, 791.
[161] App No 25546/06 (ECtHR, 24 April 2012) 132.
[162] ibid 130.
[163] App No 4250/09 (ECtHR, 29 August 2012).

protection of Article 8 extends to those who are in unlawful, as well as lawful, tenancies, determining that the state's 'legitimate interest in being able to control its property comes second to the applicant's right to respect for her home'.[164] In *Bagdonavicius and Ors v Russia,* the court found a violation of Article 8, in that the state had not examined the proportionality of the interference, nor had it consulted with the applicants in relation to rehoming options prior to the destruction and forced eviction.[165] Currently pending before the court is the case of *Cazacliu and Ors v Romania,* which is seeking to challenge the living conditions in social housing, as breaching Articles 3, 8, 6 and 14 of the Convention.[166] This case could potentially add considerably to the jurisprudence on conditions of housing provided for by the state.

The development of housing rights under the Convention is significant. While the court is steadfast in its position that the Convention does not support a general right to be housed, it has carved out exceptions. What began with placing negative obligations by way of procedural safeguards has evolved to incorporate positive obligations. These may require the state to assist in obtaining alternative accommodation in order for the eviction to be legitimate, in a somewhat paradoxical approach. This is redolent of the position taken by the European Social Committee in expanding the reach of the ESC beyond the existing textual rights, by identifying, and enunciating, the values that underpin it. The Committee has stated that 'human dignity is the fundamental value and indeed the core of positive European human rights law'.[167] In relation to housing rights, while those dealt with through the European Court focus primarily on procedural safeguards[168] the Committee proposes that the dignity of the person must be protected during evictions.[169] By requiring that the state provide alternative accommodation, and by extending procedural safeguards to unlawful tenancies, the European Court is moving more in line with the reasoning of the Committee.   [6–63]

In terms of social assistance, *Andersson and Kullman v Sweden* firmly established that Article 8 did not give rise to a right to financial support to maintain a certain standard of living.[170] As with the foregoing considerations, the individual would be required to be in a particularly vulnerable position by   [6–64]

---

[164] ibid 70.

[165] [2016] ECHR 323.

[166] App No 63945/09.

[167] *World Organisation Against Torture v Italy* Complaint No. 19/2003 [31].

[168] (2004) 40 EHRR 189.

[169] *European Roma Rights Centre v Italy* Complaint No 27/2004. The Committee stated that evictions must be conducted in a manner which respects the dignity of the persons affected in order to be compliant with the Charter obligations.

[170] (1986) 46 DR 251.

virtue of state action, or other exceptional circumstances, to engage a positive duty in this regard.[171]

[6–65] While there is no right to social security under Article 8, the court has utilised Article 14 to ensure that social security is provided in a non-discriminatory manner.[172] The landmark case of *Petrovic v Austria* dealt with parental leave entitlement of fathers.[173] The court determined that there was no obligation to provide any benefit. However, where a benefit was provided, failing to implement it in a non-discriminatory manner was a breach of Article 8, in conjunction with Article 14. Notwithstanding this, the court at the time held that the state had not exceeded its margin of appreciation, as there was no general consensus among member states,[174] a ruling illustrative of the difficulty in imposing positive obligations in circumstances where welfare provisions vary from state to state.[175]

[6–66] Despite the fact that *Petrovic* was ultimately unsuccessful, it precipitated further cases, such as *Niedzwiecki v Germany*, where the court found a violation of Article 8 in conjunction with Article 14 due to differential treatment in child benefit for those who did not hold a residence permit.[176] Further, in *Markin v Russia*, the failure to give the parental leave to servicemen that was allowed to servicewomen amounted to a breach.[177] It was noted that the foregoing case of *Petrovic* was unsuccessful on the grounds of a lack of consensus between member states, which, here, was overcome, as the majority of member states had legislation in place providing parental leave for both parents.[178]

[6–67] In terms of social welfare benefits, Article 8 is concerned with ensuring that these are implemented on a non-discriminatory basis. While the complete denial of all social security may result in a breach of Article 3, Article 8 does not yet impose positive obligations in this regard. However, this has not been explicitly outruled, and the possibility of extending these positive obligations into the sphere of private life was initially espoused in *X and Y v Netherlands*, where the court, in analysing Article 8, determined that 'in addition to the primary negative undertaking, there may be positive obligations inherent in an effective respect for private or family life'.[179] More recently, in *Soares de Melo v Portugal*, the court, in finding a breach of Article 8 for removing the children of a woman living in poverty (on the grounds that this constituted neglect), was

---

[171] O'Cinneide (n 87) 583.
[172] Palmer (n 139) 240.
[173] (2001) 33 EHRR 14.
[174] ibid [37].
[175] Kos (n 95) 129.
[176] App No 58453/00 (ECtHR, 25 October 2005) [33].
[177] App No 30078/06 (ECtHR, 22 March 2012).
[178] ibid 99.
[179] (1986) EHRR 235 [23].

highly critical of the fact that state officials knew for some time of the nature of her financial situation and at no point intervened to assist. Arguably, this is a clear movement towards imposing positive obligations.[180]

The European Court is consistently expanding the parameters and scope of **[6–68]** the ECHR, and, as more and more cases come before it involving social and economic rights, its jurisprudence in this area is evolving. It has consistently applied the principle that, if a deprivation of a social and economic right is such that it materially effects a textual right of the ECHR, then the court will adjudicate upon it, regardless of resource implications. As international consensus relating to the justiciability of these rights expands and increases, so too will the court's jurisprudence. The court has used the ECHR to indirectly incorporate social and economic rights, including health, medical treatment, conditions of housing, safeguards for evictions and non-discrimination in social welfare claims. It has further accepted, in principle, that social and economic deprivation could result in inhuman and degrading treatment. The case to prove that principle is still awaited.

Ireland and the ECHR: The European Convention on Human Rights Act 2003

As an international treaty, the status of the ECHR in domestic law is of vital **[6–69]** importance. As a creation of the Council of Europe, and not the EU, it did not automatically form part of domestic law and, until transposition, was treated as any other international treaty.[181]

The ECHR became part of Irish law by way of the European Convention on **[6–70]** Human Rights Act 2003, 50 years after Ireland became a state party to the Convention.[182] This Act did not give direct effect to rights in Irish law. Rather, it determined how and when the ECHR can be used to interpret and enforce existing rights. In other words, 'The Convention itself remains international law that is not, per se, binding in domestic law'.[183] Thus, the operation of the Convention in Ireland is limited, insofar as it can only have effect through the spectrum of the Act.[184]

---

[180] App No 72850/14 (ECtHR 16 May 2016).

[181] Raymond Byrne and Paul McCutcheon with Claire Bruton and Gerard Coffey, *Byrne and McCutcheon on the Irish Legal System* (6th edn, Bloomsbury Professional 2014) ch 17.

[182] Ireland is the last Council of Europe member to domestically incorporate the Convention.

[183] Fiona de Londras, 'Using the ECHR in Irish Courts: More Whisper Than Bang' ("Using the ECHR: Where are we Now?" PILA Seminar, the Distillery Building, Dublin 13 May 2011) 1, available at <www.ucd.ie/t4cms/pilaechrseminar130511fdelondras.pdf> last accessed 6 January 2017.

[184] Fiona de Londras, 'Neither Herald nor Fanfare: The Limited Impact of the ECHR on

Pre-Incorporation

[6–71]   The ECHR was first considered in the domestic context in *O'Laighleis*, where the applicant challenged the Offences against the State (Amendment) Act 1940 as being inconsistent with Convention rights.[185] The Supreme Court, in refusing to apply the Convention, stated:

> The Oireachtas has not determined that the Convention is part of the domestic law of the state, and accordingly this Court cannot give effect to the Convention if it be contrary to domestic law or purports to grant rights or impose obligations additional to those of domestic law.[186]

[6–72]   This decision was subsequently affirmed by the Supreme Court in *Doyle v Commissioner of An Garda Siochana*, reiterating that, due to Ireland's dualist nature, it had no role in enforcing unincorporated international treaties,[187]and, in *Gilligan v Criminal Assets Bureau,* it stated that 'there can be no question of any decision of the European Court of Human Rights furnishing in and of itself a basis for declaring legislation unconstitutional'.[188] While the ECHR, like international treaties generally, did not form part of domestic law, there was opportunity for the jurisprudence of the European Court to be used as persuasive authority, the success of which has varied widely.

[6–73]   An early attempt to rely on the jurisprudence of the European Court is seen in *O'B v S*, where the court was required to determine whether the term 'issue', used in the Succession Act 1965, could encompass children born outside of wedlock. [189] The claimant relied on *Marckx v Belgium,* where it had been found that, while the safeguarding of traditional family structure was a legitimate aim, measures which resulted in prejudice against 'illegitimate' children were a breach of Article 8.[190] The Supreme Court, however, refused to acknowledge this ruling and instead stated that it was bound to determine the case according to domestic law.[191]

[6–74]   In *Norris v AG*,[192] legislative provisions which criminalised homosexual

---

Rights Infrastructure in Ireland' in Suzanne Egan, Liam Thornton and Judy Walsh (eds), *Ireland and the ECHR: 60 Years and Beyond* (Bloomsbury 2014) 37.

[185] [1960] IR 93.
[186] ibid 125.
[187] [1999] 1 IR 249, 268.
[188] [1998] 3 IR 185, 202.
[189] [1984] IR 316.
[190] (1979) 2 EHRR 330.
[191] This situation was remedied following a ruling in the European Court of Human Rights in *Johnston v Ireland* [1986] 9 EHRR 203, where the court found Ireland in breach of Article 8 due to its treatment of illegitimate children. Thereafter, the Status of Children Act 1987 was passed.
[192] [1984] IR 36.

activities were challenged[193] as infringing the right to privacy,[194] as well as the right to bodily integrity.[195] The applicant relied on the European Court's determination that similar provisions in UK legislation violated Article 8.[196]

However, the Chief Justice concluded that: **[6–75]**

> … neither the European Convention on Human Rights nor the decision of the European Court in *Dudgeon v UK* (1981) 4 EHRR 149 is in any way relevant to the question which we have to consider in this case.[197]

It is difficult to conceive of how *Dudgeon*, a case of almost identical factual background, could not be relevant and, ultimately, the European Court agreed with Norris that the legislation in question was a breach of Article 8, just as it had done in *Dudgeon*.[198]

Thus, relying on Convention rights was predominantly an unsuccessful exercise **[6–76]** and, as such, prior to the enactment of the 2003 Act, the impact of the Convention on the furtherance and development of Irish law can only be described as minimal. Decisions of the European Court against Ireland directly were equally met with judicial hostility, with the courts deferring to the legislature for the implementation of any such ruling.[199]

Incorporation

As pressure mounted from independent human rights groups to incorporate the **[6–77]** ECHR domestically, it was the Good Friday Agreement that ultimately led to its transposition.[200] While there was no express pledge to incorporate, it rapidly

---

193 ss 61 and 62 of the Offences Against the Person Act 1861 and s 11 of the Criminal Law Amendment Act 1885.
194 Under Article 40.3 and relying on the case of *McGee v AG* [1974] IR 284.
195 Under Article 40.3 and relying on the case of *Ryan v AG* [1965] IR 284.
196 *Dudgeon v UK* (1981) 4 EHRR 149.
197 [1984] IR 36 (O'Higgins CJ).
198 *Norris v Ireland* (1988) 13 EHRR 186.
199 For example, see the ruling in *Keegan v Ireland* (n 29), where the European Court found Ireland in breach of Article 8 for not recognising the rights of an unmarried father to his child and the concept of a de facto family. In the later case of *WOR v EH* [1996] 2 IR 248, the Supreme Court ignored the Keegan decision, as the Constitution did not recognise the concept of a de facto family.
200 The Good Friday Agreement or Belfast Agreement, 'An Agreement reached at the Multi Party Talks on Northern Ireland, Cm3883 (1998)' was signed on 10 April 1998 (entered into force on 2 December 1999) and was a major agreement of the Peace Process for Northern Ireland establishing rules and governance on human rights, decommissioning of weapons, justice and policing as well as the establishment of institutions, status of governments and relationships between Ireland, United Kingdom and Northern Ireland. See Ronagh McQuigg, 'The European Convention on Human Rights Act 2003 – Ten Years On' (2014) 3 International Human Rights Law Review 61, 73.

became apparent that this step was necessary in order to ensure at least the perception of equivalent human rights protection between the UK and Ireland.[201] This was particularly so as Ireland found itself in the position of being the only Council of Europe state not to have incorporated the Convention, following the enactment of the Human Rights Act 1998 in the UK.[202]

[6–78]   Discussions on how best to give effect to these rights in domestic law were fraught with disagreement.[203] The main contention centred on whether they should be on par with constitutional rights, or below them. The Constitution Review Group recommended that they should be superior to all other legislation, and found that the only way to ensure this was by way of constitutional amendment.[204] This recommendation, echoed by the Irish Human Rights Commission,[205] was rejected in favour of an indirect, sub-constitutional approach, described as an 'interpretative' method of incorporation. McKechnie J explained the consequence of this approach, stating:

> It is a misleading metaphor to say that the Convention was incorporated into domestic law. It was not. The rights contained within the Convention are now part of Irish Law. They are so by reason of the Act of 2003. That is their source. Not the Convention. So it is only correct to say, as understood in this way, that the Convention forms part of our law.[206]

[6–79]   Fundamentally, while the ECHR may now be cognisable in domestic courts, and as per the Act, account must be taken of Convention law, as the 'meaning and operation of the Act is a matter of domestic law governed by Irish courts'.[207]

[6–80]   The Act itself, in comparison with other legislation, is relatively short and was heavily influenced by the Human Rights Act 1998, which gave effect to the ECHR in UK law.[208]

---

[201] Gerard Hogan, 'The Belfast Agreement and the Future Incorporation of the European Convention of Human Rights in the Republic of Ireland' (1999) 4 Bar Review 205.

[202] Ray Murphy, 'The Incorporation of the ECHR into Irish Domestic Law' (2001) 6 European Human Rights Law Review 622, 631.

[203] Hogan (n 201).

[204] The Constitution Review Group, *Report of the Constitution Review Group* (Dublin Stationery Office 1996) 191.

[205] See Irish Human Rights Commission, 'Submission on the European Convention in Human Rights Bill to the Joint Oireachtas Committee on Justice, Equality, Defence and Women's Rights' (June 2002) available at <www.ihrc.ie/publications/list/submission-on-the-european-convention-on-human-rig/> last accessed 5 January 2017.

[206] *Foy v Register of Births Deaths and Marriages, Ireland and AG (No.2)* [2007] IEHC 471 [93].

[207] de Londras (n 183) 1.

[208] Analysis of the Human Rights Act 1998 is beyond the scope of this chapter. See generally, John Wadham, Helen Mountfield QC, Elizabeth Prochaska and Raj Desai, *Blackstones*

Section 2[209] asserts that the court must interpret domestic law in a manner **[6–81]** compatible with the Convention 'in so far as is possible',[210] whether that law came into effect prior to the passing of the Act or not.[211] Where this is not possible, a declaration of incompatibility can be made.[212] There has been widespread reluctance to rely on this provision, most likely due to its ambiguity. This section is both broad, as it requires all law to be interpreted in a compatible manner, and narrow, in that such an obligation is restricted by being subject to the rules of interpretation.[213] Its impact would depend on the element to which the court gives more weight and, if they took a minimalist approach, it renders the provision redundant. In *Dublin City Council v Gallagher,*[214] the court

---

Guide to the Human Rights Act 1998 (7th edn, Oxford University Press 2015); Richard Gordon QC and Tim Ward, *Judicial Review and the Human Rights Act* (Cavendish Publishing 2000); David Hoffman and John Rowe QC, *Human Rights in the UK An Introduction to the Human Rights Act 1998* (2nd edn, Pearson Education Ltd 2006); Nicolas Kang-Riou, Jo Milner and Suryia Nayak (eds), *Confronting the Human Rights Act: Contemporary Themes and Perspectives* (Routledge 2012); Lammy Betten (ed) *The Human Rights Act 1998, What it Means: The Incorporation of the European Convention on Human Rights into the Legal Order of the United Kingdom* (Kluwer Law International 1999); Aileen Kavanagh, 'What's so Weak about Weak Form Review? The Case of the UK Human Rights Act' (2015) International Journal of Constitutional Law (forthcoming); Christopher Crawford, 'Dialogue and Declarations of Incompatibility under Section 4 of the Human Rights Act 1998' (2013) 25 Denning Law Journal 43; Evan Fox-Decent, 'Contextual Constitutionalism after the UK Human Rights Act 1998' (2012) 62 University of Toronto Law Journal 133.

[209] s 2(1) provides, 'In Interpreting and applying any statutory provision or rule of law a court shall, in so far as is possible, subject to the rules of law relating to such interpretation and application, do so in a manner compatible with the State's obligations under the Convention provisions', and s 2(2), 'This Section applies to any statutory provision or rule of law in force immediately before the passing of this Act or any such provision coming into force thereafter'.

[210] Meaning that the obligation is not an absolute one. See Gerry Whyte, 'Public Interest Litigation in Ireland and the ECHR Act 2003' in Egan, Thornton and Walsh (eds) (n 184) 258.

[211] This section has its origins in s 3 of the UK Human Rights Act 1998, which provides, 'So far as it is possible to do so, primary legislation and subordinate legislation must be read and given effect in a way which is compatible with Convention Rights'. For analysis of how this section has been interpreted in UK courts, see Christopher Crawford, 'Dialogue and Rights-Compatible Interpretations under Section 3 of the Human Rights Act' (2015) 25 King's Law Journal 34; Aileen Kavanagh, 'The Elusive Divide Between Interpretation and Legislation under the Human Rights Act 1998' (2004) 24 Oxford Journal of Legal Studies 259; Francis Bennion, 'What Interpretation is Possible under Section 3(1) of the Human Rights Act 1998' [2000] Public Law 77; Conor Gearty, 'Revisiting Section 3(1) of the Human Rights Act' (2003) 119 Law Quarterly Review 551; and Alison L Young, 'Judicial Sovereignty and the Human Rights Act 1998' (2002) 61 Cambridge Law Journal 53.

[212] Under s 5.

[213] Cliona Kelly, 'Maximising the Potential of the European Convention on Human Rights Act 2003: The Interpretive Obligation and the Importance of Framing' in Egan, Thornton and Walsh (eds) (n 184) 57.

[214] [2008] IEHC 354.

appeared to favour the latter, requiring adherence to existing rules of statutory interpretation.[215]

[6–82]   However, in circumstances where there is more than one possible interpretation, the court must choose the Convention-compatible option.[216] The provision extends not only to primary or even secondary legislation, but notices pursuant to legislation[217] and the common law are also encompassed.[218] This applies to law in force prior to enactment, although retrospective application is not permissible under the Act.[219]

[6–83]   Section 3[220] of the Act is concerned with ensuring that 'organs of the State' fulfil their duties in accordance with Convention obligations and, while quasi-judicial tribunals are included, the President, Oireachtas and Courts are expressly excluded.[221] It places a positive duty on state bodies to perform their functions in a manner compatible with Convention obligations by ensuring compliance with, rather than simply refraining from violating, such rights.[222] In practice, this duty has been difficult to enforce. The High Court, in *Pullen*, held that the local authority had breached Article 6(1) of the Convention through its failure to adhere to s 3 on the basis that it chose to follow an incompatible procedure.[223] On appeal to the Supreme Court, this reasoning was not upheld, as it would have set the precedent that all state organs would have to check for alternative compliant legislation and use it.[224]

[6–84]   Section 4 of the Act is closely linked with s 2 and lists the authorities which the courts shall have cognisance of when interpreting the law.[225] This section

---

[215] Paul Brady, 'Convention Compatible Statutory Interpretation: A Comparison of British and Irish Approaches' (2012) 1 Statute Law Review 1, 31.

[216] ibid 37.

[217] In *Law Society of Ireland v The Competition Authority* [2006] 2 IR 262, it was determined that a notice pursuant to the Competition Act 2002 was a rule for the purpose of the Act.

[218] s 1(1).

[219] *Dublin City Council v Fennell* [2005] IR 604 [86] (Kearns J).

[220] s 3(1) states, 'subject to any statutory provision (other than this Act) or rule of law, every state organ shall perform its duties in a manner compatible with the State's obligations under the Convention'.

[221] This section has its origins in s 6 of the UK Human Rights Act, which makes it unlawful for a public authority to act in a manner which is incompatible with a Convention right. For analysis of this section, see Merris Amos, 'Transplanting Human Rights Norms: The Case of the United Kingdom's Human Rights Act' (2013) 35 Human Rights Quarterly 386; Nicolas Kang-Riou, Jo Milner and Suryia Nayak (eds), *Confronting the Human Rights Act: Contemporary Themes and Perspectives* (Routledge 2012).

[222] Fiona de Londras and Cliona Kelly, *European Convention on Human Rights Act; Operation, Impact and Analysis* (Round Hall 2010) 97.

[223] *Pullen v Dublin City Council* [2008] IEHC 379.

[224] *Pullen v Dublin City Council* [2009] 2 ILRM 484.

[225] s 4(1) states, 'Judicial notice shall be taken of the Convention provisions and of: (a) Any declaration, decision, advisory opinion or judgment of the European Court of Human

arguably means that the court is obliged to take these authorities into account, rather than creating a discretion to do so. The court is then to take 'due account', an obligation extended to all courts, although, in practice, Convention jurisprudence has primarily been considered in the Superior Courts.[226] This vague and uncertain obligation fails to specify whether these must be considered before the court reaches its own conclusion.[227]

Finally, s 6 of the Act provides that the Human Rights Commission and the Attorney General must be notified of any claim seeking a declaration of incompatibility.[228] **[6–85]**

The scope of the Act is, therefore, quite limited. It does not confer legally enforceable rights and is only applicable in terms of interpreting existing rights. Its potential to establish new rights has dissipated considerably in light of its relegation to the status of an interpretative aid, rather than a direct incorporation of Convention rights, resulting in questions as to whether the Act is any more 'than a ruse with a very clever name'.[229] **[6–86]**

There are two remedies available under the 2003 Act: damages under s 3[230] or a declaration of incompatibility under s 5.[231] The legislative provision of two explicit remedies has been interpreted by the court to necessarily mean that remedies are restricted to those provided for, thereby excluding any other remedy, including injunctive relief.[232] **[6–87]**

Rights established under the Convention on any question in respect of which that Court has jurisdiction (b) Any decision or opinion of the European Commission of Human Rights so established on any question in respect of which it had jurisdiction (c) Any decision of the Committee of Ministers established under the Statute of the Council of Europe on any question in respect of which it has jurisdiction–And a court shall, when interpreting and applying the Convention provisions, take due account of the principles laid down by those declarations, decisions, advisory opinions, opinions and judgments'.

[226] Thomas E O'Donnell, 'The District Court, The European Convention on Human Rights Act 2003 "Cause and Effect"' (2010) 2 Judicial Studies Institute Journal 97.

[227] de Londras and Kelly (n 222) 131.

[228] s 6(1) states, 'Before a Court decides whether to make a declaration of incompatibility the Attorney General and the Human Rights Commission shall be given notice of the Proceedings in accordance with the rules of court'.

[229] Suzanne Egan, 'The European Convention on Human Rights Act: A Missed Opportunity for Domestic Human Rights Litigation' (2003) 25 Dublin University Law Journal 230, 245.

[230] s 3(2) provides that a person may 'institute proceedings to recover damages in respect of the contravention in the High Court'.

[231] s 5(1) provides that, where there is no other legal remedy available, the court may 'make a declaration that a statutory provision or rule of law is incompatible with the State's obligations under the Convention provisions'.

[232] Whyte, 'Public Interest Litigation in Ireland and the ECHR Act 2003' in Egan, Thornton and Walsh (eds) (n 184) 261.

[6–88]   Section 3 provides that an award of damages can be made where injury, loss or damage has occurred as a result of the state failing to perform its functions in a manner compatible with the Convention. Such damages can only be awarded where 'no other remedy in damages is available'.[233] Thus, the issue of when to plead the ECHR becomes centrally relevant, as remedies under the 2003 Act can only be granted in circumstances where damages cannot be awarded under another branch of law (for breach of contract, tort etc). The argument that constitutional matters must be initially exhausted prior to any claim under the 2003 Act[234] has been endorsed by the courts.[235] Further, it is within the discretion of the court as to whether the award will be made.[236] Given the rarity of a case that could fulfil these requirements, to date there have been only two cases in which damages have been awarded under this section. One exception to the rigid application has emerged in circumstances where the Act is used as grounds for an application for judicial review of a decision. In these circumstances, it appears that the court has retained the power to award more than damages:

> It is apparent that Section 3 does not exclude the availability of certiorari in judicial review proceedings for breach of the Section 3 duty on the ground that a statutory discretion was exercised in such a way as to breach the Section 3 duty.[237]

[6–89]   The second remedy, the declaration of incompatibility contained in s 5, has its origins in s 4 of the Human Rights Act 1998. The reason for its inclusion in the Human Rights Act is based on the notion of parliamentary sovereignty, a concept central to the UK legal system, which provides that Parliament is the sole body with the power to repeal primary legislation, meaning that the court cannot declare legislation invalid.[238] The declaration of incompatibility in the UK was somewhat of a compromise. The courts use its power to declare legislation incompatible with Convention law in order to bring a matter to the attention

---

[233] s 3(2).

[234] Gerard Hogan, 'The Value of Declarations of Incompatibility and the Rule of Avoidance' (2006) 1 Dublin University Law Journal 418, 416.

[235] *Law Society v Competition Authority* [2005] IEHC 455 and *Carmody v Minister for Justice, Equality and Law Reform* [2010] 1 IR 635.

[236] s 3(2) of the Act states that the Court 'may' award damages and, therefore, an award of damages is not mandatory.

[237] *Byrne v Dublin City Council* [2009] IEHC 122 [5.2].

[238] A discussion of the finer points of parliamentary sovereignty is beyond the scope of this thesis. For such analysis, see generally, Alison Young, *Parliamentary Sovereignty and the Human Rights Act* (Hart 2009); Alison Young, 'Parliamentary Sovereignty and the Human Rights Act 1998' (2002) 61(1) Cambridge Law Journal 53; Mark Elliot, 'United Kingdom: Parliamentary Sovereignty Under Pressure' (2004) 2 International Journal of Constitutional Law 545; Richard Bellamy, 'Political Constitutionalism and the Human Rights Act' (2011) 9 International Journal of Constitutional Law 86; Aileen Kavanagh, 'The Role of Parliamentary Intention in Adjudication under the Human Rights Act 1998' (2006) 26 Oxford Journal of Legal Studies 179.

of Parliament. It therefore keeps compliance with Convention obligations under review. Such considerations do not apply in the Irish context. The Irish legal system is built on the more classic model of separation of powers, with the courts playing a robust role including retaining the ability to invalidate legislative acts which are unconstitutional.[239] Thus, it was not necessary for the 2003 Act to follow the UK, particularly within the realm of remedies. Despite the option to extend the court's existing ability to repeal legislation, contrary to the Constitution, the 2003 Act provides only for a declaration of incompatibility.

This declaration is made by the High or Supreme Court,[240] where the law in question cannot be interpreted in a manner compatible with the Convention. This declaration is very different to a finding of unconstitutionality, by which the offending legislation will be invalidated. It does not affect 'the legal validity, continuing operation or enforcement' of the law in question.[241] It is primarily a symbolic remedy, more than a practical one. For this reason, the declaration has been referred to as a 'pale shadow' of the declaration of unconstitutionality.[242] The Taoiseach is mandated by the Act to put the declaration before the Dáil, but there are no subsequent procedural or substantive requirements.[243] Moreover, there is no right to compensation for the person or persons who have suffered as a result of this incompatibility.[244]   [6–90]

To date, there have been three declarations of incompatibility, which have resulted, albeit slowly, in changes being made to the law to bring it in line with the Convention.   [6–91]

Post Incorporation

Post incorporation, the most authoritative statement on the position of the ECHR in Ireland, affirmed in *O'Donnell v South Dublin County Council*,[245] was advanced by the Supreme Court in *McD v L*.[246] This case considered the enforceability of an agreement between a same-sex couple and a sperm donor as to the legal rights to the child. The agreement expressly stated that the biological   [6–92]

---

[239] Egan (n 229) 245.

[240] s 5(1) states that the High or Supreme court 'may' make a declaration of incompatibility, thus not making it mandatory.

[241] s 5(2)(a).

[242] Hogan, 'The Constitution and the Convention' in Egan, Thornton and Walsh (eds) (n 184) 85.

[243] s 5(3) states, 'The Taoiseach shall cause a copy of any Order containing a declaration of incompatibility to be laid before each House of the Oireachtas within the next 21 days on which that House has sat after the making of the Order'.

[244] s 5(4)(c) states, 'The Government in their discretion, consider that it may be appropriate to make an *ex gratia* payment of compensation to that party'.

[245] [2015] IESC 28.

[246] [2009] IESC 81. See also, Brady (n 215).

father would have no influence over the child's upbringing, nor would he have custody or legal rights. Following the birth of the child, the applicant reneged on the agreement and sought to assert his legal rights under the Guardianship of Infants Act 1964. In the High Court, Hedigan J refused the orders sought by the father and, relying on the ECHR (despite the fact that the European Court had not yet determined such), found that the couple, as a de facto family, enjoyed rights under Article 8.[247]

[6–93]   On appeal, the Supreme Court overturned this reasoning, with Murray CJ providing an in-depth analysis of the status of the Convention in Irish Law, post-incorporation.[248] He first established that the Convention only has the impact on national law that the legislation gives it.[249] He then pointed out that the state cannot be forced to comply with an order of the European Court and the only penalty is expulsion from the system.[250] In terms of the High Court ruling, the Supreme Court felt that Hedigan J had overshot the jurisprudence of the European Court, which had not yet determined that same-sex couples fell within the scope, and protection, of Article 8.

[6–94]   In holding that the High Court erred in its interpretation, and in rejecting the notion of a de facto family in this case on constitutional grounds, heavy emphasis was placed on the fact that the High Court was anticipating jurisprudence from Strasbourg.[251] At the time of the Supreme Court ruling, it was noted and accepted by the High Court that there was no jurisprudence from the European Court granting de facto status to same-sex couples, a situation since remedied in *Schalk & Kopf v Austria*[252] and in *Gas and Dubois v France*.[253]

[6–95]   In contrast, *Foy v Registrar of Births Deaths and Marriages, Ireland and the Attorney General* represented an instance in which there was a definitive ruling by the European Court on an identical issue.[254] Lydia Foy, a post-operative transsexual, claimed a breach of her rights, as she was unable to change her

---

[247] [2008] IEHC 96, referred to in the Supreme Court judgment [2009] IESC 81 (Denham J).

[248] For analysis of the High Court judgment, see Maria Cahill, 'MCD v L and the Incorporation of the European Convention on Human Rights' (2010) 1 Irish Jurist 221.

[249] [2009] IESC 81, 90.

[250] ibid.

[251] For a full analysis of the de facto family in Irish law, see Conor O'Mahony, 'Irreconcilable differences: Article 8 ECHR and Irish Law on Non Traditional Families' (2012) International Journal of Law, Policy and the Family 1, and Fergus Ryan, 'Are Two Irish Mammies (even) Better than One? Heteronormativity, Homosexuality and the 1937 Constitution' in Eoin Carolan (ed), *The Constitution of Ireland: Perspectives and Prospects* (Bloomsbury Professional) 2012.

[252] (2011) 53 EHRR 20.

[253] App No 25951/07 (ECtHR, 15 March 2012).

[254] [2002] IEHC 116.

gender on her birth certificate.[255] McKechnie J found no constitutional violation and dismissed her claim in 2002, although he did urge the Oireachtas to review the issue.[256] The matter was appealed to the Supreme Court on the basis of intervening developments, being the coming into force of the 2003 Act and the ruling in *Goodwin v UK* in the European Court.[257] The Supreme Court referred the case back to the High Court to be re-examined in light of these advancements.

It was held that, given the status of the ECHR in Irish law, the decision in *Goodwin* was not binding.[258] It was affirmed as being sub-constitutional and the principle of non-retrospectivity established in *Fennell* was upheld.[259] The applicant here sought to distinguish her case due to the 'ever present nature of her plight'.[260] In effect, her argument was that it was a continuing breach and not the single instance of refusal to change her birth gender, which occurred before the coming into effect of the Act. In rejecting this contention, the court determined that this would 'lead to great uncertainty and would place the first-named respondent in an impossible position'.[261] It was determined that the most persuasive argument being proffered by the applicant was that the failure of the statutory regime to allow a change to the birth register infringed her rights under the ECHR. Having extensive regard to the case law of the European Court of Human Rights in this area, the court concluded that Ireland was 'disconnected from mainstream thinking',[262] and non-compliant with Article 8. It therefore issued the first declaration of incompatibility under s 5 of the 2003 Act. **[6–96]**

The state, in *Foy*, argued that the declaration of incompatibility should not be granted, as the applicant was relying on state inaction (a failure to enact legislation, rather than prohibitive legislation), an argument that was criticised by the court: **[6–97]**

> In my view the failure of the State through the absence of having any measures to honour the Convention rights of the citizens, is every bit

---

[255] The background to this case is discussed at length in Michael Farrell, 'Lydia Foy and the Struggle for Gender Recognition' (2012) Socio-Legal Studies Review 153. See also Tanya Ni Mhuirthile, 'Article 8 and the Realisation of the Right to Legal Gender Recognition' in Egan, Thornton and Walsh (eds) (n 184) 201-218

[256] [2002] IEHC 116 [177].

[257] (2002) 35 EHRR 447. Here, the circumstances were almost identical to that of Lydia Foy and involved a case brought by Christine Goodwin against the UK in circumstances where Ms Goodwin was unable to change her birth certificate. The European Court of Human Rights held that this violated her right to privacy and her right to marry contained within Articles 8 and 12 of the Convention. The decision resulted in the UK enacting the Gender Recognition Act 2004 to remedy this defect.

[258] [2007] IEHC 471 [32].

[259] [2005] IR 604.

[260] [2007] IEHC 471 [36].

[261] ibid [37-38].

[262] ibid [104].

as much a breach of its responsibility as if it had enacted a piece of prohibited legislation.[263]

[6–98]   Notwithstanding that a stricter approach was taken by the Supreme Court in *McD v L*,[264] this case can be distinguished, in that the state in *Foy* was aware of the issue and had failed to remedy it.

[6–99]   The state's appeal against the declaration of incompatibility granted by the High Court in Foy was officially withdrawn in June 2010 after it pledged, in 2009, to introduce legal recognition for transsexuals. Thus, the declaration of incompatibility became final.[265]

[6–100]   In the aftermath of this declaration, the Gender Recognition Advisory Group was established in 2010 and published its report in 2011, recommending that legislation be introduced.[266] In 2013, Lydia Foy announced that she would be returning to the High Court due to continued state inaction in progressing this legislation. Her claim alleged that the inordinate delay amounted to a breach of Article 3 of the Convention and that the 2003 Act itself was in breach of the Convention for failing to provide an adequate remedy.[267]

[6–101]   Lydia Foy's proposed litigation was settled in October 2014, when the state informed the High Court of its 'firm intention' to enact the Gender Recognition Bill in 2015.[268] This legislation entered into force on 4 September 2015.[269] Despite the discontinuance of the case, it has brought the effectiveness of the declaration into question and potentially calls into question the compliance of the Act itself with the Convention. Recent developments in the European Court suggest that declarations of incompatibility alone will not satisfy Article 13 and must be coupled with prompt legislative change.[270]

---

[263]   ibid [108].

[264]   [2009] IESC 81.

[265]   Department of An Taoiseach, 'Renewed Programme for Government' (10 October 2009) 9, available at <www.defence.ie/WebSite. nsf/72804bb4760386f380256c610055a16b/2a49a2267d0f095b80257754004d3e17/ $FILE/94315182.pdf/Renewed_Programme_for_Government,_October_2009.pdf> last accessed 06 January 2017. See also Ni Mhuirthile, 'Article 8 and the Realisation of the Right to Legal Gender Recognition' in Egan, Thornton and Walsh (eds) (n 184) 201-218.

[266]   See Gender Recognition Advisory Group, 'Report to Joan Burton, TD, Minister for Social Protection' (15 June 2011), available at <www.welfare.ie/en/downloads/Report-of-the-Gender-Recognition-Advisory-Group.pdf> last accessed 07 January 2017.

[267]   Michael Farrell (FLAC), 'Briefing Note on the Lydia Foy Case and Transgender Issues in Ireland' (February 2013) 5, available at <www.flac.ie/download/pdf/foy_case_briefing_note_feb_20131.pdf> last accessed 07 January 2017.

[268]   Mary Carolan, 'Lydia Foy Settles Transgender Birth Cert Case against State' *The Irish Times* (28 October 2014).

[269]   Gender Recognition Act 2015 (Commencement) Order 2015, SI 369/2015.

[270]   *Hobbs v UK* (2007) 44 EHRR 54 and *Burden v UK* (2008) 47 EHRR 38. See also, Oran

Social and Economic Rights Post Incorporation: Any Changes?

The landscape of social and economic rights in Ireland has not been changed   **[6–102]**
drastically since the enactment of the 2003 Act.[271] Rather, there have been
distinct and subtle changes, particularly in relation to housing.

The primary impact on social and economic rights culminated in the second   **[6–103]**
declaration of incompatibility granted by the Supreme Court in *Donegan,* and
it is worth examining the history here.[272] The offending section (which was
ultimately declared incompatible) had been at the fore of several prior challenges.
Section 62 (3) of the Housing Act 1966 provides that, where an application is
made to the District Court for a warrant of repossession by the local authority
on the grounds contained within the section, the said warrant shall issue. The
court, therefore cannot investigate the merits or reasonableness of whether the
warrant should, in fact, issue. In *The State (O'Rourke) v Kelly,*[273] the Supreme
Court dismissed claims that this provision fettered judicial discretion and in both
Dublin Corporation v Hamilton[274] and *Rock v Dublin City Council,*[275] it rejected
challenges, placing considerable emphasis on the fact that the local authority
must not be unduly encumbered in dealing expeditiously with its properties.

Byrne v Scally further entrenched the position where the challenge to eviction   **[6–104]**
was based on the absence of legal representation.[276] The court held that, if the
Court had the power to examine the merits of the eviction, she may have been
entitled to legal representation. As it was not entitled to engage with the merits
of the case, the issue of legal representation was moot. This ruling is based on
the notion that one safeguard gives rise to another, and, in the absence of the
first safeguard, the second does not arise.[277]

A case which bears striking resemblance to the ultimately successful challenge   **[6–105]**
in *Donegan,* is *McConnell v Dublin Corporation.*[278] This litigation challenged
an eviction based on the undisputed anti-social behaviour of the applicant's

---

Doyle and Desmond Ryan, 'Judicial Interpretation of the European Convention on Human Rights Act 2003: Reflections and Analysis' (2011) 33 Dublin University Law Journal 369.

[271] For analysis of how similar provisions have impacted social and economic rights in the UK, see Ellie Palmer, *Judicial Review, Socio Economic Rights and the Human Rights Act* (Hart 2007).

[272] *Donegan v Dublin City Council, Ireland and the Attorney General* and *Dublin City Council v Gallagher* [2012] IESC 18.

[273] [1983] IR 58.

[274] [1999] 2 IR 486.

[275] (SC, 2 February 2006).

[276] (HC, 12 October 2000).

[277] Mark Coen, 'Fair Procedures, Local Authority Housing, the Constitution and the European Convention on Human Rights' (2009) 1 Dublin University Law Journal 423, 426.

[278] [2005] IEHC 7.

minor son. In dismissing the claim, it was held that as the behaviour was not in dispute, that an opportunity to be heard would not have changed the outcome and that the decision 'was not disproportionate to the objective of good estate management'.[279]

[6–106] The first case challenging this section, following the enactment of the 2003 Act, was *Leonard v Dublin City Council*,[280] where Dunne J found that it was compatible with the Convention. In holding that Article 6 was not violated, emphasis was placed on the fact that the applicant had the opportunity to engage with the Council prior to the eviction and failed to do so. Further, it held that Article 8 could not be read as conferring a right of possession on a tenant once it had been lawfully terminated.[281]

[6–107] In the High Court case of *Donegan*, this section was challenged once again.[282] The eviction was premised on the discovery of narcotics in the bedroom of Mr Donegan's son. The local authority requested that he apply for an exclusion order against his son on this basis.[283] He refused to comply with this request, stating that his son was an addict who was undergoing treatment and was not involved in the distribution of narcotics. In these circumstances, the Council had an option of applying for the exclusion order itself, or seeking repossession of the property under s 62.[284] The Council chose to proceed with the latter. Mr Donegan sought a declaration that this section was incompatible with Articles 6, 8 and 13 of the Convention. Laffoy J, in the High Court, referred extensively to the judgment of *Connors*,[285] as the case herein centred on the lack of procedural safeguards, and crucially, involved a factual dispute:

> A statutory regime under which possession of the home of an occupier, whether a licensee or tenant, can be recovered by a public authority which does not embody procedural safeguards whereby the occupier

---

[279] ibid.

[280] [2008] IEHC 79. This was the second challenge to the section, the first being made and rejected on constitutional grounds under Case 2007/916JR (3 December 2007).

[281] Caroline Carney, Lorna Nic Lochlainn, Siobhan O'Donoghue, Tom Power, 'I Can't Get No Satisfaction: An Analysis of the European Convention on Human Rights on the Repossession of Public Housing in Ireland' (2010) 13 Trinity College Law Review 55, 61.

[282] *Donegan v Dublin City Council* [2008] IEHC 288.

[283] This was based on a report provided by the Garda, which states, at para 8, that he was 'known to be selling heroin on the streets', referred to in the factual background section of *Donegan v Dublin City Council* (Laffoy J).

[284] s 3 of the Housing (Miscellaneous) Provisions Act 1997 had come into effect, which allowed the local authority to apply to the Court for this exclusion order if the tenant would not do so "for whatever reason". This provision also gives the Court the power to examine the merits of the exclusion order and is not granted summarily, as the warrant for repossession is under s 62.

[285] (2004) 40 EHRR 189.

can have the decision which will inevitably result in his eviction from his home reviewed in accordance with Convention recognised fair procedures (as illustrated by the decision of the court in *Tsfayo*), in my view, cannot fulfill the *Connors* test of being fair and affording due respect to the rights protected by Article 8.[286]

In granting the declaration of incompatibility, the court perceived the factual dispute as instrumental to the determination.

This decision was promptly appealed to the Supreme Court, and judgment was delivered in 2012. In the interim, however, several other cases came before the courts on the same issue, as the declaration of incompatibility does not affect the validity or enforceability of the legislation in question. In *Pullen (No. 1)*, decided relatively soon after *Donegan*, Irvine J again dealt with a challenge to this section.[287] In this case, the applicants did not seek a declaration of incompatibility. Rather, they sought a declaration under s 3 that the state organ had failed to perform its duties in a matter compatible with the Convention. In holding that there was a breach of both Articles 6 and 8, the judgment in *Donegan* was expressly approved and applied,[288] with the court concluding that, while the objective of the Council in maintaining order and good estate management was a legitimate aim, the lack of procedural safeguards resulted in summary eviction in a manner disproportionate to achieving it.[289]   **[6–108]**

Pullen (No.2) sought an injunction restraining the eviction and it was confirmed that the court did not have the power to grant injunctions under the Act. In *Pullen (No.3)*,[290] an application for damages was successful under s 3(2) of the 2003 Act.   **[6–109]**

The eviction in *Dublin City Council v Gallagher* resulted from a refusal to grant succession to an existing tenancy.[291] O'Neill J found violations of Article 8, due to the lack of procedural safeguards, and Article 6, as he was not given an opportunity to adduce evidence to establish that he was entitled to succeed to the tenancy. Further, he concluded that judicial review was not an appropriate remedy for a factual dispute.[292] The court, in granting a further declaration of incompatibility, noted that it would assist Mr Gallagher in obtaining damages for the breach of rights.   **[6–110]**

---

[286] [2008] IEHC 288 [89].

[287] [2009] 2 ILRM 484.

[288] [2008] IEHC 379 [67].

[289] ibid [59-60]. See also Padraic Kenna, 'Local Authorities and the European Convention on Human Rights Act 2003' in Donncha O'Connell (ed), *Irish Human Rights Law Review* (Clarus Press 2010) 27.

[290] *Pullen v Dublin City Council (No.3)* [2010] 2 ILRM 61.

[291] *Dublin City Council v Gallagher* [2008] IEHC 354.

[292] Carney, Nic Lochlainn, O'Donoghue, Power (n 281) 63.

[6–111]   The decision in *Gallagher* was also appealed, and the Supreme Court joined it with the appeal in *Donegan*.[293] The court dismissed the declaration in the *Gallagher* case, as it accepted that he did not meet the legal criteria to succeed to the tenancy. However, it upheld the declaration in *Donegan*. A particularly compelling part of the Supreme Court judgment is the discussion of the adequacy of judicial review as a remedy. Given the nature of judicial review, which examines how a decision is made and not the merits, it concluded that it was not appropriate in these cases, as they involved a determination based on facts:

> Was Mr Donegan's son a drug addict or a drug pusher? It is purely a question of fact, simple, I dare say to resolve. Was Mr Gallagher residing with his mother for the period in question or was he not? Again, a rather straightforward matter. It is therefore rather difficult to see how a remedy like judicial review, modeled in the manner in which it is, could in any way make a decision or reach a conclusion on these issues.[294]

[6–112]   As the District Court's sole function is to ensure that the statutory criteria had been satisfied, once it had assured itself of this, any judicial review would only confirm the decision reached.[295]

[6–113]   Since this decision, the provision has again been challenged in the High Court in *Webster v Dun Laoghaire Rathdown County Council*.[296] In this case, the court held that, given the Supreme Court had already issued a declaration of incompatibility in respect of s 62, it saw no point in making another. However, it observed obiter that the obligation to ensure procedural safeguards may potentially extend to situations where there are no factual disputes.[297]

[6–114]   This possibility was comprehensively rejected in *O'Driscoll v Limerick City Council*, wherein the court found that, as there was no factual dispute, judicial review was an adequate remedy.[298]

---

[293] [2012] IESC 18.

[294] ibid [214].

[295] This inadequacy of judicial review has been cited with increasing regularity in claims involving asylum and immigration. However, the reasoning of the Supreme Court has, so far, been confined to cases involving s 62 of the Housing Act 1966. See *JCM and ML v The Minister for Justice and Equality, Ireland and the Attorney* General [2012] IEHC 485; *Khalad Islam Khattack v Refugee Appeals Tribunal, Minister for Justice and Equality, Ireland and the Attorney General* [2012] IEHC 569; and *FE(A minor acting by her father and next friend) ME and BR (A minor acting by her father and next friend) ME, MAE (A minor acting by his father and next friend) ME and ME v The Minister for Justice and Law Reform* [2014] IEHC 62.

[296] [2013] IEHC 119.

[297] ibid [7.9].

[298] [2012] IEHC 454.

As a result of the declaration by the Supreme Court, the Housing (Miscellaneous Provisions) Act 2014 was introduced.[299] Part 3 of the Act amends s 62; under s 12(9), the District Court is empowered to hear the merits of the possession order, taking all reasonable circumstances into account, particularly the effect that such repossession order would have on the tenant.[300] Should the tenant fail to attend the hearing, the District Court can, where it is satisfied that there is a prima facie case for doing so, grant the order sought.[301] This Act was commenced on 15 September 2014 by the Minister, who expressly excluded Part 3 of the Act at that time. This section came into effect on 1 January 2016.[302]　　　**[6–115]**

In terms of placing any positive obligations for the provision of social housing or, indeed, adequate conditions of housing, there has been little progress, with conflicting cases and differentiated judgments. The cases litigated have primarily involved members of the Travelling community and the obligations on the state to furnish them with adequate accommodation. Several cases, all involving Traveller accommodation, have examined the positive obligations arising from the Convention. Restricting its considerations to lawful tenancies, the court determined that the Convention did not apply to unlawful occupation of land,[303] a decision at odds with more recent jurisprudence of the European Court.[304] The initial position of the courts was akin to that taken in *TD*: there is no obligation to provide for housing.[305]　　　**[6–116]**

One of the first attempts to litigate housing conditions under the ECHR was made in *Doherty v South Dublin County Council*.[306] The case considered the living conditions of an elderly Traveller couple, who argued that the state was obliged to provide them with a caravan containing heating and plumbing, and not an apartment, which they had refused on grounds of culture.[307] In rejecting their argument, Charleton J relied on jurisprudence from the European Court[308] in determining that the state did not have a duty to provide a particular amount of adequate halting sites.[309] It would appear that, as the Council had already made an offer of accommodation, which could objectively (though, perhaps, not　　　**[6–117]**

---

[299] Housing (Miscellaneous Provisions) Act 2014.

[300] s 12(9)(b).

[301] s 12(7).

[302] Housing (Miscellaneous Provisions) Act 2014 (Commencement of Certain Provisions) (No.2) Order 2015, SI 482/2015.

[303] *McDonagh v Kilkenny County Council* [2007] IEHC 350.

[304] See *Winterstein v France* App No 27013/07 (ECtHR, 17 October 2013).

[305] See Chapter 4 for an examination of the courts' position in relation to housing prior to 2003.

[306] [2007] IEHC 4.

[307] Whyte, 'Public Interest Litigation in Ireland and the ECHR Act 2003' in Egan, Thornton and Walsh (eds) (n 184) 272.

[308] In particular, the cases of *Chapman v UK* (2001) 33 EHRR 399 and *Codona v UK* App No 485/05 (ECtHR, 7 February 2006).

[309] [2007] IEHC 4, 45 (Charleton J).

culturally) be deemed adequate to meet their housing needs, this was sufficient to discharge their obligations.[310]

[6–118] The case of *O'Donnell v South Dublin County Council* came shortly after *Doherty* and was more successful.[311] It was brought on behalf of three minor siblings who resided in a temporary halting site provided by the defendant. The three plaintiffs suffered from a condition known as Hurler's syndrome, and alleged that the overcrowded and cramped conditions in which they resided breached Article 8. They sought an order directing the Council to provide an additional wheelchair-accessible home with toilet and shower facilities, or, in the alternative, an order that it make such funds available to them in order to purchase the caravan themselves. [312]

[6–119] In rejecting the claim of a statutory entitlement under the Housing Acts (on the basis that the applicants had not identified a particular incompatible section), Laffoy J went on to consider the European Convention. The court determined that it must balance the 'effect of having to live in overcrowded, potentially unsafe and admittedly inadequate accommodation for three and a half years, with 'the economic wellbeing of the state'.[313] In distinguishing *Doherty* on the facts, specifically the offer of alternative accommodation, the court found that there had been a violation of Article 8. Laffoy J was careful to point out that this was not to be used as a precedent to further a general right to adequate housing, but rather that it was to be confined to the facts of this particular case.[314]

[6–120] Thus, where the particular circumstances reach such severity due to illness or disability, *and* where the plaintiffs are minors *and* where the local authority had knowledge of the conditions, it can be argued that the state does have a positive duty to provide for adequate accommodation.

[6–121] Having determined the breach, the court concluded that the only remedy open to it was one of damages under s 3 of the 2003 Act and awarded the sum of €58,000. The case was then adjourned for the parties to determine how they should proceed.

[6–122] In a further case bearing the same name the following year, another breach of

---

[310] Whyte, 'Public Interest Litigation in Ireland and the ECHR Act 2003' in Egan, Thornton and Walsh (eds) (n 184) 272.

[311] [2007] IEHC 204.

[312] Under the Traveller Accommodation Scheme (Circular letter TAU4/2002), a Traveller can apply for a loan to a maximum of €6,350, repayable at €20 per week, in order to improve living conditions. In this case, Mrs O'Donnell did not apply for the loan, as she contended that it would not be possible to obtain the necessary accommodation for that amount, a contention with which Laffoy J agreed.

[313] [2007] IEHC 204.

[314] ibid.

Article 8 was found by the court.[315] The case was taken by a family in relation to their cramped and overcrowded living conditions, alleging, in particular, that it was unsuitable for the minor child, Ellen, who had cerebral palsy and was confined to a wheelchair. The case again involved a temporary halting site and the Council conceded that the conditions were, in fact, unfit for human habitation. It argued that it had discharged its obligation by providing initial (and additional) accommodation, and that it was the plaintiff's own actions in giving away one caravan and failing to maintain another, that had resulted in the current circumstances. In other words, the Council contended that the plaintiffs were the authors of their own misfortune. The success of the case effectively centred on the fourth named applicant, Ellen. As in the foregoing case, considerable emphasis was placed on her disability and it is highly unlikely, given the facts, that it would have succeeded, had Ellen been able-bodied.

This case was appealed to the Supreme Court, and judgment was delivered in March 2015.[316] The court accepted that Ellen lived in (and continues to live in) deplorable conditions, which breached her rights to autonomy, bodily integrity and privacy. The judgment of MacMenamin J interpreted the statutory obligation contained in the Housing Acts. This seemingly discretionary power, that they 'may provide' sites, became a mandatory obligation once a request had been made.[317] Having determined the case by reference to a statutory obligation, there was no need to consider Ellen's claim in light of Convention jurisprudence, and the court remitted the case back to the High Court for a determination of damages. [318]   **[6–123]**

It remains the position, however, that, in order to succeed in such a claim, there must be some compelling illness or disability, which makes the conditions at issue considerably harsher for the particular applicant and distinguishes him or her from others living in similar conditions. In addition, there must be knowledge on the part of the state and a refusal to alleviate the conditions.[319] Of particular note, in the most recent Supreme Court judgment, is the absence of reiteration that social and economic rights are non-justiciable, which may indicate some softening opinions. This follows on from the statement of MacEochaidh J, who   **[6–124]**

---

[315] *O'Donnell v South Dublin County Council* [2008] IEHC 454.
[316] [2015] IESC 28.
[317] Liam Thornton, 'Socio-Economic Rights, the Constitution and the ECHR Act 2003: O'Donnell v South Dublin County Council in the Supreme Court' *humanrights.ie* (16 March 2015) available at <humanrights.ie/children-and-the-law/socio-economic-rights-the-constitution-and-the-echr-act-2003-odonnell-v-south-dublin-county-council-in-the-supreme-court/> last accessed 6 January 2017.
[318] [2015] IESC 28 [86].
[319] *Dooley & Ors v Killarney Town Council and Kerry County Council* [2008] IEHC 242. While the respondent acknowledged the unacceptable nature of the living conditions, the court refused to determine that they amounted to breaches of Articles 3 and 8, relying heavily on the fact that alternative accommodation had been refused.

refused to allow, in principle at least, the distribution of resources argument to be definitive, determining that:

> Where state action results in a breach of human rights and where the only remedy is the expenditure of additional money, the Court, in my opinion, must be entitled to make an appropriate order, even if the consequence is that the State must spend money to meet the terms of the Order.[320]

[6–125] Thus, the jurisprudence of the European Court is having an indirect effect on the vindication of social and economic rights. By interpreting existing law through the rubric of the 2003 Act, subtle, but distinct, changes are occurring as the courts become more familiar and comfortable with Convention law.

Conclusion

[6–126] The ECHR has faced an uphill struggle in terms of having an impact in Irish law. The dualist nature of Ireland, coupled with the sub-constitutional status of the Convention, has not greatly assisted. Given that the Convention technically remains international law, and it is only through the rubric of the 2003 Act that it can affect domestic law, it has had an arduous task. However, it is significant that one of the main areas in which the Convention is having an impact is the right to housing. Once considered constitutionally sound, s 62 of the Housing Act 1966 has been deemed to be in contravention of Ireland's Convention obligations, and has been repealed to ensure specific procedural protections against evictions for local authority tenants. The Convention has also had an impact on the conditions of local authority housing, particularly for vulnerable members of society. Given the jurisprudence and reasoning detailed above, it seems that, where the Constitution does not provide a right or a remedy, the Convention can have a significant impact. Both cases in which declarations of incompatibility were made involved rights which were not protected by the Constitution, although it is arguable that they could have been with an expansive interpretation of the right to privacy and the inviolability of the dwelling.

[6–127] In the same manner, given that social and economic rights, as a whole, do not enjoy protection under the Constitution, there remains the potential for future declarations of incompatibility to vindicate the rights of the individual in the areas of health and social welfare, as is evidenced from the jurisprudence of the European Court.

[6–128] It is clear that the European Convention and the 2003 Act are underutilised in Irish courts. With some creative pleading and an open-minded, human rights-focused judiciary, the impact that the 2003 Act can have on social and economic rights in Ireland is positive.

---

[320] *CA and TA v Minister for Justice* Record No. 2013/751/JR.

CHAPTER 7

The Charter of Fundamental Rights of the European Union

The CFR: An Introduction

The European Union (EU) historically had no competence in human rights **[7–01]** issues, nor was it inclined to expand its remit into those areas. Slowly, the Court of Justice of the European Union (CJEU) began to accept and recognise the place of fundamental rights within the EU. This is evident in the evolution of the treaties, culminating in the Lisbon Treaty, which gives legal effect to the Charter of Fundamental Rights of the European Union (CFR) and places the protection of human rights at the core of EU obligations. The CFR, in affirming, once more, that all rights are indivisible, interdependent and interrelated, protects a more extensive list of rights than the ECHR including specific protection for social and economic rights. Given the legal status of the CFR, the core concepts of EU law of supremacy and direct effect and the oversight by the CJEU, it would be easy to see the CFR as the saviour of social and economic rights. Unfortunately, it suffers from a significant flaw, it can only be invoked against the state where it is implementing EU law and thus has no effect on domestic law generally. As the EU has primarily been an economic institution, there is a dearth of regulation solely protecting human rights, making the application of the CFR in this regard practically non-existent.

This chapter catalogues the evolution of the EU in the protection of human **[7–02]** rights and postulates whether the accession of the EU to the ECHR could further enhance accountability in the EU for fundamental rights and whether this will impact upon the status of social and economic rights in Ireland.

The European Union: Principles, Purposes and Key Concepts

In the wake of World War II, Europe was utterly devastated, physically, **[7–03]** psychologically and politically. Rebuilding and uniting Europe posed a formidable challenge. In 1947, the Marshall Plan was proposed, which gave monetary grants to all European nations, provided that they cooperate in the distribution of American aid and that they progressively abolish all trade barriers.[1] Stalin called this a capitalist plot and forced all countries under his control to withdraw. However, the plan did have considerable success. It restored trade and production, while, at the same time, controlling inflation. By 1951, their economies were booming. The implementation of this plan demonstrated that the best recovery path for Europe was as a single economic entity. Various inter-governmental organisations began to emerge to strengthen this European bond in economic and political matters, primarily on the basis of the Schuman Plan.[2] Robert Schuman argued that Europe was facing three problems: economic dominance by the US, military dominance by Russia and a possible war with Germany. He proposed that the way forward was through a supranational entity to oversee the production of steel and coal, the two commodities essential to a war at this time. In June 1950, a conference was held in Paris and, as a result, on 18 April 1951 the Treaty creating the European Coal and Steel Community was signed by Belgium, France, Italy, Luxembourg, the Netherlands and West Germany.

[7–04]   This first Treaty created the building blocks for what was to become the European Union. Later in Messina in June 1955, foreign ministers decided to create a common economic institution and, in 1957, the European Economic Community was born.[3] Its sole purpose was in the creation and harmonisation of an internal market. The Treaty created the three institutions of the EU: the Commission, which is the main legislator and has the power to bring states to the ECJ for non-compliance; the Council of Ministers, which discusses, amends and adopts laws; and the Parliament, the only directly elected body of the EU, which now has a co-legislative role with the Commission. Within its first decade, it also created the CJEU (or the European Court of Justice, as it was then called).

[7–05]   While the EEC had a brief surge from 1970 to 1985, it became stagnant, termed 'Eurosclerosis'.[4] International difficulties saw the resurgence in national interests, with member states acting for themselves and not within the unity of the EEC. For example, during the oil embargo in 1973, states acted alone in negotiating bilateral trade deals with Iran and Saudi Arabia.[5] In the early 1980s, renewed enthusiasm for the EEC emerged, driven by improved international economies, the appointment of a new president of the Commission and the ending of the Cold War, which saw many European countries fearful that the

---

[1]   US Secretary of State George C Marshall announced this plan at a conference in Harvard University on 5 June 1947. See Stanley Hoffman and Charles Maier, *The Marshall Plan: A Retrospective* (Westview 1984).

[2]   The Schuman Declaration (Paris, 9 May 1950).

[3]   Consolidated Version of the Treaty establishing the European Community 25 March 1957.

[4]   A term coined by German economist Herbert Giersch to describe the stagnation of the EU.

[5]   For background to this embargo, see Ibrahim FI Shihata, 'Destination of Arab Oil: Its Legality under International Law' (1974) 68(4) American Society of International Law 591.

two superpowers may enter into agreements which would be detrimental to their interests. In this regard, the European Countries were convinced that, if they were a united economic entity, they would be able to assert and protect their interests more comprehensively. The outcome of this was the introduction of the Single European Act, which came into force on 1 July 1987. This Act gave new competences to the EEC in areas of economic and social cohesion, research and development and environmental matters, necessary to achieve a working internal market. The Maastricht Treaty sees the first movement in the Treaties away from purely economic policy towards one that includes human rights under the three pillars of the Community.[6] This is also clear from the change of the name to the European Union. However, this renewed enthusiasm for Europe was not without its difficulties. The Luxembourg Accords in 1996 came into being as a result of France refusing to attend meetings, as it disagreed with using a qualified majority rather than a unanimous approval of new regulations. The Accord stated that, where the member feels that a matter is of such importance, it can insist on there being a unanimous decision, effectively creating a veto system.[7] As a result, the Commission found itself in a precarious position when presenting a new regulation which may adversely affect the interests of a member state, even though the Accord was not legally binding.[8]

The Treaty of Lisbon, which entered into force in 2009, has, by far, the most significant impact on the human rights competence of the EU, not least of which is by the incorporation of the CFR and its elevation to Treaty status. However, it is clear from the above that the reason underlying the creation of the EU was to ensure economic cohesion. Two of the ways to ensure this uniform application of law and principles throughout member states come from rulings of the CJEU, establishing the supremacy of EU law and also its direct applicability. [7–06]

The supremacy of EU law did not derive from a Treaty provision. Rather, the CJEU explained the principle and necessity in *Costa v ENEL*: [7–07]

> The law stemming from the treaty, as an independent source of law, could not, because of its special and original nature, be overridden by domestic legal provisions, however framed, without being deprived of its character as community law and without the legal basis of the Community itself being called into question.[9]

The position of the CJEU has not changed since this ruling. It is a fundamental and key concept of EU law that it is supreme to national law and that such [7–08]

---

[6] See Alina Kaczorowska, *European Union Law* (3rd edn, Routledge 2013) 18-22.
[7] For analysis of the Luxembourg Accords, see John Lambert, 'The Constitutional Crisis (1965-1966)' (1966) 4 Journal of Common Market Studies 195.
[8] Case 68/86 *UK v Council* [1988] ECR 855.
[9] [1964] ECR 585, 594.

supremacy is necessary in order for the free market to function. This supremacy is effective over national constitutions[10] and international agreements.[11]

[7–09] Thus, the law of the EU is supreme over national law and, where there is a conflict between the two, the member state is legally bound to give effect to EU law and disregard the national law. This is complimented by the second key principle of EU law, that it is directly effective in the national systems of member states. This is another creation of the CJEU, considered necessary in order to ensure, not only the effectiveness of EU law, but also that individuals deriving benefit therefrom would be protected. Arguably, this concept was first established by the Permanent Court of International Justice in *Concerning the Competences of the Courts of Danzig*.[12] Here, it was held that, where a Treaty is adopted which creates rights and obligations capable of being relied upon in domestic courts, this provides an exception to the general rule that individuals are not subjects of international law. This principle was adopted by the CJEU in the *Van Gend & Loos* case, where it justified the approach by stating that the Community 'constitutes a new legal order of international law … the subjects of which comprise not only of Member States, but also their nationals'.[13] In order for a piece of EU law to be directly effective, it must meet certain criteria, which have evolved from the CJEU over time. First, it must be clear and precise. Secondly, it must be unconditional, meaning that it does not require any implementing measures on the part of the member state. Finally, and where relevant, the deadline for implementation by a member state, where such is required, must have passed. This is restricted primarily to directives which depend upon measures being taken by the member state. This principle applies both horizontally and vertically meaning that the provisions of EU law can be relied upon in national courts against the member state, but also against private entities.[14]

[7–10] These two well-entrenched principles of supremacy and direct effect were concocted by the CJEU at a time when human rights protection was not at the fore of the EU's considerations. However, as the EU moves tentatively towards greater protection for human rights, these concepts may prove pivotal in ensuring effective and meaningful protection.

---

[10] Case 11/70 *Internationale Handelsgesellschaft* [1970] ECR 1125.
[11] The exception here is that, if the agreement were concluded and in force prior to accession to the EU, that agreement will prevail over EU law.
[12] Advisory Opinion on 3 February 1928, Series B, No. 15
[13] Case 26/62 *NV Algemene Transport-en Expedite Onderneming van Gend & Loos v Netherlands Inland Revenue Administration* [1963] ECR 1, 12.
[14] The horizontal application was confirmed in Case 43/75 *Defrenne v Sabene* [1976] ECR 455.

Human Rights Protection and the Court
of Justice of the European Union

The Court of Justice of the European Union (CJEU) was established in 1952   **[7–11]**
as the overseer and enforcer of EU Law. Primarily, it acts as an aid to national
courts in interpreting EU law and it further sanctions states where they are in
breach of the law.[15] Of importance, in this regard, is that there is no general right
of individual petition to the CJEU. Only in narrow and limited circumstances,
where an EU institution has directly breached an individual's rights, is there
a right to petition. Most cases come by way of preliminary reference from
the national court, or as an inter-state complaint. Additionally, the European
Commission can institute proceedings in the court against a state. As clearly set
out above, the EU was initially created in order to ensure economic and fiscal
stability within Europe. It was not until 1992 and the Maastricht Treaty that
human rights found their way into the treaties of the EU. Prior to this, the court
was examining cases involving human rights considerations and determining
their placement within the EU. Kaczorowska believes that the development
of the court's jurisprudence can be classified into three distinct phases.[16] The
first phase is evident in the *Stork* case, where it refused to examine whether
EU law was in compliance with the fundamental rights established in national
constitutions.[17] One reason for this outcome was based on the concept of
supremacy, stated above, but another was based on the fact that the treaties did
not contain any reference to fundamental human rights. The court therefore
focused on the economic goals, leaving human rights eminently rejected.[18]

The second phase is where the court, following pressure from member states,   **[7–12]**
began to modify its position. In *Stauder,* the court remarked obiter that
fundamental rights formed part of the general principles of EU law.[19] This ruling
was expanded upon in *Internationale Handelsgellschaft,* which is the first case
that formally recognised fundamental rights as forming part of community
law as deriving from the national constitutions of member states.[20] In *Nold,*
the court enunciated an additional basis for incorporating fundamental rights
into community law (supplementary to national constitutions), international
human rights treaties, in particular the ECHR.[21] However, the court in *Grant*
explained that there is a limitation in engaging with human rights, in that those
fundamental rights cannot have the effect of extending a Treaty provision beyond

---

[15]   Article 19 TEU gives an overview of the court functions.
[16]   Kaczorowska (n 6) 215.
[17]   Case 1/58 *Friedrich Stork & Cie v High Authority* [1959] ECR 17.
[18]   Manfred M Zuleeg, 'Fundamental Rights and the Law of the European Communities'
(1971) 8(4) Common Market Law Review 446.
[19]   Case 26/69 *Erich Stauder v City of Ulm-Sozialamt* [1969] ECR 419.
[20]   Case 11/70 *Internationale Handelsgesellschaft* [1970] ECR 1125.
[21]   Case 4/73 *Nold, Kohlen-und BaustoffgroBhandlung v Commission* [1974] ECR 491.

the competence of the EU.[22] The third and final phase is the determination that the protection of fundamental rights extends, not only to EU institutions, but also to member states. This was initially a highly controversial move, given the lack of uniform application of fundamental rights within the member states, but also because of the haphazard development of the case law. This has since been ameliorated with the entry into force of the Charter, which gives the court broad powers to scrutinise whether member states are acting in a manner compatible with the fundamental rights.

[7–13]   While the CJEU initially refused to engage with the protection of fundamental rights, it has now evolved into a central consideration. In *Kadi*, it struck down a regulation implementing a UN Security Council Resolution on the grounds that it breached the fundamental rights of the EU legal order and that the UN Charter provisions could not prevail over those rights.[23]

[7–14]   There was no categorisation of rights into social and economic rights or civil and political rights. However, it did not make any real attempt to bring social rights within the remit of community law.[24] It is somewhat surprising that the CJEU has not looked to the ESC, given that most member states had a hand in its drafting and it is specifically mentioned in the preamble to the Single European Act.[25] The second class status of social and economic rights within Community law was affirmed when fundamental rights finally found their way into the Maastricht Treaty, where only the ECHR and common constitutional traditions of member states would be seen as sources of such.[26] In *Schmidberger*, when the court commented that 'measures which are incompatible with the observance of human rights *thus recognised* are not acceptable in the community',[27] this excludes social and economic rights, as the recognised sources are national constitutions and the ECHR only. This stance is evidenced in the *Laval* decision, where, despite the ESC, the CFR and the ILO Convention was mentioned earlier

---

22   Case C-249/96 *Lisa Jacqueline Grant v South-West Trains Ltd* [1998] ECR I-621.
23   Case C-402/05P *Yassin Abdullah Kadi and Al Barakaat International Foundation v Council of the European Union and Commission of the European Communities* [2008] ECR I-6351. See also, Katja S Ziegler, 'Strengthening the Rule of Law but Fragmenting International Law: The Kadi Decision of the ECJ from the Perspective of Human Rights' (2009) 9(2) Human Rights Law Review 288; Carmen Deaghici, 'Suspected Terrorists' Rights between the Fragmentation and Merger of Legal Orders: Reflections in the Margin of the *Kadi* ECJ Appeal Judgment' (2009) 8 Washington University Global Studies Law Review 627.
24   Bruno de Witte, 'The Trajectory of Fundamental Social Rights in Europe' in Grainne de Burca and Bruno de Witte (eds), *Social Rights in Europe* (Oxford University Press 2005) 153.
25   Mark Gould, 'The European Social Charter and Community Law- A Comment' (1989) 14 European Law Review 223.
26   Roderic O'Gorman, 'The ECHR, the EU and the Weakness of Social Rights Protection at the European Level' (2011) 12(10) German Law Journal 1833, 1837.
27   Case C-112/00 *Schmidberger v Austria* [2003] ECR I-5659.

in the case. When it came to the balancing act between the right to strike and the right of the company to provide a service, the CJEU relied solely on provisions of the Treaties.[28] With the ECHR adjudicating on more social and economic rights cases, together with newer European constitutions including express provision and protection, this may pave the way for the CJEU to become more active within the realm of these rights.

However, since 2009, the Lisbon Treaty has given effect to the Charter of Fundamental Rights, which contains within its provisions specific protection for certain social and economic rights.   [7–15]

The Charter of Fundamental Rights

The CFR took less than one year to draft and it was adopted at the Nice Summit   [7–16]
in 2000. It established the rights which all citizens should enjoy and which member states should strive to protect. Although, prior to the Lisbon Treaty, it was an unenforceable document, akin to the Universal Declaration, it came to be utilised as an interpretative tool in case law. In the case of *Blaise Baheten Metok & Ors v Minister for Justice Equality and Law Reform*, the CJEU determined that Directive 2004/38, regulating the right of entry and residence of non-EU nationals, must be interpreted in light of the provisions of the Charter.[29] Thus, the CFR was acknowledged as a benchmark for human rights protection within the EU, though it lacked a legally-binding character.

The Treaty of Lisbon altered the status of the CFR, providing in one article that   [7–17]
it is legally-binding and has the same status as other treaties of the EU.[30] The very next sentence, however, qualifies its scope with the caveat 'The provisions of the Charter shall not extend in any way the competences of the Union as defined in the Treaties'.[31]

While the vast majority of the rights contained within the CFR are a reiteration   [7–18]
of the classic civil and political rights, it does contain some rights that are purely social and economic rights. Indeed, the first right, which arguably encompasses a social and economic rights dimension, is dignity; 'Human dignity is inviolable. It must be respected and protected'.[32]

---

[28] Case C-341/05 *Laval un Partneri Ltd v Svenska Byggnardsarbetareforbundet* [2007] ECR I-11767.

[29] [2008] ECR I-6421.

[30] Article 6.1 states, 'The Union recognises that the rights, freedoms and principals set out in the Charter of Fundamental Rights and freedoms of the European Union of 7th December 2000 as adapted at Strasburg on 12th December 2007 which shall have the same legal value as the Treaties'.

[31] Treaty of Lisbon amending the Treaty on European Union and the Treaty establishing the European Community [2007] OJ C306/01, Article 6.1.

[32] Chapter 1, Article 1.

[7–19]   The concept of human dignity as a human right is not well defined in scholarship or jurisprudence. In an attempt to define dignity, Bagaric and James state that it is 'a term so elusive as to be virtually meaningless',[33] Davis says that the concept of human dignity 'does not give us enough guidance'[34] and Macklin refers to human dignity as a 'fuzzy concept'.[35] In defence of the provision, Donnelly contends that dignity cannot be easily analysed or defined, but instead,, it is the 'concept that links human rights'.[36] He goes further, to suggest that our understanding of dignity shapes our practice of human rights and that such practice is justified by the ability to lead a life of dignity.[37] In this sense, the right to human dignity encompasses both civil and political, as well as social and economic, rights.

[7–20]   The CFR confirms a generally accepted, albeit somewhat aspirational, statement, that all rights are indivisible, interrelated and interdependent, and does so by cataloguing both social and economic with civil and political rights.[38] Further, Article 3(3) speaks of the EU working to 'combat social exclusion and discrimination' and to 'promote social justice'. Elevating their status and importance in the hierarchy of principles and values of the EU gives the CJEU considerable scope to examine social and economic rights in cases before it.

[7–21]   There are specific social and economic rights contained within the CFR, such as the right to education,[39] the right to cultural and linguistic diversity,[40] the right

---

[33]   Mirko Bagaric and Allan James, 'The Vacuous Concept of Dignity' (2006) 5(2) Journal of Human Rights 257, 260.

[34]   Julia Davis, 'Doing Justice to Dignity in the Criminal Law' in Jeff Malpas and Norelle Lickiss (eds), *Perspectives on Human Dignity: A Conversation* (Springer 2007) 177.

[35]   Ruth Macklin, 'Cloning and Public Policy' in Justin Burley and John Harris (eds), *A Companion to Genethics* (Oxford University Press 2002) 212.

[36]   Jack Donnelly, 'Human Dignity and Human Rights, Protecting Dignity: An Agenda for Human Rights' (Swiss Initiative to Commemorate the 60th Anniversary of the UDHR, Research Project on Human Dignity, June 2009) available at <www.udhr60.ch/report/donnelly-HumanDignity_0609.pdf> 84, last accessed 19 February 2017.

[37]   ibid 86.

[38]   See Lord Goldsmith, 'A Charter of Rights, Freedoms and Principles' (2001) 38 Common Market Law Review 1201.

[39]   Article 14(1) states, 'Everyone has the right to education and have access to vocational and continuing training',
Article 14(2) states, 'This right includes the possibility to receive free compulsory education',
Article 14(3) states, 'The freedom to found educational establishments with due respect for democratic principles and the right of parents to ensure the education and teaching of their children in conformity with their religious, philosophical and pedagogical convictions shall be respected, in accordance with the national laws governing the exercise of such freedom and right'.

[40]   Article 22 states, 'The Union shall respect cultural, religious and linguistic diversity'.

of the elderly specifically to live with dignity and to social participation,[41] the integration of those with disabilities,[42] social security and social assistance,[43] and the right to health care.[44]

The rights apply both vertically and horizontally but are limited by Article 51(1), which establishes that they only apply in the implementation of EU Law. Therefore, these rights do not apply to general provisions of domestic law and in order to invoke them there must be a clear link to EU law. Further, the CFR confirms that it does not extend the scope of EU law, nor does it create new competences.[45] Therefore, the EU will not be able to create legislation to ameliorate a breach of a right, unless the power and competence to do so is already established by the Treaties. Further limitations on rights are permissible insofar as they are proportionate and necessary in order to reach the objectives of the EU. This includes obligations, not only under the Treaties, but also under secondary EU Law.[46]

[7–22]

Article 52 of the CFR gives some guidance as to how the rights are to be interpreted. Where the right has a corresponding right in the ECHR, the interpretation given by the European Court is to be followed. Where it derives from national constitutions, they are to be interpreted in line with those national traditions. It is clear to conclude that, where the state gives effect to EU Law

[7–23]

---

[41] Article 25 states, 'The Union recognises and respects the rights of the elderly to lead a life of dignity and independence and to participate in social and cultural life'.

[42] Article 26 states, 'The Union recognises and respects the rights of persons with disabilities to benefit from measures designed to ensure their independence, social and occupational integration and participation in the life of the community'.

[43] Article 34(1) states, 'The Union recognises and respects the entitlement to social security benefits and social services providing protection in cases such as maternity, illness, industrial incidents, dependency or old age, and in the case of loss of employment, in accordance with the rules laid down by Community Law and national law and practices'; Article 34(2) states, 'Everyone residing and moving legally within the European Union is entitled to social security benefits and social advantages in accordance with Community law and national law and practices'; Article 34(2) states, 'In order to combat social exclusion and poverty, the Union recognises and respects the right to social and housing assistance so as to ensure a decent existence for all those who lack sufficient resources in accordance with the rules laid down by Community law and national law and practice'.

[44] Article 35 states, 'Everyone has the right of access to preventative health care and the right to benefit from medical treatment under the conditions established by national laws and practices. A high level of human health protection shall be ensured in the definition and implementation of all Union policies and activities'.

[45] Article 51(2) states, 'This Charter does not establish any new power or task for the Community or the Union, or modify powers and tasks defined by the Treaties'.

[46] Koen Lanaerts, 'Exploring the Limits of the EU Charter of Fundamental Rights' (2012) 8(3) European Constitutional Law Review 375, 378.

by way of domestic legislation, it is implementing EU law, and therefore must be in conformity with the CFR.[47]

[7–24] However, what is meant by implementing EU law has been the subject of some debate.[48] A number of different suggestions as to how this word should be interpreted have been proffered. The literal approach would necessarily exclude any action save in circumstances where the state acts as the agent of the EU or where there is the requirement of implementing measures.[49] The teleological approach, as explained by Trevor Hartley, draws on the inherently vague wording of the article, allowing the court to develop is case law as it has previously done, in an ad hoc developmental manner.[50] The originalist or historical approach[51] looks to the intention at a specific time and interprets based on those goals.

[7–25] The court doesn't appear to have favoured one approach over the other. Rather, it has taken to using a particularly wide interpretation of the term 'implementing EU Law'. In *DEB,* the CJEU assessed German legislation regarding the award of legal aid in light of the provisions of Article 47 of the CFR.[52] This legislation was not enacted in order to implement any EU Law. However, the claimant, a German energy supplier, alleged that it had suffered a loss as a result of Germany failing to implement an EU Directive allowing non-discriminatory access to national gas networks. In *Commission v Germany,* the court found that Germany had delayed in implementing the Directive and, as a result, *DEB* could not access the gas network, thereby losing contracts. It could not pursue a case against Germany without access to legal aid , which was heavily restricted for legal persons (as opposed to natural persons). Thus, from this case, the breach of rights does not need to come from a direct implementation of EU law. An indirect implementation will suffice to invoke Charter rights.

[7–26] A more nuanced situation arises where the state is acting within the discretion granted to it by the EU. This issue arose in the case of *NS,*[53] which involved the discretion afforded to member states in the regulation of asylum seekers,

---

[47] See Case 5/88 *Hubert Wachauf v Bundesamt fur Ernahrung und Forstwirtschaft* [1989] ECR 2609.

[48] Stephen Brittain, 'The EU Charter of Fundamental Rights and Member States' (2013) 36 Dublin University Law Journal 277.

[49] Kaczorowska (n 6) 224.

[50] Trevor Hartley, 'The European Court, Judicial Objectivity and the Constitution for the European Union' (1996) 112 Law Quarterly Review 95.

[51] See David Langwallner, 'The Incoherence of Historicism and Originalism in Irish Constitutional Interpretation' (2008) 4 Independent Law Review 17, for an analysis of the difference between old originalism and new originalism.

[52] Case C-279/09 *DEB Deutsche Energiehandels und Beratungsgesellschaft mbH v Germany* [2010] ECR I-13849.

[53] Joined Cases C411-10 and C493-10 *NS v Secretary of State* and M*E and Ors v Minister for Justice Equality and Law Reform,* Judgment 21 December 2011.

specifically under the Dublin Regulation.[54] This Regulation gives member states the power to return asylum seekers to a safe third country, through which they had travelled before arriving in the member state. The CJEU was asked to determine whether such discretion must be in conformity with the CFR. The court held that 'a member state which exercises that discretionary power must be considered as implementing EU Law within the meaning of Art 51(1) of the Charter'.[55]

Where EU law is silent on a particular issue, or where a state has derogated, **[7–27]** the CFR will not apply. In the case of state derogation, the rights are to be determined by existing obligations.[56] Lanaerts objects to this viewpoint. He asserts, following the reasoning of the court in *NS*, that derogation is, in fact, implementing EU law, as the state had to fulfil the conditions of EU law in order to derogate.[57] This, he contends, has the potential to add to the impact that the CFR can have in a significant manner and would mean that it will apply in areas where EU law has competence, regardless of whether conditions for derogation are established or discretions are afforded to the state, thereby expanding its scope.

Where EU law is completely silent on an issue, the CFR cannot apply. An **[7–28]** example of this can be seen in the *Annibaldi* case, in which the CJEU held that it had no competence to examine a national law where it had not been enacted to give effect to any EU legislation.[58] This was affirmed in the *Dereci* case, which involved the applicant's entitlement to a derivative right of residence, based on his children's status.[59] The children had never left the state of which they were nationals and therefore the fundamental right of free movement established in EU Law had not been triggered. Directive 2003/86 and 2004/38 specifically did not apply to third-country nationals who apply for a right of residence to join family members who have never exercised their right of free movement and have remained in the member state of which they are nationals. As such, the court held that, notwithstanding the fact that the applicant's family life would be affected as per Article 33 of the CFR, as there was no EU law on the area, it did not have jurisdiction in the matter. Here, the difficulty of consistently enforcing social and economic rights is manifest. Social and economic rights still fall outside the ambit of EU law in the main, as the broad guarantees are refracted through the competencies of the EU. Therefore, while the Charter

---

54 Regulation No 343/2003.
55 Joined Cases C411-10 and C493-10 *NS v Secretary of State* and M*E and Ors v Minister for Justice Equality and Law Reform,* Judgment 21 December 2011 [68].
56 Lord Goldsmith (n 38).
57 Lanaerts (n 46) 385.
58 Case C-309/96 *Annibaldi v Sindaco del Comune di Guidonia and Presidente Regione Lazio* [1997] ECR I-07493.
59 Case C-256/11 *Murat Dereci and others v Bundesministerium für Inneres* [2011] ECR I-11315

appears to endorse select social and economic rights, these rights are without effect, where jurisdiction to enforce them does not vest with the CJEU and as they do not form part of the positive law of the Union.

[7–29]   A further difficulty is in distinguishing between rights, freedoms and principles within the Charter. Many rights, the classic civil and political primarily are articulated as rights. For example, Article 6 refers to the right to liberty and security. Certain freedoms are expressed, such as the freedom to choose an occupation, in Article 15. These freedoms mean that the state cannot impose disproportionate restrictions. The principles are somewhat different and it can be difficult to determine between a principle and a right. An example of a principle can be found in Article 33, which states that 'the family shall enjoy legal, economic and social protection'. The difference between a right and a principle, according to Lord Goldsmith, is that rights refer to 'individually justiciable classic rights' while principles are 'aspirations and objectives of what states should do'.[60] This echoes the sentiments prevalent at the drafting of the ICESCR and, despite the official stance of provisions being interdependent and indivisible, appears to relegate social and economic rights to a position lower than civil and political rights. This is of concern when the optional Protocol to the ICESCR is attempting to elevate their status to an equivalent level and the European Court of Human Rights is expanding its jurisprudence in the area. Given the supremacy of EU law, this could arguably have a detrimental effect on attempts to further these rights within member states and the EU generally.

[7–30]   While the CJEU has been expanding its human rights jurisprudence considerably, it has done so with a marked lack of reference to other international human rights documents, save for the occasional reference to the ECHR.[61] Arguably, the main consideration for the CJEU in relation to social and economic rights in recent years has been the austerity measures implemented by member states in order to comply with an EU bail out. The European economic crisis saw member states turning to the EU for financial assistance to avoid becoming bankrupt. This gave the EU and unprecedented opportunity to interfere with the fiscal and economic policy of the state. The Commission, the European Central Bank and the International Monetary Fund, collectively known as the Troika, negotiated the conditions of financial assistance. These conditions were also contained in a Council Decision directed to that state, thereby making them legally binding. This concept of conditionality was hitherto unheard of in EU law, but drew on

---

[60]   Lord Goldsmith, 'A Charter of Rights, Freedoms and Principles' (Henrich Boil Stuftung, London, February 2001) 35, available at <www.gruene-akademie.de/download/europa_goldsmith.pdf> last accessed 20 September 2016.

[61]   Grainne de Burca, 'After the EU Charter of Fundamental Rights: The Court of Justice as a Human Rights Adjudicator' (2013) 20 Maastricht Journal of European and Comparative Law 168.

a well-established practice of the IMF.[62] As per the Economic Stability Treaty, these conditions may range from a 'macro-economic adjustment programme to continuous respect of pre-established eligibility criteria'.[63] Following EU Regulation 472/2013, these conditions shall aim to 'rapidly re-establish a sound and sustainable economic and financial situation'.[64] Thus, the focus of the EU in this regard is the resurgence of a viable economy, with no emphasis placed on the value of protecting social and economic rights in the process. Therefore, these bail-out packages inevitably led to significant austerity measures, resulting in massively increased levels of poverty.

In order to ensure the continued economic stability of the Eurozone, the Treaty on Stability, Coordination and Governance (Fiscal Treaty) was adopted in 2013. Within this Treaty, member states who fail to keep their budget deficits within an acceptable margin face the possibility of being brought before the CJEU by the Commission, making the court the 'enforcer' of fiscal compact.[65] This Treaty was challenged in the CJEU in the case of *Pringle v Government of Ireland*.[66] The precursor to the ESM, the European Financial Stability Mechanism was a special fund operated by the Commission, novel in terms of its structure. It was incorporated as a private company under the control of nominees from the member states but operated outside of the EU legal order. The ESM was to retain this same extra-EU character. The purpose of this Treaty was to save the single currency, which was perceived to be under significant threat given the economic crisis. The applicant in the case argued that ESM would undermine the rule of law in the EU, that the narrow focus of the Treaty would run counter to the broader objectives of the EU (including the protection of fundamental rights) and raised concerns that, as an extra-EU body, it would not be subject to the same rigorous oversight by the CJEU as other EU institutions are. Three questions were posed by the Irish Supreme Court to the CJEU, centring on the legal validity of the Treaty.[67] Exceptionally, to hear this case, the court sat at

[7–31]

---

[62] Michael Ioannidis, 'EU Financial Assistance Conditionality after "To Pack"' (2014) 74 Zeitschrift fur auslandisches offentliches Recht und Volkerrecht 61.

[63] Article 12[1].

[64] Regulation 472/2013 of the European Parliament and of the Council of 21 May 2013 on the strengthening of economic and budgetary surveillance of Member States in the Euro Area experiencing or threatened with serious difficulties with respect to their financial stability (2013) OJ L140/1.

[65] Damien Chalmers, 'The European Court of Justice has taken on huge new powers as "enforcer" of the treaty on stability, coordination and governance, yet its record as a judicial institution has been little scrutinised' (London School of Economics, March 2012) available at <blogs.lse.ac.uk/europpblog/2012/03/07/european-court-of-justice-enforcer/> last accessed 07 January 2017.

[66] Case C-370/12 *Thomas Pringle v Government of Ireland, Ireland, the Attorney General* [2012] ECR I-0.

[67] Summarised in Joe Noonan and Mary Linehan, 'Thomas Pringle v The Government of Ireland, Ireland and the Attorney General' (2014) 17(1) Irish Journal of European Law 129, 134, as: (1) Whether the ESM Treaty was compatible with the EU Treaties; (2)

full capacity, with all 27 judges present. Here, the court upheld the validity of the Treaty and, further, found that, as it was not part of EU law, the CFR could not be applied to it.[68]

[7–32] This decision has been heavily criticised, with Craig commenting:

> The Judgment unfolds like a story, and even though the reader knows or can hazard a pretty good guess at the ending – the Court of Justice of the European Union will find that the ESM is lawful – the story is compelling nonetheless, since the last part of the judgment is also the denouement in which the CJEU saves the ESM from the most potent challenge to its legality.[69]

It is clear that the CJEU would decide in this manner, as its primary purpose is to ensure the economic stability of the Union. However, it has been commented that the inconsistency which this judgment shows poses a significant threat, by adopting measures which are inconsistent with other obligations set forth in the Treaties.[70]

[7–33] Thus, with the legality of the ESM Treaty determined, plus its status as being outside EU Law affirmed, measures taken to comply with obligations under this Treaty cannot be challenged as being incompatible with the CFR. However, agreements made with the Troika under the Fiscal Treaty do fall within Union law and have been the subject of challenges in the CJEU. Aside from questions as to whether the conditionality imposed on member states in order to access a bail out is legitimate,[71] together with the significant infringement on domestic sovereignty, the impact of the measures imposed have considerable impact on the living conditions of citizens of member states affected.[72] The question becomes whether national legislation implementing austerity measures are in fact implementing EU law in order to invoke the CFR. As Poulou explains, whether the agreements themselves are classified as gentlemen's agreements or international agreements, the involvement of the Commission in formulating

---

Whether the amendment to Article 136 TFEU was lawful; and (3) Whether Eurozone states could join the ESM before Article 136 TFEU was amended.

[68] [2012] ECR I-0 [105].

[69] Paul Craig, 'Pringle: Legal Reasoning, Text, Purpose and Teleology' (2013) 20(1) Maastricht Journal of International and Comparative Law 1, 3.

[70] Jonathan Tompkin, 'Contradiction, Circumvention and Conceptual Gymnastics: The Impact of the Adoption of the ESM Treaty on the State of European Democracy' (2013) 14(1) German Law Journal 169.

[71] Deirdre Curtin, 'Challenging Executive Dominance in European Democracy' (2014) 77 Market Law Review 1.

[72] Anastasia Poulou, 'Austerity and European Social Rights: How can Courts Protect Europe's Lost Generation' (2014) 15 German Law Journal 1145, 1153.

them allows for the CFR to be applicable.[73] Once applicability is established, the next question is to what extent these fundamental rights must be complied with in times of austerity. In cases to come before the CJEU on this issue, they have refused to engage with the substantive issues, thus leaving the question open.[74] For example, the Portuguese court asked the CJEU whether wage cuts to civil servants (implemented under a bail-out programme) breached the principle of fair and just working conditions.[75] The court replied that it had no jurisdiction on the matter, as a link to EU law had not been established. Interestingly, the CESC found that austerity cuts to pensions without proper consultation breached ESC Rights. It found that, while, under certain conditions, they would not have breached the CFR, the cumulative effect, coupled with the method of adoption, was sufficient to breach Article 12 of the ESC.[76]

While the CFR appeared to be a much-needed step forward in the development of the EU and the CJEU as human rights actors, the economic crisis has shown that its core fundamental purpose is to ensure economic stability and that human rights considerations, particularly those involving social and economic rights, are far from even secondary considerations. It seems that what will be classed by the court as 'implementing' EU law is given a wide definition when the right in question is a civil and political one (as was seen in *DEB*). In contrast, where it involves austerity measures which materially affect the living conditions of citizens but are imposed in order to ensure the financial stability of the Eurozone, a much tighter interpretation is used by the court. This disparity affirms the status of social and economic rights within the EU legal order as subservient to more traditional fundamental rights and economic stability. **[7–34]**

Given that they are a lower priority for the EU itself, there is certainly no impetus on member states to elevate their domestic protection. Granted, the court has developed law and the protection of human rights in certain areas, particularly within the areas of employment and aslyum, but this gesture does very little to bolster the protection of social and economic rights in the absence of specific EU law to protect same. Moreover, it is highly unlikely that any such legislation will be forthcoming in the near future. **[7–35]**

The EU Accession Treaty to the ECHR

The EU acceding to the ECHR may not have very much effect on the furtherance of social and economic rights within domestic settings and, given that the final **[7–36]**

---

[73] ibid 1159.

[74] Case T-215/11 *ADEDY et al v Council* OJ C 26/45.

[75] Case C-128/12 *Sindicato dos Bancarios do Norte and Others v BNP* (7 March 2013).

[76] Complaint No 76/2012 *Federation of Employed Pensioners in Greece v Greece* (Decision on the merits) (7 December 2012) [83].

terms of the Treaty remain unclear, much is speculation at this point. However, for the purpose of comprehensively addressing the developing human rights protection of the EU, it is worth briefly detailing.

[7–37]   In 1996, Opinion 2/93 ruled that, as the law stood, the EC (as it was at the time) could not accede to the ECHR without a Treaty amendment.[77] In 2009, the Lisbon Treaty did just that. Article 6(2) TFEU states that the EU will accede to the ECHR. The draft agreement contained seven main features:[78]

   1. The ECHR will have jurisdiction to assess acts and measures of EU institutions;
   2. The EU will initially only sign up to the Convention and Protocol 1 (governing private property and education) and Protocol 6 (abolishing the death penalty);
   3. It creates a co-respondent mechanism whereby the EU can be named as a co-respondent where the breach of Convention rights by the member state derives from the implementation of EU Law;
   4. Other states who are party to the ECHR but not members of the EU can bring the EU before the ECHR;
   5. There will be an EU judge sitting in the ECtHR;
   6. The EU will have voting rights in the Council of Europe; and
   7. The EU will contribute to the Council of Europe's budget.

[7–38]   This draft was referred in 2013 to the CJEU for an opinion on its compatibility with EU Law.[79] The court ruled that the draft agreement was incompatible with EU law and gave five main reasons for its conclusion. First, it said that the Treaty did not have regard to the specific features of EU law in three ways: It did not curtail the possibility of member states having higher human rights protection than EU law; it did not apply the rule of 'mutual trust' (which allows states to assume that other member states are complying with EU law save for exceptional circumstances); and applying Protocol 16 of the ECHR (that will allow for national courts to make references to the ECHR on interpretation) would undermine the CJEU's preliminary reference procedure.

[7–39]   Secondly, it neglected to completely omit the possibility that the ECtHR may determine disputes on EU law matters through the inter-state complaints mechanism. The co-respondent mechanism was incompatible, as it would give the ECtHR power to assess EU law and it should not have the power to allocate responsibility for a breach of the ECHR between a member state and

---

[77]   *Opinion 2/94 Pursuant to Article 228(6) of the EC Treaty* [1996] ECR I-1759.
[78]   Council of Europe, Doc No 47 + 1(2013)008Rev2, available at <www.coe.int/t/dghl/standardsetting/hrpolicy/Accession/Meeting_reports/47_1(2013)008rev2_EN.pdf> last accessed 22 September 2016.
[79]   *Opinion 2/13 Pursuant to Article 218(11) TFEU* (18 December 2014).

EU institutions. Fourth, the rules on the prior involvement of the CJEU before the ECtHR ruled on a matter of EU law was incompatible, as it did not reserve the right for the CJEU to determine if the matter had already been decided upon, nor does it allow the CJEU to interpret EU law. Finally, the rules on Common Foreign and Security Policy were incompatible, as a non-EU court cannot be given judicial review powers over acts of an institution of the EU, notwithstanding that the CJEU equally does not have this power.[80]

As things stand at the time of writing, the Accession Treaty is being redrafted in order to address the issues raised by the CJEU and the time frame for this draft is unclear. Further, it is uncertain what measures will be taken in order to comply with the CJEU's ruling without leaving the ECtHR completely powerless over matters of EU law. It is clear that the CJEU in this Opinion is asserting its supremacy over the ECtHR in matters of EU law. Given that the text of the new draft Treaty is currently unavailable for analysis, it would be unwise to speculate as to the effect it may have on the interpretation of fundamental rights. **[7–40]**

Conclusion: Ireland and the Charter of Fundamental Rights

As already stated, international law cannot form part of domestic law unless and until a positive act of the Oireachtas incorporates it. This is confirmed in Article 15.2 of the Constitution, which affirms that the sole power to make law is vested in the Oireachtas. As a result, we have seen the majority of international human rights treaties languishing in an unenforceable manner within domestic courts. The one document that has been transposed is the European Convention on Human Rights and it is effective only in so far as the legislation permits. **[7–41]**

However, the situation within the EU is different. Several referenda amended the Constitution, resulting in primary EU law being directly applicable in Ireland without the need for positive action on the part of the legislature.[81] **[7–42]**

---

80 For detailed analysis of the consequences of this ruling, see Steve Peers, 'Opinion 2/13 – The Dream Becomes a Nightmare' (2015) 16 German Law Journal 213; Louise Halleskov Storgaard, 'EU Law Autonomy versus European Fundamental Rights Protection – On Opinion 2/13 on EU Accession to the ECHR' (2015) 15 Human Rights Law Review 485; Daniel Halberstam, 'It's the Autonomy, Stupid: A Modest Defense of Opinion 2/13 on the EU Accession to the ECHR and the Way Forward' (2015) 16(1) German Law Journal 105.

81 The following amendments were made to the Constitution, allowing EU law to be effective in Ireland: The Tenth Amendment in June 1987 allowed the state to ratify the Single European Act; in July 1992, the Eleventh Amendment ratified the Maastricht Treaty and amended Article 29 to confirm that the Constitution cannot invalidate laws enacted by reason of membership of the European Union; the Eighteenth Amendment then allowed the state to ratify the Treaty of Amsterdam, as it contained protocols that the state could choose to activate at a later date where there is approval of both houses of the Oireachtas;

Each time the EU wishes to extend its law making powers, requiring the Irish state to cede some its exclusive power, a referendum is required. This loss of sovereignty was not met with rapturous enthusiasm by all, and, as far back in 1962, the economist Ray Crotty was expressing concern about the emerging European Super State and commented on how remarkable it was that 'a people renowned for the centuries long struggle for independence should now be ready to surrender a large measure of that independence'.[82]

[7–43]   The Lisbon Treaty was first put to the people of Ireland in a referendum in 2008. Following this, Ireland was given guarantees on three issues if they passed the Treaty: That the Treaty would make no changes to taxation; that the policy of neutrality would not be affected; and that the constitutional provisions of the right to life, education and position of the family under Irish law would not in any way be affected by the fact that the Treaty of Lisbon attached legal status to the CFR.[83] Armed with these assurances, the government called a second referendum in 2009, where the Treaty was passed. Coughlan opined that:

> The Treaty of Lisbon…is the culmination of the constitutional side of this federal project. It established for the first time a legally new European Union with its own legal personality, separate from and superior to member states. We would all be made citizens of this for the first time, which is a profoundly important development. I have been opposed to the project because that is what it is all about.[84]

[7–44]   Thus, when the second referendum was passed, Ireland accepted the Lisbon Treaty and, therefore, the CFR. The state must guarantee the rights contained therein, but only in the implementation of EU law. Testing the CFR in relation to the austerity measures imposed by the Troika would appear to be a fruitless exercise, given the judgments of the CJEU in earlier cases. As it stands, the EU's primary concern of economic stability adds legitimacy to Ireland's general stance on social and economic rights and does not seem to concern itself too

---

the Twenty Eighth Amendment allowed the ratification of the Treaty of Lisbon at a second referendum; and, finally, the Thirtieth Amendment allowed the state to ratify the Treaty on Stability Coordination and Governance in the Economic and Monetary Union, which gives a certain element of control over national budgets. See generally, Michael Forde and David Leonard, *Constitutional Law of Ireland* (3rd edn, Bloomsbury Professional 2013) ch 9.

82   Raymond Crotty, 'Economist suggests 20% tariff reduction' *The Irish Times* (10 May 1962).

83   Tony Brown, *"Saying No"- An Analysis of the Irish Opposition to the Lisbon Treaty* (The Institute of International and European Affairs 2010) 15, available at <www.iiea.com/publications/saying-no—-an-analysis-of-the-irish-opposition-to-the-lisbon-treaty> last accessed 19 February 2016.

84   Evidence of Anthony Coughlan to the Oireachtas Sub-Committee on Ireland's future in the EU (21 November 2008).

much with the breaches of rights arising from austerity. It is clear that, in times of economic distress, the CJEU's role as a human rights protector is secondary.

To end on a cautiously optimistic note, perhaps once the economic stability [7–45] of the Eurozone has been established and the competence of the EU into the forays of human rights extends, the court may enhance its protection of these rights. Should they do this, then the possibility of enhancing the status social and economic rights in all member states of the EU becomes real.

CHAPTER 8

Conclusion

While many areas of this book are critical of the legal status afforded to social and economic rights, it is important to be aware of the subtle but distinct changes that are occurring. It has been argued that justiciability is not a magic wand that will ensure all social and economic rights are vindicated, and this is a correct assertion. However, the importance of justiciability cannot be overstated. Without justiciability, there can be no accountability when these rights are breached and there can be no enforcement and determination of a breach. Justiciability, therefore, provides the backstop – it is the assurance that the state must provide a basic, minimum core. **[8–01]**

As Chapter 1 shows, the political arms of many western states advocate strongly for the non-justiciability of these rights. The reasons proffered by those in opposition show a clear and persistent misunderstanding of these rights and of fundamental rights generally. Rights cannot be neatly divided into those which contain positive or negative obligations, as all rights contain an amalgamation of both. Further, many decisions involving civil and political rights are equally polycentric in nature. Therefore, the arguments of democratic legitimacy, capability and classification can be dismissed. **[8–02]**

Notwithstanding this, it is evident from the development (or lack thereof) of social and economic rights on the international stage that these arguments once carried such great weight that they relegated social and economic rights to a subservient position. Resultantly, as the international norm confirmed these rights as lesser in nature, it became inordinately difficult for social and economic rights to be furthered. While the placement of these rights in the non-justiciable Article 45 of the Constitution cannot be attributed to this international stance, perhaps the prevalent arguments and the dominance of the neo-liberal political ideology at the time influenced the court in its interpretation. **[8–03]**

This book has focused quite significantly on the shortcomings of Ireland and the various treaties to which it is a party. However, each comes with relatively unexplored potential. It is clear that, within the domestic context, there is ample opportunity for these rights to be constitutionalised, either directly or indirectly. While the political will may not be there, it has become clear in recent years, with increasing austerity measures, that the citizens of Ireland want to have a minimum core of these rights protected. This is evident in the recommendations of the Constitutional Convention, although these recommendations would **[8–04]** require a referendum to implement and, given the current political climate, this is highly unlikely to happen. However, given that the courts retain a wide power of judicial discretion, it is possible that the Supreme Court could revert to the activism of the O'Dhalaigh era. Some obiter remarks from Superior Court Justices entertain the future possibilities.

[8–05] However, as that has not yet happened and the stance is one of non-justiciability, we must look to international obligations and enforcement mechanisms to determine whether this can enhance the domestic position. Within the ICESCR, the legacy of the initial debates is most clearly felt. Significant attempts have been made by the UN to approximate both sets of rights but, with similar issues being raised during negotiations for the optional Protocol, the practical effect of these efforts has been left waning. Bowing to pressure from primarily Western neoliberal opposition, the wording of the optional Protocol was watered down. At the date of writing, the Committee had yet to deliver a decision in a case brought before it, alleging violations of rights under the ICESCR and so it remains to be seen precisely how it will interpret, inter alia, progressive realisation of rights, minimum core entitlements, retrogressive steps taken in the name of austerity and the reasonableness of steps taken by the state. It may be that the Committee here will take a more activist approach, but it is feared that this may be constrained by the wording of the optional Protocol and the Treaty itself. Indeed, even if it does take a hard-line approach to violations of social and economic rights, it is not a court. It has no power to enforce its decision or to impose sanctions against the state. Notwithstanding criticisms, the introduction of the optional Protocol is an incredibly positive step forward in the protection of social and economic rights. One of the main differences in international law between civil and political rights and social and economic rights was the availability of a forum where breaches of rights could be heard. The first optional Protocol to the ICCPR was opened for signature the same day as the ICCPR itself. Although it did not enter into force for another decade, it was a powerful indicator that the UN would not tolerate breaches of civil and political rights. While the Human Rights Committee suffers from many of the same flaws as the CESCR, it provided an international stage where breaches of rights could be heard. The approximation of rights through the introduction of the optional Protocol goes some way to bridging the gap between the two sets of rights created during the transposition of the UDHR.

[8–06] As no determinations have yet been made by the Committee, it remains to be seen what, if any, impact the optional Protocol will have on furthering domestic justiciability of social and economic rights. Should they follow the example set by the CESC in taking a holistic and expansive approach in an attempt to secure effective protection, the impact may be more keenly felt. However, as is all too keenly felt by the CESC, these efforts can be in vain, given their limited power and weak wording of the treaties which they are trying to enforce. As can be seen from an overview of the concluding observations against Ireland, there is considerable room for improvement. The Committee has reportedly expressed concern at a number of issues, including the status of social and economic rights in national law. Arising from the recommendations, little has changed, likely due (at least in part) to the fact that the Committee possesses no enforcement or sanction powers. Ireland has not yet ratified the optional Protocol to allow for individual complaints, but even in circumstances where a successful case was heard before the Committee, the claimant would be unable to enforce this judgment in the domestic courts, rendering it of little practical use. It is likely that, in these circumstances, the state would offer compensation to the victim of the breach, much in the same way it has done with Amanda Mellett, following her successful case in the HRC.

The CESC has been relatively active in its attempts to protect social and [8–07] economic rights. However, like the CESCR, it is not a court, cannot enforce its decisions and has no power to sanction the state, making its effectiveness questionable. The fact that the state chooses which rights it will be bound by further subjugates these rights, as in no other human rights treaty does a state do this. Rather, they must expressly derogate from a right. In addition, the exclusion of an individual complaints mechanism in favour of a collective complaints procedure limits its applicability and the specified groups have earned it the accolade of being known as the workers' charter. Ireland, as can be seen above, does not pay too much heed to either the concluding observations or the jurisprudence of the CESC.

Moving, then, to treaties which are overseen by courts and are therefore legally [8–08] binding on the state, we are faced with an entirely different set of problems. The CFR, which is given treaty status under Lisbon, contains specific reference to social and economic rights. However, the excitement of their inclusion was relatively short lived. The rights apply only in the application of EU law and, given that the EU is primarily an economic institution, human rights (and specifically, social and economic rights) are not necessarily its paramount concern. Further, nothing in the CFR allows the court to create or expand EU law to cover an area where it does not currently have competence.

Thus, the CFR may not be the ideal forum to have breaches of social and [8–09] economic rights considered. The CJEU, while it has expanded its scope over the years to include protection of human rights, it has so far been hostile to social and economic rights, as can be seen in the austerity cases, with its primary function of economic stability of the EU rising to the fore. Further, there is no right of individual petition to the CJEU and it would require a preliminary reference from a national court. Given the status of social and economic rights in Ireland at present, very few cases come to the courts in the first instance, as the chance of success is severely limited. As such, there is no opportunity to have a case referred. Even in cases where the court may refer to the CJEU in order to invoke the CFR, it must be shown that the violation occurred through the application of EU law. Given that EU law generally does not concern itself with social and economic rights, this may be a very tenuous link to prove, and the *Pringle* case illustrates the lengths to which the CJEU will go to ensure economic stability.

[8–10] The European Convention on Human Rights provides possibly the best chance of enhancing judicially the status of social and economic rights in Ireland. Although the ECHR textually protects only civil and political rights, the court has, from its earliest days, set two precedents which are pivotal. First, it has repeatedly noted that all human rights are interrelated and interdependent, thereby refusing to exclude social and economic rights from its purview. Secondly, the dynamic interpretation of the Convention means that any given explanation of a right is not stagnant and is liable to change as societal and human rights norms evolve, and with this, the margin of appreciation afforded to member states may diminish. These two key concepts have paved the way for an expanding body of jurisprudence protecting social and economic rights, primarily in the areas of healthcare, housing and social security. Ireland transposed the ECHR into domestic law in 2002 and thereby afforded it a different status to other human rights treaties (with the exception of the CFR–as an EU treaty it is directly effective in all member states). The Irish courts are required to interpret domestic law, in as far as possible, in a manner which is compatible with the jurisprudence of the European Court.

[8–11] While the direct impact of the ECHR on national law was minimal, it did have an indirect effect. The looming presence of the ECHR in cases where the domestic law fell short caused the court to interpret the Constitution in light of the jurisprudence of the European Court, as required by the 2003 Act. This, primarily within the realm of criminal law and procedure, sees the court interpreting the right to a fair trial contained within the Constitution in light of ECHR law to expand the contours of constitutional protection.[1] It is argued that the same approach could be taken to social and economic rights to indirectly constitutionalise them. The primary articles under which social and economic rights have been deemed justiciable in the European Court have comparable protection within the Constitution. Article 2, which protects the right to life, has its counterpart in Article 40.3.2.[2] Article 3 is arguably protected through the unspecified right to bodily integrity[3] and Article 8 may be encompassed within

---

[1] For example, see *O'Leary v AG* [1993] 1IR 102, where regard was had to the ECHR in determining that the Constitution implicitly contained a presumption of innocence, and also *Heaney v Ireland* [1994] 3 IR 593, where ECHR jurisprudence was instrumental in finding that the Constitution contained a right to silence.

[2] 'The state shall, in particular, by its laws protect as best it may from unjust attack, and in the case of injustice done, vindicate the *life*, person, good name and property rights of every citizen'.

[3] Created in the case of *Ryan v AG* [1965] IR 294.

an extension of the unenumerated right to privacy[4] and also within protection of the dwelling contained with Article 40.5.[5]

It is entirely plausible, therefore, that indirect constitutionalisation of social and economic rights by the interpretation of the Constitution in light of ECHR jurisprudence, as required by the 2003 Act, could occur, should there be a willing judiciary. **[8–12]**

More likely, however, is the incremental legalisation of these rights rather than constitutionalisation, which is not the preferred option. As the *Foy*[6] and *Donegan*[7] cases illustrate, the declaration of incompatibility does not affect the validity of the law and legislative action is required in that regard. The legislature has been inordinately slow to implement the changes necessary to bring Ireland in conformity with its ECHR obligations. The court has previously stated that, where it makes a declaration, this creates an expectation that the state will act.[8] The question arises as to the power of the court to compel action where the state fails to do so. Given that the 2003 Act was designed to give effect to the ECHR within Ireland, it is arguable that the court retains the power to grant mandatory orders where the state fails to abide by the declaration of incompatibility. Any other interpretation would render the Act meaningless and without effect. As such, once the mandatory order issues and legislation is forthcoming, the right becomes legalised and, therefore, is justiciable. This makes the right justiciable, but only within the confines of the legislation, which may be repealed or altered by successive ministers. **[8–13]**

The optimum manner in which the social and economic rights could be protected would be through direct inclusion into the Constitution by way of a referendum. As seen from South Africa, this does not automatically mean that all claims will automatically be vindicated. Rather, they will be subjected to the same tests of proportionality as every other constitutional right. As this option does not look likely, it seems that the best way forward for the justiciability of social and economic rights in Ireland is through some creative use of the ECHR, the potential of which is underexplored in Irish law at present. **[8–14]**

---

4   Beginning with the case of *McGee v Ireland* [1974] IR 284.
5   'The dwelling of every citizen is inviolable and shall not be forcibly entered save in accordance with the law'. This article has been determined to have wider application and refers to general private life. In *Herrity v Associated Newspapers (Ireland) Ltd* [2009] 1 IR 316, the court affirmed that there is a general right to privacy, which is not absolute and may be balanced against other competing rights.
6   *Foy v Registrar of Births Death and Marriages, Ireland and the Attorney General* [2007] IEHC 470.
7   *Donegan v Dublin City Council, Ireland and the Attorney General* and *Dublin City Council v Gallagher* [2012] IESC 18.
8   *Foy v Registrar of Births Death and Marriages, Ireland and the Attorney General* [2007] IEHC 470 [110].

INDEX